D0206125

Management for the Human Services

Richard T. Crow

Charles A. Odewahn

The University of Alabama

PRENTICE-HALL, INC., *Englewood Cliffs, New Jersey 07632*

Library of Congress Cataloging-in-Publication Data

CROW, RICHARD T.
    Management for the human services.

    Includes bibliographies and index.
    1. Social service—Management.   I. Odewahn, Charles A.,
(date) .   II. Title.   [DNLM: 1. Social Work—
organization & administration. HV 91 C953m]
HV40.C75   1987   361'.0068   86–21187
ISBN 0–13–548652–1

Production editor: Carole Crouse
Interior design: Joan Stone
Cover design: Wanda Lubelska Design
Manufacturing buyer: John Hall

Printed in the United States of America

10   9   8   7   6   5   4   3   2   1

ISBN   0-13-548652-1   01

PRENTICE-HALL INTERNATIONAL (UK) LIMITED, *London*
PRENTICE-HALL OF AUSTRALIA PTY. LIMITED, *Sydney*
PRENTICE-HALL CANADA INC., *Toronto*
PRENTICE-HALL HISPANOAMERICANA, S.A., *Mexico*
PRENTICE-HALL OF INDIA PRIVATE LIMITED, *New Delhi*
PRENTICE-HALL OF JAPAN, INC., *Tokyo*
PRENTICE-HALL OF SOUTHEAST ASIA PTE. LTD., *Singapore*
EDITORA PRENTICE-HALL DO BRASIL, LTDA., *Rio de Janeiro*

To Carol and Toppy

Contents

3

The Manager as Figurehead and Spokesperson, 37

4

The Manager as Leader: The Personnel Process, 46

5

The Manager as Leader: The Function of Motivation, 62

6

The Manager as Liaison, 81

7

The Monitor Role, 95

8

The Manager as Disseminator, 108

9

The Manager as Entrepreneur, 117

10

The Role of the Disturbance Handler, 134

Preface

Within the past few years there have been several books written on the subject that this book addresses: managing the human service organization. What, then, might this book offer that cannot be found elsewhere? Indeed, such a question has a great deal of merit, and we hope that the pages that follow will answer the question. We would not be so presumptuous as to assume that what we have written is the *magna carta* for managers in the human service organization. Yet, what we have tried to do is present the art of management in a practical and useful context.

The encouragement for investing the untold number of hours required to pull together our thoughts came from those managers in the human services. Having spent the past nine years training such individuals, we agreed to put the pen to paper. Since 1975, we have been involved with the training of approximately 2,500 managers. Initially, our involvement was the result of being at the right place at the right time. Back in the mid-1970s the Department of Health, Education, and Welfare was interested in funding a training program for managers. The University of Alabama responded to the Request for Proposal and was subsequently funded to develop and deliver a management development training program for managerial personnel within the eight states of Region IV. Thus, our initial effort began with the states in the southeastern portion of the country. The success of the initial activity was rewarded with continued funding through 1980. During this same period of time we were contractually involved with a number of states to develop and deliver developmental training with a specific emphasis on the respective states' needs. The Department of Health, Education, and Welfare also designated the Management Institute of The University of Alabama as a training center with the responsibility of providing training and technical assistance to states throughout the country. Although the University is no longer involved in this activity, we have continued to work with states to improve the management skills and abilities of their managerial personnel.

The original impetus for the training activity that we have been engaged in was the same impetus for writing this book. Individuals move into managerial positions in the human services with little or no preparation for being managers. Most have demonstrated good technical skills and, thus, were promoted; any developmental or preparatory focus was often merely a coincidence rather than a planned decision. What we attempt to do in the training that we offer is what we attempt to do in the book: provide individuals with information that can lead to more effective management. Throughout the book we have provided numerous illustrations that we hope will be helpful in applying a particular concept, technique, or theory. We have purposely avoided weighing the reader down with repetitive reports on research findings and technical jargon. Our prevailing thesis was to give the reader something that he or she could use.

With our illustrations we have attempted to broaden the application and usefulness of the book to include managers in medical settings, corrections, and the social services. It was our intention that the book would be equally useful to the uninitiated student and the practicing manager. We believe that it can be used as a text in the classroom as well as a resource for in-service training programs in hospitals, correctional agencies, and social service organizations.

Beginning with Chapter 3, we have directed the reader to consider the various roles that the manager must fulfill, and we have avoided focusing exclusively on the functions of management. The functions have been interwoven throughout in what we hope will be a more pragmatic manner. The cases at the end of the text have been included to provide the reader with the opportunity to try his or her hand at applying what has been discussed.

If those who read the book find it to be a helpful resource for them in being better managers, then we will have achieved our intended purpose for writing the book. We sincerely hope this will be the result.

Acknowledgments

Whenever anyone sits down to "write a book," it becomes apparent that it is easier to talk about it than it is to do it and that it cannot be accomplished without the assistance of others. We would not have had the opportunity to engage in this endeavor without the support of Ludwig Guckenheimer. It was Ludwig who carried the need for training human service managers to the officialdom in Washington. Although he has retired from federal service, we will always be indebted to him for giving us the opportunity to have the experiences that provided the motivation to write the book. We would be remiss if we failed to express our appreciation to Eulene Hawkins for her foresight and encouragement in the initial training program in Region IV. To Bill Pugh we extend our thanks for his untiring support with the administration at The University of Alabama. A good typist is a blessing, and we have been blessed. The early drafts could not have been completed without the help of Margaret McCrary, and as panic set in to complete the final draft, Laila Liddy was truly a blessing. Her assistance and attention to detail were extremely helpful.

Any undertaking of this magnitude could not be accomplished without the support of our respective families. The nights and weekends spent away from them cannot be recaptured, but we say thanks for your understanding and patience. We do hope that it was not all in vain.

Introduction to Management

The management of human service organizations has become a field requiring specialized training and preparation to effectively and efficiently meet the challenges and responsibilities facing the manager. Whether in public, tax-supported organizations, in private organizations, or in private-voluntary agencies, knowledgeable and skilled managers are needed at various managerial levels. With increasingly limited resources and specific program guidelines, the human service manager must be responsive to the growing demands for greater accountability and improved program effectiveness. In essence, in today's human service organization, managers are expected to do more with less. That places an awesome responsibility on them. Thus, they must have an understanding of what management is and what is involved in being an effective manager. Being a manager is more than having a title.

The purpose of this chapter is to provide an overview of management and the art of managing. Over the years there have been significant technological gains that assist the manager, yet the difference between successful managers and unsuccessful ones can be observed and studied and will be the primary focus of this text. What makes the difference? Often, it can be reduced to the individual manager's perception of his or her role and of how best to carry out that role.

WHAT IS MANAGEMENT?

Definitions of management are as numerous as those who write about the subject. Massie (1971), for example, defines management as "the process by which a cooperative group directs actions toward common goals" (p. 4). Peter Drucker (1974) defines it as three tasks "equally important but essentially different, which management has to perform to enable the institution in its charge to function and to make its contribution: the specific purpose and mission of the institution, whether business enterprise, hospital, or university; making work productive and the worker achieving; managing social impacts and social responsibilities" p. 40). Sisk (1977) adopts a more technocratic approach with his definition: "Management is the coordination of all resources through the process of planning, organizing, leading, and controlling in order to attain stated objectives" (p. 9).

These definitions may seem very different, even contradictory. Upon closer examination, however, several common elements appear. First, the stated or implied activity described by each definition is universally applicable. All organizations, large or small, attempting to achieve a common purpose require management.

Second, management is goal oriented. Management has no life separate from the goals for which the agency is established. That principle must constantly be kept in mind, since the temptation is ever present to manage an organization "for the sake of management." When that happens, both the organization and its clients, patients, or customers are poorly served.

Third, management is a cooperative venture. The organization achieves its goals primarily through the efforts of people. Successful management motivates individuals to join in a cooperative partnership in which organizational goals and personal goals converge.

Finally, management is task oriented. The manager engages in a number of activities related to the establishment of a plan, the development of an organization, the provision of leadership and direction, and the evaluation and control of performance.

Figure 1-1 is an example of a management system and illustrates the various relationships and aspects of the system. Several elements are critical. First, the manager must recognize the role of social, political, economic, and cultural values. Figure 1-1 clearly demonstrates that the values that influence policy formulation also affect the implementation of programs to fulfill the policy. Second, policy creates the need for resource allocation, thus stipulating the primary function of management's allocation and coordination of resources. Third, the management system is oriented toward a purpose. The process receives its direction from, and is organized around, the purpose or mission declared by the policy. Fourth, the system involves the performance of a series of functions (planning, organizing, leading, evaluating) that transform resources into specific services designed to accomplish the mission declared by the policy. Finally, each element of the system is constantly feeding back information and results. For example, feedback about the outcome of service delivery (desired social change) affects both the inputs (i.e., values, policy, resources, and so on) and the management process (i.e., planning, organizing, and so on).

With this understanding of what management is and of the importance of the interrelationships that exist in a management system, let us now turn our attention to the roles, activities, and functions of management.

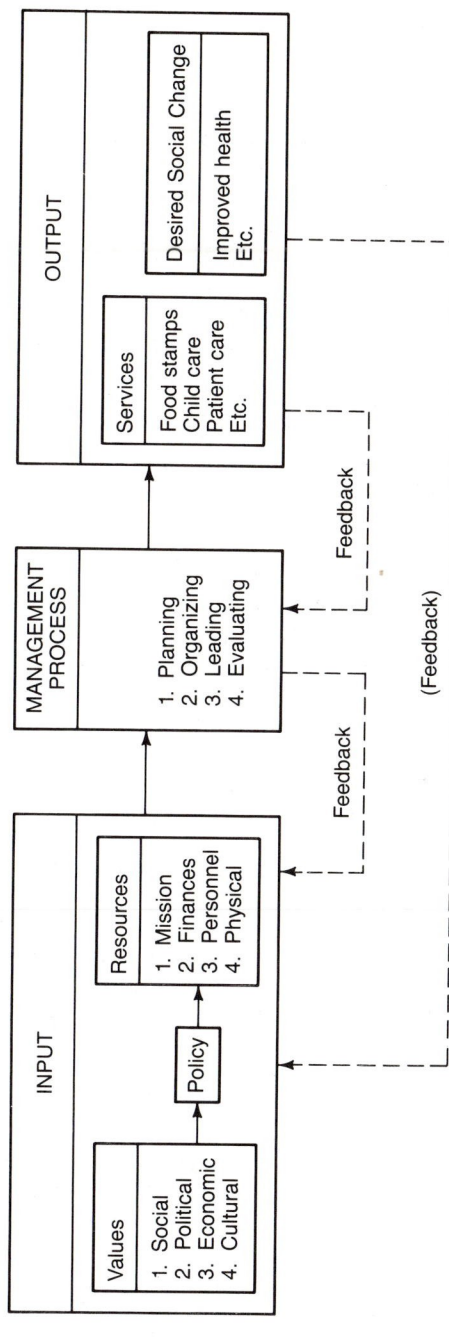

FIGURE 1-1 The Management System

WHAT DO MANAGERS DO?

The manager's primary responsibility is to coordinate the work of others, not to personally perform tasks. On some occasions the manager will perform tasks, but success as a manager does not depend primarily upon knowledge or skills in the field being managed. Rather, the manager is concerned with the functioning of the organization. The manager is responsible for creating an environment that will enable subordinates to achieve agency goals efficiently and in a personally rewarding manner. How well that environment is designed and maintained will determine the ultimate success or failure of an agency. The environment, at minimum, must provide individuals within the organization with (1) an understanding of agency goals and objectives and (2) an understanding of how they and their jobs contribute to the accomplishment of those goals and objectives. In addition, the environment must contain a system to motivate individuals to maintain a high level of performance. The statements of mission or objectives found in policy pronouncements are customarily broad statements of purpose with which the majority can agree. For example, the purpose of a public policy may be to provide superior health care to every citizen. That statement, while laudable, is not very operational. With that as your only guide, you could not be expected to move very far toward its accomplishment. It is up to the manager to clarify and develop operational objectives toward which everyone can work. Further, the manager must ensure that the statements of objectives are clearly understood by all individuals involved in the pursuit of those objectives. We encourage managers to enlist the input of subordinates in the formulation of goals and objectives. The more subordinates are involved in this process, the more committed they become to working toward the accomplishment of the agency's stated objectives.

It is crucial that management ensure that all individuals and units within the organization understand the overall goals and objectives of the organization. They must also be made aware of how they as individual units fit into the master scheme. This requires that a set of subgoals be established that, when taken together, will result in the accomplishment of the larger organizational mission. Each person in the system should be provided with a set of clear and verifiable objectives against which his or her performance will be measured. Similarly, the manager must ensure that each individual has the necessary information and a scope of authority to perform the tasks assigned.

The management environment should create a setting in which individuals strive to achieve the organization's goals and objectives because they have accepted them as their own. In short, the manager must focus on an individual's knowledge, skills, talents, and aspirations toward the accomplishment of the organizational mission. A tall order, indeed!

How does the manager accomplish those goals and objectives? To answer that question, we will have to look at the roles a manager fulfills, the activities that occupy a manager's workday, and the functions a manager must direct.

THE ROLES OF THE MANAGER

The human service manager has many identities. Henry Mintzberg (1973) has identified ten separate roles that a manager is likely to be called upon to perform (pp. 55–99). He has delineated three interpersonal roles, three informational roles, and four decisional roles.[1]

Interpersonal Roles

The figurehead role.   As the head of an organization or a unit within the organization, a manager must perform some duties of a ceremonial nature. The presentation of a gold watch to a long-service employee is an illustration of this role behavior.

The leader role.   In this role the manager is responsible for ensuring that the people assigned to the unit perform in a satisfactory manner. As leader the manager must motivate and encourage subordinates to achieve organizational goals.

The liaison role.   In this role the manager is concerned with establishing an external information and mutual assistance system.

Informational Roles

The monitor role.   Here the manager receives and filters information useful to the organization. The information flows both from the formal organizational communications network and from the external information system developed in the liaison role.

The disseminator role.   In this role the manager transfers important information that has been gathered to subordinates who would not otherwise have access to that information.

The spokesman role.   The manager, in this role, speaks on behalf of the organization or organizational unit to the external environment. This may be a reporting session with the superior, or it may be a speech to the local Rotary Club.

Decisional Roles

The entrepreneur role.   Through decisions to implement new programs or to change existing procedures, the manager acts as an entrepreneur.

---

[1]List and adapted definitions of Ten roles of Management from *The Nature of Managerial Work* by Henry Mintzberg. Copyright © 1973 by Henry Mintzberg. Reprinted by permission of Harper & Row, Publishers, Inc.

The disturbance handler role.   In any organization some situations have the potential of becoming crises. The manager must respond to such situations.

The resource allocator role.   The manager must decide how resources will be allocated among the various unit functions within the organization.

The negotiator role.   No organization or unit within the organization is self-sustaining or "an island, entire of itself." Every unit must interface with other parts of the organization as well as with outside forces. The manager is responsible for the negotiations that maintain the proper environment with those other units or external forces.

It is obvious that while these ten roles must be performed by any manager, they cannot be separated and neatly placed in a logbook. The manager may perform several of the functions simultaneously. For example, when a bureau chief is having lunch with a group of peers and the topic of next year's budget comes up, is the bureau chief acting as liaison, monitor, resource allocator, or negotiator? It is quite likely that the chief is performing all of those roles. This suggests yet another approach for understanding the task of management, the manager's tasks or activities.

ACTIVITIES OF MANAGERS

A second way to better understand the job of a manager is to view how managers spend their time—that is, to look at the specific tasks that compose the job of manager. The following discussion illustrates what the human service managers do as they carry out their job responsibilities. Rino J. Patti (1977) has reported on the activities of ninety social welfare managers in the state of Washington. He has categorized thirteen functional groupings of managerial activity, which are presented in Table 1-1 together with the average number of hours per week spent in each activity.

In addition to asking the respondents how they spent their time, Patti asked each manager to rank the activities in order of importance to the effective performance of the manager's job. He reported several findings as particularly significant. For example, "Over two thirds of the managers in this sample judged activities subsumed under controlling, supervising, and planning as the most important ones they had performed during the prior week. Somewhat less than one half of the respondents ranked coordinating as significant, while one quarter or less of the managers felt that activities associated with representing, information processing, direct practice, and evaluating were important to effective job performance" (p. 8). It can be seen from Table 1-1 that the three activities ranked most significant—planning, controlling, and supervising—occupied approximately 40 percent of these managers' time each week. That statistic, however, masks the fact that each manager engaged in a wide variety of tasks and activities throughout the survey week. A chief requirement in the job of manager is

**TABLE 1-1.   Mean Hours Spent in Each
Activity by Managers**

ACTIVITY	MEAN HOURS
Planning	3.9
Information processing	6.2
Controlling	5.4
Coordinating	3.8
Evaluating	1.5
Negotiating	.7
Representing	1.8
Staffing	.9
Supervising	6.7
Supplying	.3
Extracurricular	1.9
Direct practice	4.1
Budgeting	1.0

Source: R. J. Patti, "Patterns of Management
Activity in Social Welfare Agencies," *Admin-
istration in Social Work* (New York: The Haworth
Press, Spring 1977), p. 7.

the ability to deal with and adjust to rapid change from one task or activity
to another. To provide insight into the breadth of activity subsumed under
the thirteen categories, Table 1-2 presents a summary of the specific activities engaged in by a typical manager in the performance of the major
functions.

So far, we have approached the topic of management from the per-
spectives of managerial characteristics and activities. The intent has been to
provide an overview of the nature of the management process. With that in
mind, let's turn our attention to the processes that constitute management—planning, organizing, leading, and controlling. The intent is to provide a brief overview of each of those areas; a more in-depth treatment of
them will follow throughout the text.

Planning

In a very real sense, planning may be considered the essence of management. Planning is the initial step or function performed by an
administrator.

Plans are the means by which managers extend and make operational
the mission stated in a social or organizational policy. This planning function may be dichotomized into the broad categories of strategic planning
and operational planning. Strategic planning is customarily carried out at
the highest administrative level within an agency. It begins with the determination of the major objectives of the organization. In that context, an
objective is the specific target an agency must achieve in order to continue
to exist. Included in strategic plans are matters such as the types of service
to be provided, type and number of personnel necessary to provide those

TABLE 1-2. Categories of Management Activity

Planning	Determining goals, policies, and courses of action. For example: strategy setting, staff work scheduling, grant development.
Information processing	Time spent in communicating information (reading, writing, compiling, telephoning), where the manager or interviewer was unable to specify the function those activities filled.
Controlling	Collecting and analyzing information as to how the total operation of major segments of the organization are progressing.
Coordinating	Exchanging information with persons within or outside the agency other than subordinates or superiors in order to relate and adjust programs.
Evaluating	Assessing and appraising proposals and reported or observed performance.
Negotiating	Conferring, bargaining, or discussing with a view to reaching an agreement with another party.
Representing	Advancing the interests of the agency through contacts with individuals, groups, or constituencies outside the organization.
Staffing	Recruiting, interviewing, hiring, and promoting staff.
Supervising	Obtaining space, equipment, supplies, and other nonfinancial resources required for the work of the agency.
Extracurricular	Activities done during the workweek that would not be a part of a job description, such as partisan political activity or attending classes.
Direct service	Giving counseling, treatment, or advice directly to a client.
Budgeting	Planning expenditures and allocating resources among items in the budget.

Source: R. J. Patti et al., *Educating for Management in Social Welfare* (unpublished report, The University of Washington), p. 17.

services, capital expenditures, and costs associated with each of those activities. Strategic plans tend to be long-range and are stated mainly in broad terms to provide coordination of the various elements composing the organization. The outputs of strategic planning are statements of principles that constitute guides for movement toward the accomplishment of agency objectives. We call those statements of principles *policies*. Policies act as guideposts for decision making throughout the organization.

Operational planning, on the other hand, involves the translation of objective statements and policy guidelines into action statements. This type of planning has a much shorter time frame than strategic planning, usually one year or less, and is conducted by middle- and lower-level managers. Operational plans are derived from the objectives or strategic plans originating with the upper levels of management. They are concerned with definite actions that must be taken in order to accomplish the goals established for the unit by the strategic plan.

Operational plans, then, provide the specific program direction necessary to carry out policy statements. Examples of these types of plans are found in documents such as procedure manuals, rules, and the unit's budget.

Whether one is attempting to develop an agencywide strategy or a plan of action for next week, the rudiments of the planning process are the same. According to Grover Starling (1982),

> A planner would be acting rationally if he/she undertook five interrelated steps:
>
> 1. Identify the problems to be solved and the opportunities to be seized upon.
> 2. Design alternative solutions or courses of action (i.e., policies, plans, and programs) to solve the problems or seize upon the opportunities and forecast the consequences and effectiveness of each alternative.
> 3. Compare and evaluate the alternatives with each other and with the forecasted consequences of unplanned development and choose the alternative whose probable consequences would be preferable.
> 4. Develop a plan of action for implementing the alternative selected, including budgets, project schedules, regulatory measures, and the like.
> 5. Maintain the plan on a current basis through feedback and review of information.[2]

This sequence describes a process not too unlike the one you and your family face when attempting to decide upon a vacation trip. First, you must consider each family member's preferences, for example, beach versus mountains. Second, you must choose the goals to be accomplished by the trip, for example, rest and relaxation or sightseeing and activity. Third, you must consider the basic premises affecting the final decision, for example, length of vacation possible. Fourth, you must identify and compare vacation alternatives that will satisfy the goals set to determine the best choice, that is, which vacation plan will satisfy the greatest number of family members. Next, you must select the actual trip to be taken, and then formulate supporting plans, for example, develop an itinerary, purchase needed materials, make reservations. Finally, during and after the vacation, all members of the family will evaluate the plan for future vacation planning.

Organizing

The plans discussed in the previous section result in a "road map," leading the agency toward the objectives established by a social welfare policy. If that is the case, then the structure of the organization is the vehicle that transports the agency to the objective. Through the formal organizational structure, responsibility, authority, and accountability are allocated to individuals within the agency. Within the organizational structure each individual is made responsible for a group of tasks that constitute a job. Each individual is granted the authority to make decisions within the assigned area of responsibility. Finally, through the structure each indi-

---

[2]Grover Starling, *Managing the Public Sector*, rev. ed. (Homewood, Ill.: Dorsey, 1982). pp. 190–191.

vidual is made accountable to a higher authority for the results achieved in the performance of the job.

From this it may be concluded that the initial task of organizing consists of determining what activities will constitute a basic job. Once again, it should be noted that the activities to be performed must flow from the basic objectives set for the agency. The collection of activities or tasks that we describe as a job then becomes the foundation of organizing.

Following the grouping of activities or tasks into jobs, a framework must be constructed to specify the relationships between those elements. That is, jobs must be grouped so that the performance of each of the specialized activities fits into a "chain of command," in which responsibility, authority, and accountability are understood.

Organizationally, the agency will have a wide choice of patterns that will accomplish this organizational framework. For example, a functional pattern may be chosen that logically reflects occupational specialization. Under this pattern all jobs containing like activities are placed in the same department, for example, all fiscal activities. A second structural pattern may group all jobs related to the same service program into the same department. For example, all personnel related to providing day care for children of working mothers may be grouped into one department. Another possibility is to base the pattern of organization on the location of a given set of activities, for example, a county welfare department. Yet another structure might be the organization of the agency by client group. All child-care activities, for example, may be placed in a single department.

These structural patterns, while not constituting all the available organizational forms, are representative examples of useful bases for developing effective and efficient work structures. In practice, you are likely to find a mixture of the patterns within any given agency. You may find functional grouping at the statewide level and client grouping at the local level. In the final analysis, the form of organizational structure will depend on the pragmatic consideration of workability.

Whatever the pattern of structure selected, it must clearly establish for each individual within the organization the flow of authority and responsibility, while ensuring accountability of each person for his or her performance of organizational tasks.

Leadership and Direction

The two previous sections have shown us that the plan provides the organization with a map of its objectives and that the structure provides the transportation to the objective. In this section, we will see that it is leadership that provides the energy to reach the organization's goals.

The difference between simply "minding the store" and actively striving to achieve goals is the level of motivation found among the personnel in the organization. The administrator, through his or her abilities as a manager-leader, has the responsibility of motivating employees to strive for high performance. Thus, the manager-leader must understand the factors that influence human work behavior.

Managers must think about the people within their organizations, but they must also think of the goals to be attained. Managerial leadership, then, may be defined, as it is by Starling (1982), as "the process of influencing the activities of a group in efforts toward goal attainment in a given situation. The key elements in this definition are leader, followers, and situation" (p. 430). Those three variables interact to affect leader behavior and may result in a variety of styles. Tannenbaum (1981) has posited a leadership style continuum (see Figure 1-2) that varies from a task-oriented, highly autocratic style to a people-oriented, highly participative style. The factors of leader, follower, and situation will indicate where on this continuum an individual manager is likely to fall.

The leader's actions at any given time are influenced by his or her own personality and the environment. Since the manager often deals with uncertain situations, the manager's own feelings of security about his or her position will influence leadership style. The leader's feelings of security also influence the level of confidence placed in subordinates. The higher the level of confidence, the higher the degree of freedom granted subordinates. Similarly, the leader's own philosophy of leadership will affect the type of leadership. The leader, for example, who believes subordinates to be naturally lazy will likely be much more authoritarian and directive than the leader who believes subordinates have a high degree of commitment and a natural inclination to achieve work goals. The latter manager is more likely to permit subordinates a greater area of freedom and to be more participative in leadership style.

The follower is also influenced by personality and environment. Each

FIGURE 1-2 Leadership Style Continuum. From R. Tannenbaum et al., *Leadership and Organization: A Behavioral Approach* (New York: McGraw-Hill, 1961), p. 69. Reproduced by permission of the publisher.

| Manager makes decision, announces it. | Manager sells decision. | Manager presents ideas, invites questions. | Manager presents tentative decision, subject to change. | Manager presents problems, gets suggestions, makes decision. | Manager defines limits, asks group to make decision. | Manager permits subordinates to function within limits, defined supervision. |

of us responds to direction in a different way. Some subordinates have a relatively high need for structure and do not wish to take responsibility for making decisions; they prefer to remain dependent upon the leader. Others, however, feel a high degree of identification with the organization and feel they possess the ability to deal with most situations. The latter type of subordinate is likely to be very receptive to a democratic leadership style and to reject the highly authoritarian style.

Situational factors influence leader behavior. The number of individuals involved in a problem requiring action will affect the degree of participation possible. For example, it is unlikely that even the most democratic leader could consult with two hundred field staff about a new program. The pressure of time is also likely to increase the degree of authoritarianism in leadership style. In a crisis, it is more difficult to involve others. Geographic proximity and the ease with which people can interact also are situational variables that affect the style of leadership. Widely dispersed units or highly mechanized kinds of operations make interaction difficult and thereby reduce the chance for participative decision making.

Evaluation and Control

Throughout the discussion of administration, we have placed great emphasis upon ensuring that each activity is consistent with the objectives and goals of the agency. How are we to ascertain the extent to which those objectives are being attained? How are we to determine if an alternative program might improve overall service delivery? How are we to provide flexibility in service delivery to meet the changing needs of clients? How are we to respond to the legislative call for accountability? The answer to each of those questions is, through evaluation and control systems.

A primary problem facing all administrators is how to determine the extent to which their units are accomplishing what they were established to do. A good program evaluation system, coupled with adequate managerial control, is an essential element of the administrative system. Such a system contains four critical elements: establishing standards of performance, information gathering, information analysis, and deviation correction.

Establishing standards for performance involves translating the goal or goals of a program into measurable indicators of success. Care must be taken to ensure that indicators are developed for all identifiable outcomes, both those intended and those not intended. For example, the goal of increasing client purchasing power by 50 percent may have the unintended consequence of increasing price levels, thereby negating the higher income. Unless both of these indicators are considered in evaluating the program, incorrect conclusions will result. A second major factor to be considered is that the goals of many social programs tend to be ambiguous and, therefore, create difficulties in establishing measurable standards. The temptation is great in such cases to substitute hunches and unsupported claims for more objective criteria. That temptation must be resisted if we are to improve the operation of social welfare delivery systems.

The compilation, analysis, and comparison of information necessary to evaluation make use of most of the commonly used research methods. Information for analysis may be collected from a wide variety of sources, including budgets, published statistics, client records, and interviews. Similarly, there is a wide variety of experimental designs and statistical techniques available for the purposes of evaluation. A word of caution is necessary. Many times, the evaluator is faced with "information overkill" and must pause to evaluate the contribution of given bits of information. For example, the manager may put a great deal of time and effort into the accumulation of very precise financial data related to supplies purchased for a program, only to discover that total funds expended on supplies account for less than one percent of total costs. In such a situation, the costs of supplies contribute little to the evaluation of the program. Similarly, the sophistication of the statistical tests performed in evaluation should be comparable to the level of sophistication of the information being measured. Again, much time and expensive effort can be spent in performing intricate and complex statistical comparisons that add little to our basic understanding of the program being evaluated.

The final and, perhaps, key element in the evaluation process is that of correction. It must be remembered that evaluation is a tool of management control and, as such, should result in improved program administration. Finding out what is wrong with a unit or program is meaningless unless such knowledge is used to correct the problem and improve the service. It is in this way that evaluation is a means of control. It controls the movement of the organization toward the objective by providing the information to correct the course when there is deviation from the planned progress toward the objective.

Implementation and Decision Making

Throughout our discussion of the administrative process we assumed an important element—implementation. A plan must be placed in operation; organizational structure requires decision; leadership implies direction; and evaluation must lead to action. Thus, the decision-making ability of an administrator-manager weighs most heavily in the ultimate success of the organization.

Managerial decision making, like any situation requiring problem solving, contains four basic elements. First, the manager must assess the situation and find the element that needs action. This requires an investigation into the causes of unsatisfactory performance to determine what outcome is necessary to determine a satisfactory solution. Second, the manager must formulate alternative solutions that may yield the desired outcome. The third step in the decision-making process is the analysis of the alternatives. This analysis may range from a simple listing of the advantages and disadvantages of each alternative to highly sophisticated mathematical formulations. The final critical element in decision making is the choice and implementation of a solution. This involves putting together a definite plan of attack and communicating it to all those with a role in the implementation.

A Final Word

As you consider and weigh what has been discussed, you may question if it can be done. Certainly, you know of some managers who have achieved a measure of skill in fulfilling their managerial and organizational responsibilities, and, indeed, you know of some who have failed. Is success a realistic expectation? We suggest that it is and that the organization's success is directly related to its management. Simply, managers can make or break the organization. Those human service organizations that are characterized as successful are those that have effective managers. Keep in mind that management does not occur in a vacuum. It occurs within the organizational context. Let's consider one way of looking at that relationship.

MANAGERIAL EFFECTIVENESS
AND ORGANIZATIONAL SUCCESS

In their recent book, Peters and Waterman (1982) report on their findings after studying several organizations throughout the country. They propose that those organizations that were most successful were those that met the following criteria:[3]

1. A bias for action
2. Close to the customer
3. Autonomy and entrepreneurship
4. Productivity through people
5. Hands on, value driven
6. Stick to the knitting
7. Simple form, lean staff
8. Simultaneous loose-tight properties (pp. 13–16)

Let's briefly look at each of the eight criteria and consider its application to the human service organization.

A Bias for Action

Basically, this means getting on with it. How often managers within human service organizations are prone to delay action by forming a committee to "study" the matter. Rather than being a creative and innovative device, all too frequently the committee gets bogged down in minutiae and the committee's meetings become an end rather than a means to an end. What is suggested is that there is a need for action—to keep moving rather

---

[3]List and adapted definitions of Eight attributes from *In Search of Excellence: Lessons from America's Best-Run Companies* by Thomas J. Peters and Robert H. Waterman. Copyright © 1982 by Thomas J. Peters and Robert H. Waterman. Reprinted by permission of Harper & Row, Publishers, Inc.

than holding to the status quo. Obviously, there will be occasions when the "action" will be in error, but most of the time such situations are not irreversible. Necessary in meeting the criterion of action are open lines of communication. If there are such, the likelihood of making major errors is reduced.

Close to the Customer

It is necessary for human service organizations and the managers within the organizations to keep in touch with those who use the services provided. It is not enough to take the position that "we know what is best" for the clients or patients. Managers should provide the opportunity for the recipients of the services to react to and have a say in decisions. Listen to what they have to offer. If managers are more responsive to what the recipients have to say, it can prevent a number of problems. Clients and patients want and deserve quality service, and by listening to them, management can get a better feel for the quality of the service being delivered.

Autonomy and Entrepreneurship

The human service manager should allow decision making to be spread throughout the organization. One person cannot do it all. The only way to develop individuals throughout the organization who are able to make decisions is to give them authority along with responsibility. They will make mistakes, but it is by taking risks that people learn. As the manager encourages and practices decision making, he or she will allow others to be creative and innovative, and that can only lead to more successful organizational performance.

Productivity through People

The human resources of any organization are its most critical asset. The human service organization is no different. Successful managers recognize that and treat people throughout the organization with respect. Those who work in the organization can either support or undermine what the organization is seeking to accomplish. The greater the awareness of that reality, the greater the probability of success. As mentioned before, people will make mistakes, but that should not lead to castigating the individual; practice the golden rule of management: "Do unto your subordinates as you would have them do unto you."

Hands On, Value Driven

Managers need to be seen. It might be more comfortable to hide behind a secretary and closed doors, but such behavior is counterproductive. Managers who recognize the need to be seen and to be involved from time to time with those throughout the organization will be more successful. By keeping in touch, the manager conveys to the workers that he or she cares about what they are doing. Further, by such activity the manager can be aware of the extent to which the basic philosophy of the organization is being carried out. For example, if the manager is attempting to convey to the line workers the need to treat clients and patients with respect and to deliver quality service, what better way to see if that is happening than by getting out of the office and observing?

Stick to the Knitting

Human service organizations ought to do what they know best. It is management's responsibility to keep the organization on track as to where priorities and emphases should be placed. It is easy to be seduced by the possibility of obtaining additional funding by moving off into an area that is new and foreign. The result might well be catastrophic failure and can lead to compromising the integrity of the organization. Hospitals should focus on patient care and let the social service organizations deal with the other areas of need that a patient may have. We do not mean to imply that organizations should not seek new ways to be creative. What we are suggesting is that you should stay in your own ballpark.

Simple Form, Lean Staff

There is much to be said for keeping the structure of the organization simple. One of the most significant advantages of a simple structure and the corresponding lean staff is that communication is enhanced and decisions can be made more quickly and easily. The more layers communication has to go through, the greater the chance for distortion and miscommunication and, similarly, the longer it takes for a decision to be made. As resources become more scarce, managers will bear the burden of streamlining the structure and reducing the number of staff needed to carry out the mission of the organization. The payoff to this is the potential for increased efficiency and effectiveness.

Simultaneous Loose-Tight Properties

To be effective, the human service organization must find a balance between centralization and decentralization. As we have already mentioned, autonomy should be spread throughout the organization, thus leading to a decentralized format for decision making. At the same time, areas must be centralized. For example, if there is an organizational and management commitment to quality service, then there is no room for compromise or deviation. That particular orientation comes from the top down, and all employees throughout the organization must subscribe to it.

These eight criteria form the nucleus for a well-run, successful human service organization. They are not meant to be hard-and-fast rules; rather, they suggest a formula for success. The more managers pay attention to what has been discussed, the greater the likelihood that the outcome will be efficient, effective, and responsive service delivery to the recipient groups.

PLAN OF THE BOOK

This book does not follow the traditional format of management textbooks. Many texts deal with the sequential flow of management functions such as planning, organizing, staffing, directing, coordinating, reporting, budgeting, and evaluation. Other management books focus on the behaviors of individuals and groups within the organizational environment. What we seek to do is combine the two approaches by integrating those managerial behaviors and the functions of management and focusing upon the roles into which the manager is cast according to his or her responsibilities.

To accomplish that objective the authors have divided the text into four major parts. First, we will set out the basic environmental and structural concepts of the human service organization, dealing first with the relationship between the organization and societal values and mores, followed by discussion of the basic structural considerations of the organization. The remainder of the text is organized around the format provided by Mintzberg (1973) in his study of the roles of a manager. We direct the reader's attention to the interpersonal roles of the manager. In that section we combine the roles of figurehead and spokesperson and also discuss the roles of leader and liaison. The basic functions of staffing, leadership, motivation, and coordination will be dealt with in that section. Next, we focus on the informational roles of monitor and disseminator. We then introduce the reader to the decisional roles—entrepreneur, disturbance handler, resource allocator, and negotiator. The discussions of these roles include the basic functional skills associated with their performance. The final section of the book includes several cases that have been selected for their relevance to the substance of managerial performance.

REFERENCES

DRUCKER, P. F. (1973). *Management: Tasks, responsibilities, practices.* New York: Harper & Row.

MASSIE, J. L. (1971). *Essentials of management.* Englewood Cliffs, N.J.: Prentice-Hall.

MINTZBERG, H. (1973). *The nature of managerial work.* New York: Harper & Row.

PATTI, R. J. (1977, Spring). Patterns of management activity in social welfare agencies. *Administration in Social Work,* pp. 5–17.

PETERS, T. J., & WATERMAN, R. H., JR. (1982). *In search of excellence: Lessons from America's best-run companies.* New York: Harper & Row.

SISK, H. L. (1977). *Management and organization* (3rd ed.). Cincinnati: South-Western.

STARLING, G. (1982). *Managing the public sector* (rev. ed.). Homewood, Ill.: Dorsey.

TANNENBAUM, R., ET AL. (1961). *Leadership and organization: A behavorial approach.* New York: McGraw-Hill.

QUESTIONS FOR DISCUSSION

1. Why should administrators be concerned with social, political, economic, and cultural values? Is it not likely that those things have already received enough attention in the policy formulation and planning process?

2. The authors state that administration is a cooperative venture with staff. In your experience, is that statement a fair description of the true state of affairs?

3. Do you agree that administrators should generally not provide direct services to clients or patients? Would it not make sense for administrators to "get their hands dirty" with some of the work of the agency?

4. Evaluate Mintzberg's ten administrative roles. Can you add to the list?

5. React to Patti's finding that 40 percent of the manager's time is spent in planning, controlling, and supervising. Does that use of time seem appropriate?

6. Of the styles discussed, what kind of leadership seems most appropriate in social agencies? Why?

7. Discuss the implications of the authors' idea that evaluation is a means of improving program administration. What are the positive aspects of evaluation? In what ways can evaluation be misused?

8. Could health and welfare agencies operate without administrators? What kind of an organizational structure would be possible if there were no administrators or managers?

SUGGESTED PROJECTS

1. Using the Mintzberg model of roles, discuss and analyze the managerial functions of a selected administrator in a human service agency.

2. Propose and discuss an administrative system for a local human service organization.

The Organizational Context

chapter *2*

The major purpose of management is to make certain that the organization fulfills the purpose for which it is established. The focus of the manager's concern, therefore, must be on the organization rather than on a single activity or small group of activities. This holistic approach requires that each manager develop a broad understanding of the organizational environment, both internal and external, and ensure that his or her activities, as well as those of subordinates, are consistent with the organization's activities.

In this chapter we will develop a framework for the analysis and understanding of the organizational contexts of the human service activity. We will explore the macroconcepts that affect the structural and design aspects of the organization. The chapter will close with a discussion of the specific organizational strategies used by operating agencies. Both discussions will be organized around the major factors that directly affect the philosophy and style of management within the human service organization.

A DEFINITION

Miles (1980) defines an organization as "a coalition of interest groups, sharing a common resource base, paying homage to a common mission, and depending upon a larger context for its legitimacy and development" (p. 5). Subsumed within this definition are the four major considerations necessary to the understanding of the operation of the human service agency. First, every organization is established with a central purpose, such as the elimination of poverty, the improvement of health care, or the protection of society. Those broad statements of purpose must then be translated into specific goals for the agency. Second, the organization is composed of individuals and groups whose responsibility is the fulfillment of the established goals. Third, the organization exists in a larger community upon which it depends for its ultimate continuance. Finally, the organization represents a system with rules for the distribution of resources, both internally and externally.

Organizational Goals

Every agency derives its legitimacy from its formally stated goals. These may be stated through legislation in the case of a public agency or by charter in the case of a private organization. The purpose of the formal statement is to provide boundaries within which the organization may legally operate. Thus, the goal statement gives direction to the members of the organization and limits their scope of activity to an intended purpose. Theoretically, all the members of the organization accept and are committed to the ultimate goals of the agency.

The formally stated goals are often misleading in their simplicity. For example, the formal goal of a hospital may be to "provide quality patient care." The question the hospital must then answer is, How will this goal be reached? In short, whose definition of the goal will be accepted—the physicians', the nurses', the administrators', the patients'? Each organizational subgroup may have a different interpretation of the appropriate strategy for accomplishing the ultimate goal of the hospital. For example, the doctors may deem it essential to provide a wide range of care, requiring sophisticated equipment. On the other hand, the administrator, concerned with rising costs, may seek to limit the range of care by narrowly defining the patient group.

As suggested previously, within every organization the formal goals, which are typically long-range, must be given operational meaning through the establishment of more short-term goals. Many times, the relationship between the formal and the operational goals may be relatively ambiguous, creating uncertainty and placing upon the manager a responsibility "for giving leadership to the matter of defining, redefining, interpreting, and utilizing agency purposes as guides for programs and services" (Trecker, 1971, p. 25). This task requires an understanding of the other factors influencing the organization.

Organizational Participants

Talcott Parsons (1960) provides a convenient scheme for the analysis of participants in the human service organization. He delineates three subgroups within the organization, each with a somewhat different perspective and approach.

The first of Parsons's subgroups is the institutional component. Its primary focus is upon the external environment. That is, it is concerned with relating the agency to the larger community. Internally, it is concerned with the development of policies and programs necessary to meet the needs of the larger community. Since those activities require a consensus among diverse groups, the modus operandi of the institutional subgroup centers on negotiations and the development and use of political skills. Philosophically, its concern is to achieve equity among the various publics associated with the agency. For example, the commissioner of a state welfare agency must give attention to the state and federal legislatures, from which the agency receives both its legitimacy (legislatively mandated goals) and the funds necessary to carry out the mission of the agency. Further, the commissioner must balance the concerns of the larger community with those of specific client groups in the development of specific agency policies and programs. In summary, the institutional component, in the terms of the systems concept developed in Chapter 1, focuses its attention primarily upon the inputs of the system, since they are derived from the external community.

The second subgroup identified by Parsons is the technical component, whose primary responsibility is to dispense services offered by the agency. The primary focus of this subgroup is the client and the provision of professional services to the client. Philosophically, it is primarily committed to a professional discipline rather than to a particular agency or organization. Generally, it is more attuned to a collegial form of organization and feels that the decision-making apparatus of the organization should focus upon the professional services needed by a particular client group. Further, the standards of service should be determined by "standards of the profession" rather than through control mechanisms set up by the organization.

Management, the third subgroup in Parsons's scheme, has the organizational responsibility to provide a link between the institutional and the technical components. Thus, its responsibilities are to interpret policies flowing from the institutional subgroup and to allocate resources among the various service delivery units. Within the systems concept the managerial concern is principally with the transformation process.

The External Environment

Each human service organization exists in a unique environment; however, several factors external to the organization influence the agency's operations. Those factors include current social mores and values, current political practice, the current state of economic activity, and the influence of client groups. All those factors are interrelated, yet an understanding of each will aid the astute manager in attempting to cope with the external environment.

American society has a long tradition of concern for needy people, but the approach to providing human services has varied tremendously as American society has developed. At any given time the attitudes prevalent in society with respect to the human service activity provide a setting within which the human service organization exists. From the standpoint of the organization, the changes in society's values provide a degree of uncertainty. For example, during the 1960s there was strong societal support for the so-called War on Poverty and, as a result, human service activities grew and prospered. On the other hand, the movement toward conservatism, which gained strength in the early 1980s, led to decreasing emphasis on those activities, and fewer of society's resources were devoted to the human services. That period of change resulted in increased uncertainty and substantial changes in approach among agencies.

The general public's wishes are partially fulfilled through the political process; thus, that process becomes an important facet of the external environment for the organization. The political process, through legislation, interprets and gives specific meaning to the perceived desires of the majority. Many times, the link between legislation and the desires of the majority is tenuous and at times may appear to be contrary to the voiced consensus of the general populace. Since the political apparatus operates at different levels (federal, state, local) and through various branches (executive, legislative, judicial), each level or branch may have a somewhat different interpretation of societal desires. For example, early in the Reagan administration the decision was made to reduce the level of funding for federally sponsored human service activities and to rely more upon the private sector to provide needed services. State and local governments varied in their response to that federal action, some choosing to follow the lead of the federal government and others increasing state or local support for government-sponsored programs. Such actions mean that the manager in an agency must be attentive to all aspects of the political process.

The economic system provides the resources that enable society to provide any level of human services. The factors that affect the economy, therefore, also have an impact on the agency manager. During periods of inflation, the costs of service delivery increase, and a corresponding dollar of direct aid is worth less to the recipient. During periods of recession, society is able to afford less of all services and is likely to seek a reduction in expenditures on human service functions. This presents the human service manager with a paradoxical situation, since recession is accompanied by increased demand upon the organization at a time when resources are typically at a low ebb.

A fourth environmental element influencing the work of the human service manager is that of the ultimate consumer. Is the consumer the client who receives direct aid, or the taxpayers who provide the funds, or some other special interest group? The answer to that question may seem intuitively obvious, but the manager must examine the facts of operation carefully before taking action. The answer lies in determining who are the primary beneficiaries of the services of the organization. A shift in this focus of the organization will result in changed patterns of influence and resource allocation among groups within the organization. For example, consider the situation of institutions for the mentally retarded. Historically, society viewed the role of such organizations as custodial. Under that environmentally imposed goal the dominant force within the institution was the medical staff. With a shift in emphasis to a goal of "normalization and deinstitutionalization," the primary beneficiary became the client. Thus, special education, psychology, nursing, and social work became major forces of the internal organization, creating new pressures upon both the organization and the community.

The System of Rules

Every organization exists within a system of rules that govern its operation. For example, there are systems for resource allocation, there are standards of service, and there are criteria for eligibility, all of which affect the job of the human service manager. The effective manager will be aware of both the present system of rules and the process by which those rules are made or altered. For example, the director of a department of public welfare needs to have a working knowledge of the political process involved in legislative action. He or she must be aware of the committee structure, the relationship between the executive and the legislative branches, the prevailing attitudes among legislators toward the agency, and so on. If it is a state agency, the director must also be familiar with the federal processes, both legislative and administrative.

THE IMPACT ON THE MANAGER

The forces discussed in the previous section are not independent variables; rather, they interact and change over time to affect the human service manager. For example, during the 1960s the external environment was such that it dictated an expansion of all types of human services. Thus, the goal structure, the participant groups, and the system of rules were in general agreement. That consistency eased the task for managers, allowing them to concentrate upon the traditional managerial concerns of coordination and control. With the change toward greater conservatism during the 1970s, however, basic changes occurred that complicated management's tasks. The external environment began calling for greater accountability from agencies and sought to reduce the level of resources devoted to providing human services. Those demands led the institutional subgroup to seek basic changes in both the number of services offered and the ways that those services were provided. That placed the subgroup in direct conflict with the technical component, which maintained its traditional concern for professional standards. In that situation, management was faced with the additional problem of accommodating what appears to be irreconcilable views. To cope with such situations, management must develop strategies for reducing the uncertainty faced by the organization.

ORGANIZATIONAL COPING STRATEGIES

As management scans the environment and identifies the sources of uncertainty for the organization, it must decide upon a strategic response. The responses of human service organizations to environmental uncertainty may be grouped into two broad categories: organizational definition and organizational design.

Defining the Organization

The human service organization may deal with environmental uncertainty through the definition of its service domain. As Miles et al. (1974) point out, "An organization's domain consists of those activities it intends to pursue, and, in choosing a domain of activity, the organization simultaneously determines its pattern of interdependence with elements of the environment." Thus, the organization defines its environment by deciding what client groups it will serve, what services it will provide, and how those services will be delivered. For example, the American Cancer Society has defined a narrow environment through its attention to a particular malady, thereby reducing the degree of environmental uncertainty. Public organizations have sought to reduce uncertainty through regulation and legislation. For example, a state welfare agency is empowered by legislation to provide aid to families with dependent children, the extent of the aid to a particular family being governed by regulation.

The organization may also act to limit environmental uncertainty through the use of contracts and joint ventures. For example, the response of a state agency to the need for day-care services may be to establish contracted services. That assures that the service will exist, yet it reduces the state agency's uncertainty associated with the development of an in-house delivery system. Similarly, where it is unclear whether a program or service lies within an agency's domain, but where action is required, the agency may create a joint venture. For example, the uncertainty associated with fund-raising for community service agencies acting individually led to the creation of United Way as a joint venture.

A final response by human service organizations to environmental uncertainty is diversification. Faced with a high degree of uncertainty about a particular program or service, the organization may opt to expand activities into other areas. For example, the existence of the American Society for Crippled Children was threatened by the development of polio vaccine. Once the goal of developing a vaccine had been reached, the response of this group was to diversify and expand its concerns and services into other childhood-related conditions.

Organizational Design

A way organizations attempt to deal with uncertainty brought on by environmental dependencies is through organizational design and structure. Later in this chapter we will discuss in detail the concepts associated with the internal structuring of the human service organization. The concern of this section is with the environmental influences upon the process of design and the organizational responses to the uncertainty created by those factors.

"The basic effect of uncertainty is to limit the ability of the organization to preplan or to make decisions about activities in advance of their execution. Therefore it is hypothesized that the observed variations in organizational forms are variations in the strategies of organizations to (1) increase their ability to preplan, (2) increase their flexibility to adapt to their inability to preplan, or (3) decrease the level of performance required for continued viability" (Galbraith, 1974, p. 64).

As we shall see, many of the concepts of organizational structure are directed toward increasing the organization's ability to preplan its activities. Kotter (1979) suggests that "(1) organizations will usually create separate subunits to deal with each major source of external dependence, (2) they will generally staff and organize these subunits differently so that each is capable of effectively understanding and managing its environmental entity, and (3) they establish mechanisms for resolving conflicts among the different subunits, and thus for dealing with the conflicting demands made by those external entities they are dependent upon" (p. 90). The desired result of those activities is the ability to increase the preplanning of activities based upon the increased specialization and knowledge of the environment found within each of the subunits. For example, a general hospital will establish various units, such as surgery or intensive care, and will staff them with individuals possessing expertise in those specialties. Further, the hospital will maintain a mechanism for resolving conflicting demands from the various units. Since each unit is relatively self-contained, it should be able to more accurately determine its needs and the activities necessary to respond to the contextual environment it faces.

A second strategy for responding to uncertainty suggested by Galbraith is the creation of slack resources within the organization. Through this strategy the "organization increases its flexibility to respond to environmental demands by reducing the number and type of constraints placed upon the various subunits." Slack may take such forms as inflated budgets, reduced standards, and lengthened schedules for completion of tasks. For example, an agency starting a new adult services program may have a great deal of difficulty in projecting the extent of demand for such a program. To deal with the uncertainty, the initial budget may be established at the outside limits of expected demand.

Organizations may also deal with environmental uncertainty by increasing their capacity for processing available information. Within every organization there exists more information than typically can be effectively entered into the management process. Thus, by increasing its capacity to collect, store, analyze, and disseminate pertinent information, the organization decreases the uncertainty within its operations. The development of computer-based information systems (discussed in detail in Chapter 7) permits the organization to process a greater amount of information more rapidly, allowing improved data handling and decision making. For example, the public welfare system was long plagued with rumors and suspicions of fraud. It was not until the advent of sophisticated computer information systems, however, that the scope of the problem could be identified; then the problem began to be dealt with.

A final method employed by organizations to deal with environmental uncertainty is the creation of organization boundary roles. The activities performed by these roles, according to Miles (1980), include "(1) representing the organization to its external constituencies; (2) scanning and monitoring environmental events that are potentially threats; (3) protecting the organization from environmental threats; (4) information processing and gatekeeping; (5) transacting with other organizations for the acquisition of inputs and the disposal of outputs; and (6) linking and coordinating activities between organizations" (p. 320).

The representing role includes activities involved in the development of the "public face" of the organization. For example, the director of an agency may appoint a media representative, whose task is to create and maintain a favorable image of the agency. The scanning and monitoring function involves the identification of trends or anticipation of events that are likely to have an impact upon the organization. For example, a health-care planning unit has the responsibility for identifying new developments in health care and demographic changes in its area and for gathering information related to present health-care facilities as well as those that will be needed in the future. The "legislative-liaison" is responsible for monitoring the activities of the legislature to identify legislation that may be either potentially helpful or potentially harmful to the organization.

All human service organizations are subject to a number of environmental threats. Sanctions (such as loss of funds for failure to comply with eligibility requirements), penalties for not complying with affirmative action requirements, and so on are continuing threats to organizational safety. Organizations attempt to protect themselves from those sanctions by creating specialized functions whose purpose is to ensure that the organization is meeting its requirements. For example, the quality control division of a state welfare agency is charged with the task of monitoring how well the agency is complying with federal standards.

As we noted earlier, the quantity of information flowing into a complex organization can be enormous. In addition, the quality of information received by the organization may vary greatly. The organization may establish buffer roles to filter, interpret, and condense information to a useful form. While there are many gatekeeping mechanisms, a good example is the regional office structure. For example, the decision makers in the Department of Human Resources could not possibly deal with all the information from the vast number of agencies with whom they have a relationship. Thus, the ten regional offices serve, in part, as a mechanism for filtering, interpreting, and condensing information, which is then forwarded to the Washington office.

Organizations must acquire resources and expend resources on a regular basis. To facilitate those exchanges, they frequently establish transacting roles, which include the purchasing function, the grantsmanship function, and so on. The most critical transacting role in the human service organization, however, is that of the direct service provider. The direct service provider occupies the boundary between the client and the organization and is frequently called upon to resolve the conflict between the needs of the client and the needs of the agency. That is particularly difficult if the organizational objectives are not entirely compatible with the client's objectives.

Finally, boundary roles include the function of linking and coordinating. The proper functioning of many programs requires that two or more organizations combine, with each providing a piece of the program. For that to operate effectively, the organizations involved must develop and maintain strong working relationships. For example, the child support enforcement division has the responsibility for locating and dealing with the parent responsible for providing child support. To perform that function, however, the division needs the cooperation and support of other agencies—the police and the courts.

This discussion of boundary roles has treated them as though they are separate functions performed by different individuals. While that may often be the case, especially in large organizations, it is not always true. In a small agency one person may perform all the functions associated with the boundary role. Similarly, not all the boundary role functions will be required in all organizations.

THE ORGANIZATIONAL STRUCTURE

The discussion thus far has correctly implied that a formal set of relationships exists within the organization that facilitates the performance of necessary activities and functions. It is that structural arrangement of the organization that provides the context in which the managers perform their job of managing others. Management, by definition, is working through others to accomplish the overall purpose of the organization, and it is the organizational structure that outlines the relationships between the people and functions they perform that facilitate the accomplishment of organizational purpose. In the discussion of organizational structure we will concentrate on four possible forms: traditional (bureaucratic) and three more contemporary forms (matrix, System 4, and contingency designs).

Bureaucratic

The bureaucratic form of organization design is attributed to Max Weber. He believed that such a design would assure predictability of the behavior of the employees within the organization (Weber, 1947). He proposed the following design strategies, which would assure the precision, stability, reliability, and stringency of discipline required for optimum organizational performance:

1. All tasks necessary for the accomplishment of goals are divided into highly specialized jobs.
2. Each task is performed according to a system of rules covering the rights and duties of employment.

3. Each member or officer of the organization is accountable to a superior; thus there is a well-defined hierarchy of authority.

4. Each individual in a superior position carries out his or her responsibility in an impersonal, formalistic manner, thereby maintaining a social distance from the subordinates and clients.

5. Each member of the organization is selected and promoted on the basis of technical competence and is protected from arbitrary dismissal.

The preceding strategies present the ideal type of bureaucracy. No organization exhibits all of those characteristics, but all organizations, including those in the human services, are structured in a form that incorporates aspects of the bureaucratic model. The term *bureaucracy* has developed a negative connotation among the general public and even, to some degree, among those who work within such a structure. The general perception of the bureaucracy is that it is buried in "red tape" and is impersonal. Managers within human service organizations would do well to reevaluate what is being said about their organizations.

Matrix Design

In recent years there has been an emerging organization design known as the *matrix organization*. Although this design has been used in the private sector with a measure of success, it has recently been adopted by public health and social service agencies (Knight, 1976). The matrix design focuses on both goal and process aspects of the organization. Individuals may be assigned to a goal-oriented project while at the same time maintaining their permanent organizational affiliation within a functional or process unit. The assignment to a project is on an ad hoc basis and once the project is completed each participant returns to his or her functional area full time. A simple matrix design is shown in Figure 2-1. A project director will be assigned to each project and, typically, will report to the highest level of management. As is noted in Figure 2-1, each project draws from functional areas, and the required number of members from those functional areas will be temporarily assigned to the project. In situations where coordination of activity and tasks is critical, the matrix design might well be the appropriate solution. However, such a design is not without its problems. While it is conducive to drawing upon the expertise of specialists, it does foster communication and reporting difficulties. The members of functional units who are assigned to specific projects are responsible to two superiors, and that can lead to conflict. On the one hand, they report to their superior in their functional area; on the other hand, they are also responsible to the project director. How priorities are established for their activity is crucial if the matrix approach is going to function effectively. With the establishment of clear guidelines, concern about responsibility can be kept in proper perspective. Members of the project should be advised of their responsibility to the project and the expectations relative to their participation. At the same time, they must be aware of their responsibility to their functional area. If the expectations in such areas are realistic and practical, the matrix design can work. One of the primary outcomes of such

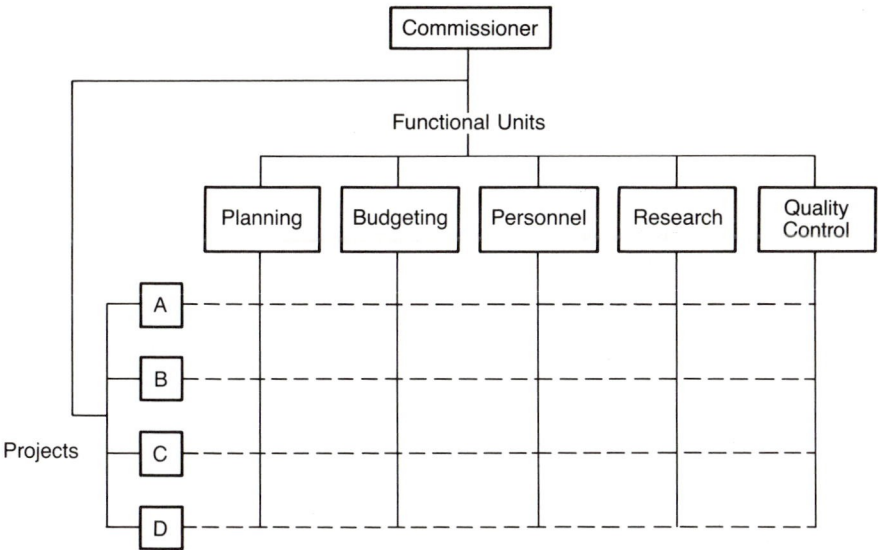

FIGURE 2-1 Matrix Design

a design is the improvement of motivation and commitment of those who work within the organization. When they are assigned to various projects, their contributions are recognized and that fosters the development and growth of members of the organization.

System 4 Design

The System 4 design was conceived by Rensis Likert and is based on extensive research he conducted at the University of Michigan (1961). He argues that there is a marked difference between effective and ineffective organizations and proposes eight dimensions by which areas can be assessed. Each of the eight dimensions is a continuum, with classical design organizations (System 1 organizations) at one extreme and System 4 organizations at the opposite end. Table 2-1 describes the eight dimensions and their extreme points. As noted in Table 2-1, the System 4 organization has the potential to be more adaptable to change, thereby overcoming a problem of the more classical-type organization. Within System 4, managers are encouraged to provide an environment that taps the full potential of human motivation and capabilities. A basic premise of System 4 is that individuals want to be more involved in such matters as decision making, goal setting, and control over their areas of work. An organization will be effective to the extent that its processes are

> . . . such as to ensure a maximum probability that in all interactions and in all relationships with the organization, each member, in the light of his background, values, desires, and expectations, will view the experience as suppor-

TABLE 2-1. Classical and System 4 Designs

CLASSICAL DESIGN ORGANIZATION	SYSTEM 4 ORGANIZATION
1. *Leadership process* includes no perceived confidence and trust. Subordinates do not feel free to discuss job problems with their superiors, who in turn do not solicit their ideas and opinions.	1. *Leadership process* includes perceived confidence and trust between superiors and subordinates in all matters. Subordinates feel free to discuss job problems with their superiors, who in turn solicit their ideas and opinions.
2. *Motivational process* taps only physical, security, and economic motives through the use of fear and sanctions. Unfavorable attitudes toward the organization prevail among employees.	2. *Motivational process* taps a full range of motives through participatory methods. Attitudes are favorable toward the organization and its goals.
3. *Communication process* is such that information flows downward and tends to be distorted, inaccurate, and viewed with suspicion by subordinates.	3. *Communication process* is such that information flows freely throughout the organization—upward, downward, and laterally. The information is accurate and undistorted.
4. *Interaction process* is closed and restricted. Subordinates have little effect on departmental goals, methods, and activities.	4. *Interaction process* is open and extensive. Both superiors and subordinates are able to affect departmental goals, methods, and activities.
5. *Decision process* occurs only at the top of the organization; it is relatively centralized.	5. *Decision process* occurs at all levels through group process; it is relatively decentralized.
6. *Goal-setting process* is located at the top of the organization, discourages group participation.	6. *Goal-setting process* encourages group participation in setting high, realistic objectives.
7. *Control process* is centralized and emphasizes fixing of blame for mistakes.	7. *Control process* is dispersed throughout the organization and emphasizes self-control and problem solving.
8. *Performance goals* are low and passively sought by managers, who make no commitment to developing the human resources of the organization.	8. *Performance goals* are high and actively sought by superiors, who recognize the necessity for making a full commitment to developing, through training, the human resources of the organization.

Source: Adapted from R. Likert, *The Human Organization* (New York: McGraw-Hill, 1967), pp. 197–211. Reproduced by permission of the publisher.

tive and one which builds and maintains his sense of personal worth and importance. (Likert, 1961, p. 103)

The System 4 organization design must be characterized by the following concepts: (1) the principle of supportive relationships, (2) group decision making and group methods of supervision, and (3) high performance goals (Likert, 1967, p. 47). The structure of the organization is depicted as a set of groups linked by managers. This "linking-pin" function is illustrated in Figure 2-2. Some managers are members of more than one group; in this dual capacity they serve as a link between the groups. They represent their groups to those at higher levels of the organization and coordinate their groups with those who are in lower-level positions.

Contingency Design

What should influence the design or structure of the organization? That question is answered with varying approaches, as we have seen. Each of the three designs proposes principles, concepts, and processes which, if followed, will lead to an effective design. Yet, there is a problem with that orientation. Organizational design cannot be viewed as an either-or proposition as Likert postulated in the dichotomy between System 1 and System 4. Rather, it is appropriate to consider the reality of the situation. A particular design may be effective in one situation and totally ineffective in

FIGURE 2-2 The System 4 Organization. From R. Likert, *Human Organization: Its Management and Value* (New York: McGraw-Hill, 1967), p. 50. Reproduced by permission of the publisher.

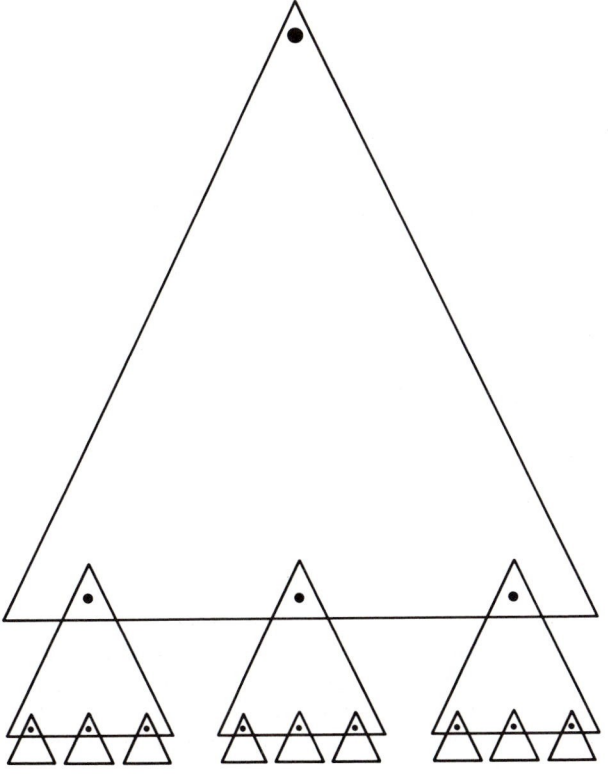

another. All human service organizations are not the same, so the structure for each will vary. Whatever the approach, it should be based on some sense of practicality and on realistic assessment of the particular situation.

As the study of the impact of design and structure has continued, there has been a movement away from the either-or approach and toward a contingency approach.

> The essence of the contingency design approach is expressed by the question: Under what circumstances and in what situations is either classical theory or System 4 organization more effective. The answer to this question requires the manager to specify the factors in a situation which influence the relative effectiveness of a particular design. (Gibson et al., 1982, p. 358)

There are two lines of thought that have attempted to identify the key situational factors. One proposes that differences in technology will determine the appropriate design, and the other states that differences in the environment and the requisite processing of information (Lawrence & Lorsch, 1969) are the crucial factors. The two approaches are not incompatible and, combined with systems theory, can lead to a general model of organization design. The integration of the findings of Woodward and Lawrence and Lorsch with systems theory is best captured by Gibson, Ivancevich, and Donnelly (1982, pp. 375–379). They propose that there are four subenvironments (input, output, technology, and knowledge) of an organization, as illustrated in Figure 2-3.

The output subenvironment. Frequently, there is a limited degree of choice as to the output of a human service organization. That is, the intended outcome of an organization's activity is prescribed by the stated purpose of that organization. In other words, what is the organization created to do? For example, a state department of public welfare is created to provide services to those in need as defined by federal and state laws and regulations. That is also true in the areas of mental health, vocational rehabilitation, and corrections. Similarly, many hospitals have been established as public institutions, although it is recognized that there are numerous private hospitals in existence. However, even a private hospital will have to make decisions that will be affected by the regulations and laws of a given state or the federal government. Whether to accept Medicaid patients is an example of such a decision. In any event, the outcome environment focuses on what it is that the organization hopes to accomplish.

A reality in this subenvironment is the frequency of change in the programs and the activities of the human service organization. As fiscal resources decrease, decisions must be made that may affect the type of client or patient to be served. For example, the emphasis on block grant funding in the human services versus categorical assistance will necessitate making some critical choices. As a state is provided with a smaller amount of fiscal resources by the federal government, the number and type of clients provided services will be affected. The frustration for many managers in that situation is that the demand for services continues to escalate

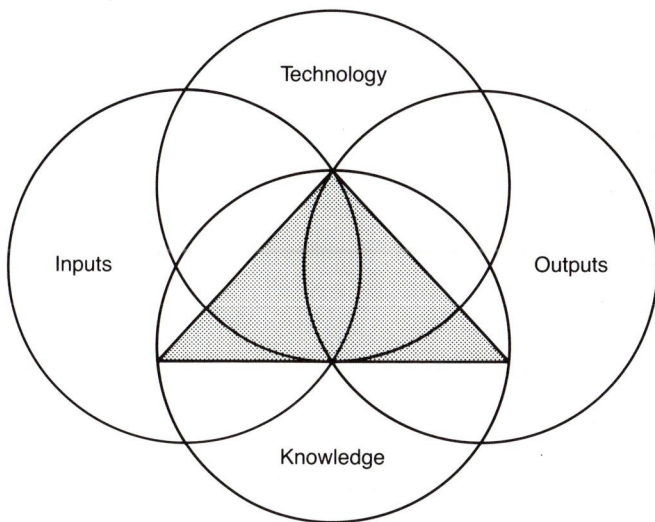

FIGURE 2-3 Subenvironments of an Organization. From J. L. Gibson, J. M. Ivancevich, & J. H. Donnelly, Jr., *Organizations: Behavior, Structure, Processes,* 4th ed. (Plano, Tex.: Business Publications, Inc., 1982), p. 375.

while the resources are diminishing. This requires careful attention to the priority of decisions and the manner in which those decisions are made. The responsibility placed upon management to be effective and efficient at the same time has led to the need to better define the expected outcomes that the organization seeks to achieve.

The input subenvironment. This subenvironment focuses on what comes into the organization. When a patient enters a hospital, that person is an input into that system. Similarly, when a person enters a local office of public welfare, he or she is an input, which must then be processed. If people and problems never changed, it would be simple to design an organization that handles such inputs very routinely; however, that is not the case. If the federal government mandates that states are to seek out those in need, as they did with the food stamp outreach program, then the organization must adjust. If the focus is placed on a specific problem, such as unemployment of specific client groups, then the organization must adapt to the change in emphasis, such as occurred with the Work Incentive Program. The more diverse the elements in the input subenvironment, the more complex the decisions to be made as to the structure and design of the organization. The critical point here is that the manager must understand the nature of the people coming into the system and the problems they bring with them. Recognizing that point, the manager can more effectively influence how the agency will carry out its mission and purpose. As is evident in Figure 2-3, the four subenvironments are interrelated; thus, they influence and have impact on one another. That is especially true of the interaction between inputs and outputs, because decisions made in those areas will affect the technology subenvironment.

The technology subenvironment.   It is this subenvironment that converts inputs to outputs. A sick person enters the hospital and, it is hoped, leaves well. An individual enters a prison and leaves better able to adjust to societal expectations. An abusive parent becomes a client in a protective service unit and leaves the unit when he or she has learned how to handle the responsibility of being a parent in a less abusive manner. What has happened in all those situations is that some action has been taken to change the circumstances that existed when the individual became known to the organization. The more routine the technology for dealing with the people and problems presented, the more structured or bureaucratic the design of the organization. That is, if there is a designated procedure to be followed whenever a specific problem is evident, then there is limited variation that needs to be built into the organization's design. A patient entering a hospital with symptoms indicating that he has suffered a heart attack will require a specific type of treatment. In many human service organizations, there is a stated procedure that should be followed; there are also those situations in which the routine application of the known technology is not useful. If those types of situations characterize the business of the organization, then a less structured design would be more effective. If the action to be carried out cannot be prescribed prior to the performance of the action, a System 4 design will be better able to handle these kinds of situations. If a person enters a local welfare office and does not fit into any of the various categories but is in obvious need of assistance, then some flexibility is indicated. In the System 4 design, there is reliance upon the group process in decision making, and where flexibility is required, the System 4 approach would be the appropriate one to follow. Keep in mind that the function of the technology subenvironment is to engage in activity that will change the person or problem indicated, thus achieving the expected output. It should be evident that there is a very straightforward relationship between the outputs expected, the technology available, and the inputs.

The knowledge subenvironment.   This subenvironment pervades the other three. Each of the other three subenvironments is subject to significant changes. Knowledge about the people or problems coming to the agency may change. A different kind of client may be coming to the local welfare office for assistance or to the hospital for treatment. The increase in the number of older citizens has required some shifting in emphasis as the nature of the problems and the needs of the individuals change. Changes are also taking place in the developing knowledge people have of the technological environment. New techniques and approaches have changed the complexion of human service organizations. In the mental health field, there is continued emphasis being placed on deinstitutionalization of the population in mental health facilities. That has led to more attention being given to short-term treatment and to greater use of community-based programs such as group homes and foster homes. We have come a long way from bloodletting in the field of medicine, banishment of the mentally ill to obscure warehouses, and public flogging of the indigent poor. The expectations of society, client groups, and practitioners have also brought about changes in the human service environment. As the expectations change, either the organization must adapt its output or the organization will be replaced. The manager must be aware of the rate of change and the focus of the change. Change can occur between and among the subenvironments, so the focus of the knowledge may be oriented toward the development of new inputs, outputs, or technology. It is the manager's task to know where the emphasis should be placed in the development of a design that takes into account the interaction occurring within the four subenvironments.

SUMMARY

Much of the literature of management in the human services has been devoted to the specific functions performed by managers, such as planning and controlling. This chapter has attempted to focus your attention upon a broader conceptualization of the organization and the role of the manager. The discussion has demonstrated the dependence of the human service agency upon elements of the external environment. This dependence paradigm is useful for both the prediction and the explanation of many facets of organizational behavior. For example, the reorganization of a state agency following the election of a new governor and the appointment of a new director is better understood if one considers the political process and the environment faced by those new officials. Similarly, the seemingly disproportionate influence of medical doctors on the operation of a hospital is more readily understood through an examination of the external environment. Finally, the factors discussed in this chapter influence the shape of the internal organizational structure. Many of the concepts discussed are directed toward creating a structure for the organization that is compatible with and supportive of the needs of the external environment. Thus, we have discussed several forms of organizational structure that are found among human service organizations.

REFERENCES

GALBRAITH, J. R. (1974, May). Organization design: An information processing view. *Interfaces.*

GIBSON, J. L., IVANCEVICH, J. M., & DONNELLY, J. H., JR. (1982). *Organizations: Behavior, structure, processes* (5th ed.). Plano, Tex.: Business Publications, Inc.

KNIGHT, K. (1976, May). Matrix organization: A review. *Journal of Management Studies,* p. 111.

KOTTER, J. P. (1979, January). Managing external dependence. *Academy of Management Review,* pp. 87–92.

LAWRENCE, P. R., & LORSCH, J. W. (1967, June). Differentiation and integration in complex organizations. *Administrative Science Quarterly,* pp. 1–47.

LIKERT, R. (1967). *Human organization: Its management and value.* New York: McGraw-Hill.
LIKERT, R. (1961). *New patterns of management.* New York: McGraw-Hill.
MILES, R. E., SNOW, C. C., & PFEFFER, J. (1974, October). Organization-environment: Concepts and issues. *Industrial Relations.*
MILES, R. H. (1980). *Macro organizational behavior.* Santa Monica, Calif.: Goodyear.
PARSONS, T. (1960). *Structure and process in modern society.* New York: Free Press.
TRECKER, H. B. (1971). *Social work administration principles and practices.* New York: Association Press.
WEBER, M. (1947). *The theory of social and economic organizations* (A. M. Henderson and T. Parsons, Trans.). New York: Oxford University Press.

QUESTIONS FOR DISCUSSION

1. With the help of your instructor, identify the major goals of your school or agency. How have those goals affected the structure of the organization?
2. For an organization with which you are familiar, develop a list of the major environmental factors that have an influence upon it. What influences have those factors had upon the organization's structure?
3. Within your school or agency, what is the primary system of rules that govern its operation? Discuss some strategies the effective manager may employ to cope with that system.
4. Discuss some ways the manager may cope with the differing organizational viewpoints held by those in institutional and technical levels of the organization.
5. Discuss the advantages and disadvantages of using the matrix form of organization as opposed to the classical organization form in the human service organization.
6. Discuss the advantages and disadvantages of the bureaucratic structure to the unit or department manager in a human service organization.

SUGGESTED PROJECTS

1. Interview a local human service administrator to determine
    a. the goals of the agency
    b. the criteria of agency effectiveness
    c. problems encountered in gaining acceptance of goals by organizational participants
2. Using the matrix or System 4 design, develop a plan for reorganizing an organization that is presently in the classical or bureaucratic form.

The Manager as Figurehead and Spokesperson

chapter 3

The manager in the human service organization is frequently called upon to act as the representative for the organization or to speak on its behalf. As the *figurehead*, the manager is a symbol and, by virtue of his or her formal authority, is obliged to perform a number of duties (Mintzberg, 1972, p. 58). Those duties may range from signing certain documents to representing the organization before the public. The local county welfare director may be expected to sit on the boards of a number of agencies within the community. The director of nursing services must be present to participate in the "pinning" ceremonies of graduating nursing students. The chief probation officer of a large urban county has been asked to be a member of the governor's advisory council on juvenile crime. Those are but a few examples of situations in which the manager fulfills the role of *figurehead*.

In a similar vein, the human service manager must be the *spokesperson* for the organization within the external environment. As the manager, he or she possesses the information to keep a variety of audiences informed. The Commissioner of Social Services meets with the members of the legislature's finance subcommittee to present the agency's budget. A hospital administrator asks the director of nursing services to join him or her in a meeting with the state health planning and development council to plead their case for increasing the bed capacity of the hospital. The court administrator joins with a group of other administrators to lobby for the passage of a piece of legislation of particular interest. In many instances, only the chief executive officer can represent and speak for the organization. The administrator of a state mental hospital holds a press conference to explain and to answer questions about why a mental patient was released and subsequently committed murder. In dealing with the external environment, it is crucial that information be controlled. That is not to suggest that there is anything to hide, rather that there needs to be "one voice." Failure to provide for such control can lead to the dissemination of misinformation, rumors, and conflicting information.

In this chapter we will focus on the roles of *figurehead* and *spokesperson*. While they may seem to be time consuming and of minimal importance, they are significant in the totality of managerial performance. Human service agencies are often on the defensive because management has not given enough attention to those two roles. The effective manager will be the one who recognizes that, takes a more anticipative approach, and avoids being reactionary and crisis oriented.

FIGUREHEAD

Symbolism

The manager is the symbol of the agency or of a particular unit within the organization. As such, his or her presence at a variety of functions is required. For example, the director of the agency escorts a group of dignitaries who are touring the agency. Such an activity can consume an inordinate amount of time, but the presence of the manager gives the event a sense of importance. Failure to make time for this type of activity could lead to problems and unexpected consequences. Let us assume that the dignitaries are a group of state legislators. Obviously, they will be voting on legislation that could substantially affect the programs and missions of the agency.

The manager's role as the symbol of the organization also has implications for those within the organization. As a manager, you create the climate for the agency or unit therein. To be present at the wedding of a loyal, hardworking employee conveys that you care; failing to attend can be interpreted to mean that you do not have the time for such an event. Taking time to stop by the hospital to visit your secretary who was seriously injured in an automobile accident will mean more than almost anything else you could do. Your secretary will remember forever that "the boss took time from a busy schedule to come to see me." The key here is that the *boss* did it. Writing a personal note to the widow of your associate director, who died suddenly, will have immeasurable benefits. How? Simply, people tell others.

In their book *A Passion for Excellence,* Peters and Austin (1985) devote an entire section to the importance of symbolic behavior. In studying successful organizations they found numerous examples of such behavior and concluded that ". . . leadership (management) is symbolic behavior . . ." (p. 271). They emphasize the point by stating: "Every minute is a symbolic opportunity. It's an opportunity that you consciously, or more likely, unconsciously, choose to grasp or squander" (p. 271).

Indeed, as the *boss* you are a symbol. Whether you are communicating with the outside environment or within the organization, it is you who should be there, not someone else representing the agency. The upset parent of a child who has been attacked while in the juvenile detention center wants to talk with the superintendent—the person in charge. If the superintendent refuses to talk with the parent, it could be construed that he or she is not in charge. Certainly, the manager cannot spend all of the time answering telephone calls, attending weddings, or giving tours, but he or she should realize that there are situations in which only the manager can represent the organization. How can this be done selectively? Answering the following questions will provide some direction:

1. What are the potential benefits of my participation to the organization?
2. What are the potential consequences if I do not participate?
3. Is there someone else who could better represent the agency?
4. Will it be beneficial or counterproductive to use someone else?
5. How much time is involved? Do I have the time?
6. Will multiple benefits result from my participation?
7. Will others see my failure to participate as a lack of concern and commitment?
8. Will my credibility as a manager be enhanced or damaged by my participation?
9. Will the credibility of the organization be enhanced or damaged by my participation?
10. Why shouldn't I participate?

Status and Prestige

In addition to being a symbol of the organization, the manager also has status and prestige. It is the executive director who is *expected* to be on the dais at the annual recognition dinner. Whether any words are spoken or not, the mere presence is what is important. Often, the manager's presence lends credibility and importance to a particular event. Not only is it a responsibility of a manager, but it is also appreciated. The perception of most people is that the manager is a busy person, and his or her participation in a ceremonial function carries a great amount of value. In the same vein, the absence of the manager when he or she is expected to be present can easily be interpreted as a lack of interest or to mean that a particular function was not viewed as important.

Must the manager always be present for the organization to benefit? Of course not. A timely letter, a brief phone call, or a telegram of congratulations can have a value similar to that of personal presence. The message conveyed is that the boss cared enough to recognize a particular event as worth his or her time.

The status included in the managerial position also carries with it the *authority* of the position. There is a relationship between the behavior of an individual and the presence of an authority figure. Many of us can recall having had sweaty palms or shaky knees in the presence of certain individuals. It was not fear that produced those reactions but respect—respect for the position that the person occupied. The effective manager recognizes that that is so and uses it to his or her advantage. In fulfilling the figurehead role, the manager does represent the agency by virtue of the position that he or she fills.

At times, the agency may be involved in negotiations that require the presence of the manager. In a later chapter we discuss the negotiating role of the manager, but we do want to mention that the status of the manager's position is important in negotiating activity. For example, in labor negotiations the manager's presence is mandated by the very nature of what is being negotiated—only he or she can sign the labor contract. Similarly, if an agency is negotiating with another agency for contracted services, the manager must sign the agreement. It is the position, not the person holding the position, that is significant in those situations.

In concluding our discussion of the figurehead role, we should note that the significance of the role tends to diminish as you move down the hierarchy of the organization. For example, the Commissioner of Social Services spends more time formally fulfilling the figurehead role than does a supervisor in the Division of Family and Children Services. Often, a more informal fulfillment as opposed to a formal one is found among lower-level managers and supervisors. That is not to detract from the value of the role, but the significance is not as great.

SPOKESPERSON

In fulfilling this role, the manager is the "voice" of the organization or of a particular unit in the organization. It is not uncommon within the human service environment that only "word" from management carries any significance or influence. Indeed, a considerable amount of a manager's time may be spent in what is commonly referred to as PR—public relations. While this may or may not be something that a given manager looks forward to or holds in high regard, it can be crucial to the survival of an agency or a program.

A Conduit to the External Environment

The external environment views the manager as the one to speak for the organization. Granted, the larger the organization, the more likely it is to have specialists to deal with the media, but often there comes a time when the media want to hear it from the boss.

In conveying information to the external environment, it is imperative that the manager be fully informed about the issues being discussed. Nothing is as detrimental to an organization as to have the manager speak on something about which he or she is uninformed. This requires the manager to be aware of developments within the organization. That is not to suggest that the manager must know every little detail about everything that goes on, but it does mean that he or she should be on top of developments, problems, and issues. If a program manager of a local mental health center has been in the community looking for property for a group home, the director of the center had better know that that is happening. The placement of such a facility can be a volatile issue, and it is quite likely that the director will be asked questions that he or she must be prepared to answer. Although the director can and should delegate to the program manager the responsibility to locate an appropriate facility, that director cannot delegate the ultimate responsibility to represent the center to those in the external environment.

The manager is also in a position to serve as a link between certain special interests and special sources of information. There are those outside of every human service organization who have a special interest in the programs and services of the organization. There are those who consider themselves to be "watch dogs" over the activity of the agency. That can be especially true with those organizations that are funded by public dollars. How often have articles appeared in a local newspaper, written by an enterprising investigative reporter, about food stamp fraud or children who are returned to abusive parents. The reporter may believe that it is his or her professional, as well as civic, responsibility to report such matters and that he or she is the guardian of the trust that the public has placed in the local welfare department. As those situations are brought before the public, the director of the department will be the one who speaks for the agency, the one who is looked to as the expert, the link between the agency and the special interest of the media and the public. Certainly, he or she must be prepared to answer probing and sometimes embarrassing questions. In short, the manager must be prepared and informed.

Similarly, there are special interests that are supportive of the activities of the agency. It is to the manager that they look for information. The prudent manager relies upon the expert knowledge and understanding of a competent staff, but it will be to him or her that the special interest groups turn for answers. If the local chapter of the Association for Retarded Citizens wants to raise money for the state school for the retarded, it is to the director of the school that they will turn for suggestions for worthwhile fund-raising projects. A school of nursing may elicit the support of the professional nursing community for the school's nursing program. At some point they will expect to talk to the Dean of the School. Such contact strengthens supporters' commitment and should never be sold short as a waste of time. Without such support the school may cease to exist.

There are also sources of information that the manager must cultivate. A few questions will serve to highlight this important area. Who are the "power brokers" in the community? Who could be most helpful to the mission of the organization? Who has given some evidence of interest in what the organization is attempting to do? How can I cultivate a relationship that would be beneficial to the organization? There are individuals in every community, large or small, who are very influential. The successful human service manager will make an effort to nurture good relations with those individuals. A timely invitation, a short note of congratulations, and a phone call to express condolences are just a few ways to initiate such a relationship. We emphasize that this must be handled by the manager, not by a secretary or someone else in the organization. In such matters, the manager must be the one to represent and speak for the organization. When dealing with influential business people, civic leaders, legislators, and the power elite, the manager should not delegate this responsibility. It belongs to him or her.

One final comment about being a conduit to the external environment. Every manager should remember that the image of the organization projected to the external environment is in large part the image that he or she projects. How one looks or acts says a great deal about the organization. A fair measure of common sense concerning appropriateness will be a tremendous asset to the total mission and purpose of the organization. The human service manager should not underestimate the significance of the image he or she conveys to the variety of publics within a given community. It is important for the manager to know the community and the toleration level therein. A small conservative southern town is a much different environment from that of a large northeastern city. Behavior that is acceptable in the urban area might be offensive in a small town. The fact that the county welfare director is living with a man to whom she is not legally married may create nary a ripple in the urban center but is scandalous in a small town. The criteria we suggest are these: Know where you are and be sensitive. When the manager's behavior infringes upon the image of the organization, it must be examined and a decision rendered as to the future of the organization as well as to the future of the manager.

Public Relations

As we have already noted, a significant amount of the manager's time is spent dealing with the external environment. In this section we will focus specifically on the responsibilities the manager has to promote a positive image of his or her program, unit, or agency. The key word is *promote*. The purpose of public relations is to achieve mutual understanding and goodwill, and it should be viewed as a vital part of effective promotion of an organization's purpose, mission, intent, program, and reason for existing (Engel et al., 1983, p. 516). As we have stated previously in the text, a successful manager is one who takes a proactive approach to carrying out the mission and purpose of the organization. He or she is not one who sits back waiting for something to happen and then reacts to the events.

Starling (1982) identifies two purposes of public relations: (1) to inform and (2) to constructively influence the public (p. 145). Regarding the first, does it not make sense to keep the various publics informed about the activities of the organization? In the process of disseminating such information, it is vital, as Starling (1982) states, to avoid distorting the information. It might be expedient at the moment to speak in generalities and share only bits and pieces of information, yet this may be discovered later and lead to distressing consequences. A few years ago, an administrator of a large state agency was appearing before a state senate finance committee, presenting the case for increased appropriations for the department. In the course of the hearing, the administrator was asked about several million dollars that were being held back, which completely negated the creditableness of the requests. The results were that the additional money was not appropriated and the governor asked for the administrator's resignation. That state agency is still reeling from the effects of that incident. Managers of public agencies must be forthright when imparting information to whatever public needs to be kept informed. "Organizational accountability demands credibility in dealing with the public" (Engel et al., p. 531). As noted previously, the manager is the voice of the organization; he or she sets the tone and conveys the image. If the manager is viewed as one who gives conflicting information, it is the organization that will pay the price. Legislators will not support appropriation requests, the media will popularize the inconsistencies, the agency clientele will be suspect, and the employees will be embarrassed to be identified with the agency.

Informing the public can be done in many ways. Certainly the various media can be used with some degree of success. Reporters can be encouraged to write a special series about the needs of a particular group, be it health care for the poor or adoptive homes for handicapped children. Radio and TV reporters, likewise, can be enlisted to bolster the image of the agency—to report the good news as well as the bad news. Such coverage by whatever media source can be used effectively and to the benefit of the total human service endeavor.

Recently, a large municipal police department has engaged in a proactive public relations campaign. As new residents move into neighborhoods, they are visited by two uniformed officers. The purpose of the visit is to provide a packet of information and to elicit the residents' support for the police department—to show police as a "helping force" and not just a controlling force in the community. Similarly, some state social service agencies have successfully used the media to find adoptive parents for hard-to-place children. The intent of these illustrations is simply to suggest that there is room for creativity and innovativeness in keeping the public informed.

Patti (1983) emphasizes the need for agencies to keep the client/patient population informed. He stresses the need to reach out to the "population-at-risk" and not to rely exclusively on the popular media. The thesis he promotes is that it is the responsibility of the agency to let the clientele know of the services that are available to them. Individuals within a community have a right to know what is available to them. That may mean that there will be doors to knock on, leaflets to distribute, and meetings to attend. The consumer public's image of the provider agency will be markedly enhanced if they know that there is a caring attitude as evidenced by outreach activity. Again, we stress that the manager is responsible to encourage such activity.

The second purpose of the public relations program is closely related to the first: to constructively influence the public. The expected consequence of keeping the public informed is the gaining of their support. The successful manager spends time with the most influential people and keeps them informed. To illustrate that point, let us return to the example of the mental health center that wants to set up a group home. It would be very beneficial for the director of the center to take the time to meet, both formally and informally, with key leaders in the community. That may mean lunching with a city councilman to explain the purpose of and the need for the group home and to seek his support. It might mean having a drink with the city manager one evening to discuss the proposed project. It might also mean scheduling an appointment with the municipal judge to answer his questions about the center's intent to establish the group home in his neighborhood. In effect, the director is lobbying for the establishment of the group home. Further, it would be to the advantage of the center's program for the director to identify and meet with various groups (civic, social, religious, fraternal) and seek a coalition of support. All of this will take time, but it can be time well spent.

Lobbying, by definition, is influencing. It is geared toward seeking support for a particular activity, a particular program, or additional funding. To be an effective lobbyist, the manager must be knowledgeable and informed. He or she must be prepared to respond to questions and to do so specifically, not in vague generalities. He or she should avoid being defensive, should highlight and emphasize the positives and strengths. Preparation cannot be overemphasized. Be able and ready to deal with probing and critical questions. Be honest and forthright; do not be misleading. If you do not know the answer, assure those present that you will find out and then make the information available. Do not rule out compromise. Very little is ever accomplished from a win-lose approach. Quite simply, such an approach has not only a winner but also a loser. The consequence can be a more entrenched position among those who do not support what the manager is seeking.

A final word about the public relations responsibility has to do with the relationship of the manager to members of the board of directors or an advisory board. Keep board members informed of developments, plans, and activities. By doing so, you will have a better chance of enlisting their support for the total mission and purpose of the organization. Seek their counsel and suggestions. Listen to what they contribute. Act upon their recommendations. Following their advice does not mean acquiescing to the board; rather, it shows the members of the board that they are involved and that what they have to say is important. Identify particularly influential board members and foster your relationship with them. It would be unwise to antagonize and isolate them. Successful relationships with board members can spell the success or failure of the organization's total mission.

In this chapter we have dealt with the roles of *figurehead* and *spokesperson*. Whatever the size of the organization, the manager must recognize the importance of the multiple responsibilities involved in fulfilling those roles.

REFERENCES

ENGEL, J. F., WARSHAW, M. R., & KINNEAR, T. C. (1973). *Promotional strategy: Managing the marketing communications process* (5th ed.). Homewood, Ill.: Richard D. Irwin.

MINTZBERG, H. (1973). *The nature of managerial work.* New York: Harper & Row.

PATTI, R. J. (1983). *Social welfare administration: Managing social programs in a developmental context.* Englewood Cliffs, N.J.: Prentice-Hall.

PETERS, T., & AUSTIN, N. (1985). *A passion for excellence: The leadership difference.* New York: Random House.

STARLING, G. (1982). *Managing the public sector.* Homewood, Ill.: Dorsey.

QUESTIONS FOR DISCUSSION

1. "The value of the services performed by a human service organization is obvious, therefore, there is no need for these organizations to maintain a public relations program." Do you agree with that statement? Why or why not?

2. As a spokesperson, how may a manager in a human service organization benefit the clients of that organization?

3. As a manager in a human service organization, discuss the steps you would take to improve the public image of your agency.

SUGGESTED PROJECTS

1. Assume you have been invited to a local civic group to make a presentation about your agency. Prepare a twenty-minute presentation designed to gain support from your audience.

2. Prepare a news release for a new project being undertaken by your agency.

The Manager as Leader
The Personnel Process

chapter 4

"I must follow them, I am their leader!" For there to be a leader, there must be followers. In other words, there cannot be leadership without "followship." Within the human service organization the process of leadership is vitally important. The tone and climate of the organization will be significantly affected by the leaders. The extent to which individual and organizational needs complement each other will be determined largely by those in leadership positions. The kind of people attracted to the organization and those that remain will be influenced by the leaders. A manager's style of leadership permeates his or her every action. Will a subordinate be praised or criticized? Will a program be included in the budget or not? Will an idea be supported or cast aside? By virtue of his or her position in the organization, the manager possesses a great amount of liberty to affect the direction and emphasis of the agency. The manager has the authority to ask questions, meddle in activities, identify problems, and initiate solutions. As resources available to human service organizations become fewer, the role of the manager as a leader takes on an even greater significance. Leadership requires individuals with imagination, creativity, and a willingness to take risks. Of equal significance in such an environment is the attention given to the wedding of the needs of those in the organization with the goals of the organization.

Before moving on to the consideration of the activities of leadership, let us say a word about management and leadership. Frequently, the terms *manager* and *leader* are used synonymously. Do they mean the same thing? The answer is no. Simply having the title "manager" does not mean that an individual is a leader. Conversely, without the title, some individuals are extremely effective leaders through the informal system. A supervisor of a protective service unit can have great influence on the actions of employees throughout the local welfare department, even though the supervisor does not have the title of director. Similarly, a nurse's aide can alter the manner in which patients are treated, much to the dismay of the director of nursing services. The point is that leadership and management are not the same. However, to be an effective manager, one must effectively lead. We do not mean to suggest that managers have to "do it all." Quite the opposite: Leadership means that the manager brings together the pieces to make the organization work optimally. In this chapter we will discuss those leadership activities associated with staffing responsibilities: hiring, training, evaluating performance, rewarding, promoting, and dismissing. In the following chapter we will consider those activities that relate to such motivational problems as the needs and desires of employees, the perception of fairness, the question of satisfaction and dissatisfaction, and the effect of all of that on performance.

STAFFING

The initial concern in the staffing process is twofold: who is needed and how to find them. In answering the first question, the manager must assess the staffing needs of the organization, which requires a specification of the type of individual needed. What skills or abilities are necessary to do the job? The manager must give careful thought to the nature of the job and the type of person to be recruited and hired. If, for example, a state department of mental health is looking for a director of the community-based programs, what is expected of the individual? What will he or she do, or what is it anticipated that he or she will do? The interrelationship between the type of job and the type of person should be evident. Many personnel problems can be avoided if there is thoughtful attention given to the "person-job mix." In that regard, McClelland (1973) strongly urged organizations to identify the competencies needed to perform a specific job and then locate individuals who possessed them. While that is a cumbersome process, it emphasizes the need for locating those people who will fit organizational needs. It cannot be assumed that because a person has an M.S.W. degree he or she will work out in an agency that hires social workers. Similarly, some registered nurses will function quite well in general medical hospitals but be unsuccessful in a state hospital for the mentally ill.

Recruitment

Once the type of job and the type of person have been identified, attention must be given to the recruitment and hiring process. Where will proper, qualified individuals be found? There is the "flypaper" approach, which simply states that people will be attracted to the job once they know it is available. This is a reactionary orientation that does not always lead to attracting the "best" people. Conceivably, organizations may be faced with hiring the best of a mediocre lot. When the supply of qualified people exceeds the demand for jobs, in most localities, perhaps the flypaper approach will result in a pool of "good" people. However, it would be better if managers aggressively went out to find the people they needed. The manager who does that will be more successful as a leader than one who simply reacts to what he or she gets.

Effective recruitment means that potential sources of applicants be identified. Advertisement in professional sources is a typical approach and one that must be considered to comply with federal and state laws, such as the Equal Employment Opportunity provision of the Civil Rights Act of 1964. However, if that is the extent of the effort, then it will fall short. Advertising does not have to be limited to professional sources. Locating prestigious minority sources will improve the chances of locating qualified minority applicants. Further, there are a number of resources available to make the opportunity known to women. The manager should go out and locate the media sources that would reach the widest possible audience of potentially qualified candidates.

If a college degree is a prerequisite to the job, then efforts should be made to recruit on college campuses. Realizing that funds may not be available to allow that, we suggest some modifications that the manager could consider:

1. Contact by telephone those colleges where potential applicants are located. Speak to the proper individual, such as a dean, a department chairperson, or the director of a program.
2. Use contacts that have been made at meetings or conferences. Frequently, such contacts are made and then forgotten, but they could prove to be an invaluable source of applicants.
3. Draw upon the backgrounds of present employees. Use them if they are returning to their respective campuses for any reason. Every organization has individuals in its employ who maintain contacts with professors or friends "back on campus."
4. Make the most out of trips taken to other areas of the country. If you are going to attend a conference in New York, make appointments with colleges in the area. The trip is going to be taken anyway; make the most of it.

Those are just a few suggestions that, if followed, could provide the manager with valuable resources to draw upon now and in the future.

Another valuable resource is the people working for you. Do they know of anyone seeking to make a change in employment? It is advisable to seek out those "good" employees and let them know of the opportunity that is available. In our mobile society many people have friends and acquaintances who would be interested in relocating.

A variation of on-campus recruiting is field recruiting. Although this is used with success in the private sector, it is not a practical approach for most human service organizations. It is expensive and time consuming. Yet, the manager should not totally disregard this approach if it is feasible. Field recruitment means what it implies. You go into a city and set up recruitment interviews in a hotel room. Potential applicants are informed of the interviews through advertisement in the local media and appear at the appointed time. There is a way to engage in this type of recruiting without incurring substantial costs. Again, if you are going to attend a conference of the American Hospital Association, you can place announcements in strategic places at the conference site, advising individuals that you will be in your hotel room at specific times for the purpose of interviewing. You are there anyway; capitalize on the situation.

Selection Process

Locating and identifying the "right" people is only the beginning of the selection process. Once they are identified, a fair selection process must be developed. The Civil Rights Act, the Age Discrimination in Employment Act, the Vocational Rehabilitation Act, and VEVRA all have provisions that guard against discrimination in employment. Those laws state that no one can be discriminated against because of sex, race, creed, national origin, age, or physical or mental handicaps. Any human service organization that receives federal funds must have an affirmative action plan that outlines how such discrimination will be precluded. Therefore, within the guidelines of federal and state laws, how will people be selected?

There are traditional approaches to conducting the initial screening of applicants, such as letters of recommendation, assessment of applications completed by prospective employees, and interviews. Each has merit, but there are other techniques and methods that could be considered. Let us assume that the Director of Nursing Services needs to hire a head nurse. Several people have applied for the position and he or she must try to select the best of the applicants. One method that has been extremely successful is the assessment center. This method has been used extensively in the private sector by such companies as AT&T, IBM, Westinghouse, and Western Airlines. Recently, it has been adopted by organizations in the public sector, such as police departments, federal agencies, and state departments of public welfare.

The success of the assessment center lies in its objectivity and job relatedness. Before conducting the center, the organization undertakes a thorough job analysis, which is aimed at identifying the exact nature of the specific job and the various skills or abilities required to do the job effectively. Once the skills or abilities—dimensions—are known, then the assessment center can be organized. When the job analysis has been completed and the dimensions identified (usually eight to twelve), the dimensions are ranked in order of importance to the specific job. Table 4-1 depicts an ordering of eight dimensions. The ranking of the dimensions is done in cooperation with individuals in higher levels of management.

Several simulation exercises, usually three or four, are selected that will provide the opportunity for the applicants (assessees) to demonstrate how they would function in a real supervisory or managerial situation. While assessees go through the exercises, trained assessors record their behavior.

The assessors are trained to do the following: observe, record, classify, and rate behavior. While observing during the exercises, they record the behavior of the assessees. After the exercise is completed, they classify

**TABLE 4-1.   Priority of
Dimensions**

RANK	DIMENSION
1	Leadership
2	Delegation
3	Planning and organizing
4	Problem analysis
5	Judgment
6	Decisiveness
7	Oral communication skill
8	Sensitivity

the behavior by the dimensions selected for the center. For example, they rate leadership behavior, evidence of sensitivity, and so forth. The next step is to rate the behavior according to a predetermined rating scale. One method is a five-point scale, illustrated in Table 4-2.

On this scale, a rating of 3 or better indicates that the individual has given enough behavioral evidence of ability to do the respective job. A rating of 5 is not necessarily better than a rating of 3. Each assessor brings to the integration session his or her ratings and supporting evidence for each of the dimensions being assessed in a specific exercise.

Specifically, behavior is what a person actually says or does in an exercise. Typically, no assessor observes an assessee in more than one exercise; therefore, if there were four exercises, there would be four assessors for the applicant. An assessor may observe different assessees through the course of the assessment but should not observe the same person more than once. That compensates for various errors such as the halo effect, the reverse halo effect, and likes-dislikes. Once the applicant has completed all the exercises, each assessor who has observed the individual meets with the center administration, and a consensus is recorded about the individual's performance on each of the dimensions included in the center. From that session a profile emerges that identifies the individual's strengths and weaknesses. On the basis of the profile, the "best" person for the job will be evident. Table 4-3 illustrates the profiles of two applicants. On the basis of these two profiles, Applicant B would be the best person for the position.

The assessment center method can be quite costly in both time and money, but it is one of the best methods available to identify individuals who give evidence of having the ability to do the job. A word of caution: It has the greatest utility at the level of supervisor or above. It is too costly to use for lower-level positions.

Another method that has been used with some success is a selection panel. After the initial screening of applicants, a panel interviews and assesses the final list of applicants and rates each of them according to a prescribed rating system. The individual with the highest rating would be the preferred person to hire. The rationale for using a panel is that there is a greater degree of reliability in having several people, usually three to five,

TABLE 4-2. Rating Scale

RATING	DESCRIPTION
5	Much more than satisfactory
4	More than satisfactory
3	Satisfactory
2	Less than satisfactory
1	Much less than satisfactory

rate the applicants. An incentive for using this approach has been the desire to avoid discrimination against specific groups of people. This selection method can take a great deal of time. However, if such a panel is limited to the selection of key staff and professionals, the time factor is not as important.

The use of tests is a selection method that is used quite extensively, especially in the public sector. A test may serve to obtain information about an applicant's general knowledge in the area of employment, the personality of the individual, or the aptitude of the individual to do the job. Another approach is to use a work-sample test; this places the individual in the position of performing some aspect of the job, on which he or she is evaluated. If a test is to be used, it should be constructed in such a way that it is job related and valid. Many of the tests that have been used do not meet these criteria and have been declared discriminatory by the courts. Another point to keep in mind is that a test should not be the only factor that influences the decision to hire someone. There are people who are good at taking tests and others who have difficulty with them. The concern of the manager should be to hire the person who would be the "best" employee. A score on a test may have no relationship to a person's ability. Again, the level of the job is an important factor. Certainly, the typing skill of a clerical worker can be assessed by a typing test, but the counseling skill of a social worker is much more difficult to ascertain from a paper-pencil test. If a test is to be used, attention should be given to (1) its validity, (2) its reliability, (3) its potential for discrimination, (4) its job relatedness, and (5) its fairness.

TABLE 4-3. Applicant Profiles

DIMENSIONS	APPLICANT A RATING	APPLICANT B RATING
Oral communications skill	4	3
Leadership	3	3
Planning and organizing	2	4
Delegation	2	3
Sensitivity	4	5
Problem analysis	2	3
Judgment	3	3
Decisiveness	4	5

The key concern about the use of tests is whether they do bring together the right person and the right job. David McClelland proposes that what should distinguish the "right" person for a job is whether an individual possesses the requisite competencies (Goldman, 1981). McClelland makes the point that every job has competency levels and that the good and poor performers can be identified. While this is a creditable proposition, the extensiveness of his approach is financially prohibitive for most human service organizations. Yet, the issue of the level of competency needed to effectively carry out a job should not go unheeded. The selection process can be significantly improved if attention is given to what the organization is looking for in an applicant.

Training.   This is an area in the staffing process that all too often is neglected or, at best, given a "lick and a promise." When budget cuts are made, it is not uncommon for the training unit to be hit hard or, in some cases, eliminated. The training of staff is, in the eyes of many, a luxury rather than a necessity. Perhaps we would do well to ask, "What do we want an employee to do, and can this be accomplished through an effective training program?" In human service organizations, as in most organizations, it is assumed that if an individual enters the system with the proper credentials, he or she can do the job. While that may be generally true, there are enough exceptions to warrant giving careful attention to the needs of the organization as well as to the preparation of the individual. If selection is finding the right people, then training is making them into what you want them to be. Is there a difference between being a social worker in a large metropolitan welfare department and being a social worker in a suburban mental health center? How do you prepare the worker? You train him or her. Is there a difference between being a staff nurse in an intensive coronary care unit and being a floor nurse on a pediatric ward? Indeed. Therefore, the manager in the human service organization must view training as an important part of the total functioning of the organization or of his or her unit.

The training must be related to the job to be performed. It must be perceived by the trainees as worthwhile and worth their investment of time. The response of the trainee cannot be, "Oh, hell, another useless training program." In one state, probation officers were required to take training that was designed for police officers. How many probation officers do you know who have to fill out traffic accident reports? While that example may be a bit bizarre, it is not unique. Take a moment and reflect on your training program. Is is relevant to the job? Is it worthwhile? What are your employees' perceptions of the training you provide for them? What priority does it have in your scheme of management?

As you reflect on your training program, give some thought to who the trainers are. Are they some of your better people, or are they the "lames" whom you did not know where else to put? "They'll be harmless and won't be able to screw too much up down there." Is that who is "down there?" We encourage you to think about the purpose and expected outcomes of your training program. They should be designed to improve the functioning of those within the organization regarding their skills, abilities, or knowledge. If the trainers are losers, then the training will generally produce more losers.

To have an effective and useful training program, it is necessary that the management of the organization have some idea as to why they are training individuals and what the expected outcomes are. That requires assessment of the training. The basic question is, Where are the gaps that training can fill? Too often, training has been what someone thinks or believes is needed rather than a well-planned program that is based on sound data. A training program should focus on the following: (1) improvement of specialized *skills*, (2) enhancement of *abilities* to perform a job, or (3) increasing an individual's *knowledge* in an area relevant to a specific job. If organizations focus on those three areas, the success of the training will be assured.

Through training, the organization makes its employees into the kind of people it wants. However, each organization must know the kind of people it already has and the kind it still needs. No one comes into an organization fully prepared—he or she must be trained well by effective trainers.

Judging.   Every manager has the responsibility of appraising his or her employees' performance, of determining who is performing well and who is not. What distinguishes the good performers from the poor performers? Do you, as a manager, know what distinguishes person A from person B? Every human service organization has some type of performance appraisal system, but many systems are not effective. The annual review is a typical method of appraisal. "Among the archaic practices which hang on with amazing persistence in most large organizations is the annual performance review. . ." (Schrader, 1969, p. 20). Both the appraiser and the appraisee too often find the experience to be useless and a waste of time. The manager sits down with the employee and goes through a checklist, and then it's over. Judging an employee's performance is not a once-a-year activity; it is a process. Stop and think of this! A person in a superior position in the organization is constantly assessing the work of his or her subordinates. How often does a manager say, "She really did a good job with that patient," or "Tom should have known how to deal with that situation." Is that not judging the individual's performance?

In appraising an individual's performance, the manager should focus on two areas, one *judgmental*, the other *developmental*. The purpose of the appraisal is to determine if the person is doing the job he or she was hired and trained to do. That's *judgmental*. Yet, the appraisal process does not stop there. It should also identify areas where the employee could be helped, developed, or trained. That's *developmental*. The two purposes must work together, and they support the thesis that appraisal is continuous. If the manager takes this approach, the fundamental activity of judging an individual's performance will have a new and meaningful purpose for people within the organization.

A key ingredient in the appraisal process is knowing specifically what an individual is to be held accountable for within the context of his or her job. That should be made clear when the person begins employment. The protective service worker needs to know not only what the job is that he or she is to do but also how well it is to be done. A *standard of performance* should be developed that can be used as the basis upon which performance will be assessed. A standard of performance indicates how *well* an employee is doing a particular job or aspect of a job or how *much* is expected of that employee. Frequently, a standard can be written as a performance *objective* or a *target* to achieve. For example, if a public welfare office is attempting to reduce the error rate among food stamp recipients, then each worker in the program should be expected to contribute to the organizational goal by having no more than a 3 percent error rate among his or her caseloads. To illustrate further, if a hospital director of nursing is concerned about the extent to which staff nurses are being responsive to physicians' medication orders, an established target would be that all medications should be given within fifteen minutes of the prescribed time, 95 percent of the time. The significance of those two examples is that they are stated in quantitative terms. The manager can periodically determine if expected performance is being achieved. Further, both the manager and the employee know what is happening, and corrections can be made if so indicated. Again, we emphasize that evaluating performance is a continuous activity and that setting a standard or target allows for it to be meaningful and job related.

Ideally, the employee should have a role in establishing the standard. Research has shown that the more employees participate in setting job expectations, the more committed they are to achieving the expected outcome. Preferably, the performance standard should be put in writing. "The advantage of writing out performance standards for each job . . . is that each person knows specifically what is expected of his or her performance in terms of targets or goals" (French, 1978, p. 181). We strongly urge managers to invest the time and effort required, for the results can be well worth the investment. In that regard, it must be recognized that it will take time for the investment to begin to show any return. It is unfortunate that many organizations have attempted to employ such a method but have failed to let time work out the "bugs." The best evidence indicates that it takes from three to five years before the investment of time, money, and effort begins to pay off. What is proposed is closely aligned with the management-by-objectives philosophy of management (discussed in Chapter 7). Those organizations that have successfully used MBO have been willing to "ride it out." It does work if managers are patient.

Remuneration.   Employees must be adequately and properly rewarded for their work. There should be a direct relationship between performance and reward. The better an individual performs, the more he or she should be rewarded. How well an individual performs is often related to how well he or she perceives his or her performance is being recognized. As illustrated in Figure 4-1, satisfaction, motivation, performance, and rewards are all integrated. It is essential that the manager recognize the interrelationship among those elements. It is not uncommon to

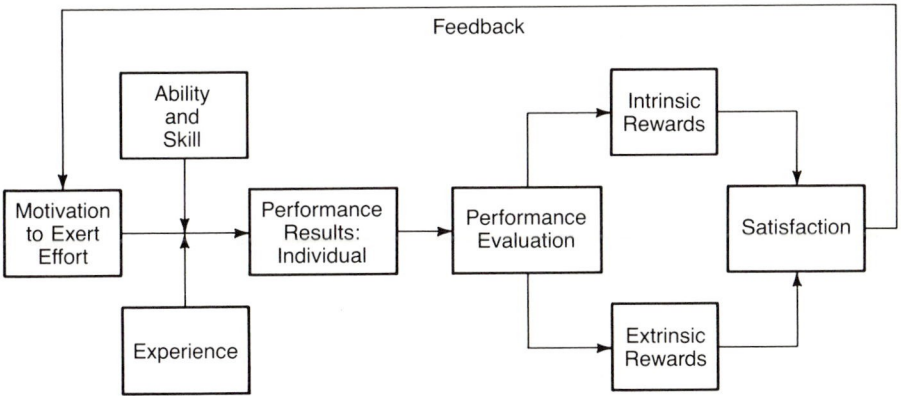

FIGURE 4-1 The Reward Process: Individual Level Only. From J. L. Gibson, J. M. Ivancevich, & J. H. Donnelly, Jr., *Organizations: Behavior, Structure, Processes,* 5th ed. (Plano, Tex.: Business Publications, Inc., 1985), p. 184.

hear an employee say, "Why should I work any harder? Everybody gets the same raise anyway." If at all possible, avoid across-the-board pay increases; they do not take into account the performance of each individual. Yet, without a creditable and equitable performance evaluation system, it is extremely difficult to differentiate among individual employees. Hence, basing the reward system on merit is defensible *only* if an adequate performance appraisal system is in place. For a reward system to be fair, it must not be based on a "good old boy" approach or on personality. It should be based on performance. Individuals within the organization must believe that their level of input (effort) is directly related to outcomes (rewards). If that is not so, then there is perceived inequity, which leads to dissatisfaction, which either adversely affects performance or causes employees to leave and go to an organization where they will be appreciated. Employees do compare their experience with others, and they will view their situation as either equitable or inequitable, as illustrated in Figure 4-2. This tendency to compare should not be underestimated by the manager.

Rewards are classified into two broad categories. Each employee is going to value either *extrinsic* or *intrinsic* rewards more highly. *Extrinsic* rewards are those external to the job, such as salary, promotions, fringe benefits, and working conditions. *Intrinsic* rewards are those associated with doing the job itself and include the satisfaction of needs, such as accomplishing worthwhile duties, being challenged, being responsible, and having autonomy. The importance of all of this is that as a manager you must have some notion of what your employees value in order to meet their needs. For example, a chief probation officer cannot assume that all probation officers will value an increase in salary any more than he or she can assume that all of them will be motivated by being given additional job responsibilities. The manager must know his or her employees. We recognize that there is a limit to how far managers in the human services can go

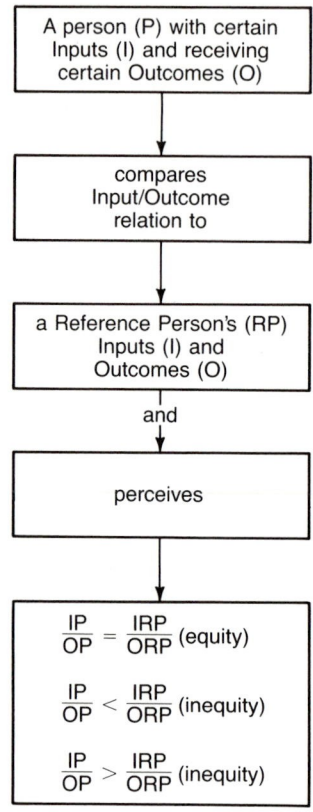

IP   = Inputs of the Person
OP   = Outcomes of the Person
IRP = Inputs of Reference Person
ORP = Outcomes of Reference Person

FIGURE 4-2   The Equity Theory of Motivation. From J. L. Gibson, J. M. Ivancevich, & J. H. Donnelly, Jr., *Organizations: Behavior, Structure, Processes,* 5th ed. (Plano, Tex.: Business Publications, Inc., 1985), p. 161.

with that, but efforts should be made to move in that direction. It is not uncommon for the manager to assume that all employees will value the same reward. The R.N. on the floor might be more motivated by having the opportunity to attend an out-of-state conference than by being transferred to a more responsible position in an intensive care unit. The key is for the manager to know his or her people. To reemphasize a point made earlier, if the performance appraisal system is working properly, then this will be more likely.

Promoting.   Promotion is one form of reward, but a manager should not assume that all employees want to be promoted. Some individuals value promotions highly and some do not want them at all. As was stated previously, the manager must know whom he or she is dealing with.

The system of promotion must be perceived as equitable. While seniority is a factor, it cannot be the only criterion. If the performance appraisal system is working, then promotions should be tied to performance. All organizations have to be careful not to promote people to their level of incompetence. For an organization to be effective, it should identify those employees most capable of handling promotion. Earlier in this chapter we discussed the assessment center technique. That technique can be used quite effectively in identifying individuals for promotion. The same procedure is followed, and the individual demonstrating the greatest potential for success will be identified. The value of the approach is that it is the best method available to eliminate subjective judgments.

Granted, the manager must have a significant role in assembling his or her team, but, at the same time, any manager should desire to have a team that has the best chance of succeeding. No manager should want a cadre of "yes people." The promotion process in the organization is vital to achieving the organizational mission. To promote individuals who are incapable or who have no desire to assume additional responsibilities serves no one. "The purpose of a promotion is to staff a vacancy that, in general, is worth more to the organization than the incumbent's present position" (French, 1978, p. 281). Those responsible for implementing the promotion system should keep that in mind. The basic question is, Who will best serve the needs of the organization?

Dismissal. Terminating someone's employment is never a pleasant task, and we strongly warn that it not be done capriciously. Dismissal should be based on well-documented information. An employee is discharged either for violating organizational rules, policies, or procedures, or for inadequate performance.

A blatant violation commonly leads to termination. For example, if an R.N. is found to be feeding his or her own drug habit out of the drug cabinet, then in most states the manager has no choice but to discharge the individual. In such instances, the necessary action is obvious. If an employee is habitually tardy or absent, then a decision has to be made as to whether the employee should remain or be dismissed. Every organization must have policies and rules that all employees are expected to follow. Those should be made known to the employees at the time they are hired. Included in any orientation program should be a discussion of the consequence for failure to abide by stated rules and policies. As mentioned earlier, there are some actions for which the only alternative is dismissal; there are other actions that may not require immediate termination.

Failure to perform at an acceptable level can also be grounds for dismissal, but it is not as easy to identify, and it, too, must be supported with documentation. As discussed earlier in this chapter, there should be, for each position, a standard of performance that is understood by all employees. If the performance evaluation system functions properly, inadequate performance can be identified and efforts made to correct the problems. Having a creditable appraisal system reinforces the developmental aspect of the performance evaluation. Yet, there may come a time when all reasonable efforts have been made and termination is the only course of action available. Managers must be sensitive to the provisions of the Civil Rights Act, the Age Discrimination in Employment Act, EEOC rulings, and court decisions that are designed to protect employees from arbitrary and capricious actions. Also, in most union contracts there are additional protections that state that an employee cannot be dismissed without "just cause" (French, 1978, p. 136). That does not mean that an employee cannot be dismissed; it simply means that there must be documented evidence to support the dismissal.

Efforts should be made to keep the employee on if at all possible. It is costly to hire new employees. Therefore, from an economic perspective, it is desirable to attempt to correct whatever problems are evident. A principle that has been widely used in this regard is *progressive discipline.* Simply put, this means that management responds to a first offense with some minimal action, but if unacceptable behavior or performance continues, management's actions become more severe. A sequence of disciplining actions might be as follows (French, 1978, p. 136):

1. Oral warning
2. Written warning stating the consequences of further offenses
3. Disciplining layoff or demotion
4. Discharge

If such a procedure is followed, then management will be protected from most subsequent actions, such as lawsuits and grievances, that the employee might choose to take.

Dismissals may also occur when the organization is forced to reduce its staff. In the human services, that is typically influenced by budgeting constraints. For example, in one state the newly elected governor acted on his campaign promise to reduce the number of state employees by 20 percent during his first two years in office. Needless to say, that had serious consequences to all state agencies, including the Department of Human Services. Another state, faced with a 15-percent reduction in the budget, reduced personnel in the staff development division from twenty-two to four. Reductions in staff may also be caused by advances in technology. The effective use of computers may adversely affect some clerical staff. If a reduction in staff is necessary, how can it be handled fairly?

Seniority should be a factor but not the only factor. Using seniority as the sole criterion means that many of the younger, recently hired personnel will be the first to go. Usefulness to the organizational mission must be included in any personnel decisions. Is June or Martha more useful? Who will best serve the organization? It should be obvious that without an acceptable performance evaluation system, the answers to those questions become quite subjective. Additional questions should be raised. What has been the performance of June compared to Martha since each has been with the organization? Of the two, which one has the requisite skills most needed? Which one gives the best evidence of potential for development? As such questions are answered, the necessary decisions that accompany the reduction will become more obvious.

A Word about Affirmative Action

Earlier in this chapter we mentioned the need for human service organizations to have an affirmative action plan. The following outline has been adapted from *Affirmative Action and Equal Opportunity: A Guidebook for Employees* (U.S. Equal Opportunity Commission, 1974, pp. 18–63) and should be helpful in the development of a plan.

A. *Issue a Written Employment Policy Statement and Affirmative Action Commitment.*
   1. Must be enforced by top management.
   2. All employees must be aware that Equal Employment Opportunity is basic recognized policy.
   3. The statement should include the following elements:
      a. Equal employment opportunity for all persons, regardless of race, creed, color, sex, national origin, or age, is organizational policy.
      b. Such a policy will require specific affirmative action to overcome the effects of past discrimination.
      c. The policy requires new goal-setting programs with measurement and evaluation factors.
      d. Affirmative action will affect all employment practices.
      e. An individual representing top management should be assigned the responsibility of the plan and be held accountable for its success.
B. *Appoint a Top Official with Responsibility and Authority to Implement the Program.*
   1. The responsibilities of the affirmative action program manager include:
      a. Developing a policy statement, a written affirmative action program, and internal and external communication procedures.
      b. Collecting and analyzing relevant employment data, identifying problem areas, setting goals and timetables, and developing new programs to remedy past discrimination.
      c. Designing, implementing, and monitoring internal audit and reporting systems to track the success of the program.
      d. Reporting at least quarterly to the Chief Executive Officer or highest ranking manager.
      e. Serving as liaison between groups within the organization, government regulatory agencies, minority and women's groups, and other community groups.
      f. Assuring that current legal information affecting affirmative action is properly disseminated.
   2. The responsibilities of other department heads and managers include:
      a. Carrying out the plan in his or her area.
      b. Participating in the development of the plan.
C. *Publicize the Affirmative Action Program.*
   1. Internally:
      a. Managers and supervisors should be fully informed in writing.
      b. All employees should be informed of the organization's policy.

      c. Where relevant, union officials should be invited to cooperate in developing and implementing the program.

   2. Externally:

      a. Through regular recruitment sources.

      b. Developing new recruitment sources.

      c. Notifying all subcontractors, vendors, and suppliers in city.

D. *Survey and Analyze Minority and Female Employment by Department and Job Classifications.*

   1. Identify present areas and levels of employment.

   2. Identify areas of under-utilization and concentration.

   3. Determine extent of under-utilization of minorities and females.

E. *Develop Goals and Timetables.*

   1. Set long-range goals.

   2. Set annual intermediate targets.

   3. Identify causes of under-utilization.

F. *Develop and Implement Specific Programs to Eliminate Discriminatory Barriers and Achieve Goals.*

   1. Recruitment.

      a. Analyze and review recruitment procedures for each job category to identify and eliminate discriminatory barriers.

      b. Establish objective measures to analyze and monitor the recruitment process.

      c. Select and train persons involved in the development process to use objective standards and to support affirmative action goals.

      d. Institute affirmative action programs to recruit for all jobs where under-utilization has been identified.

   2. Selection standards and procedures should be reviewed and analyzed in the following areas:

      a. Job-related, validated standards.

      b. Applications forms and pre-employment inquiries.

      c. Testing.

      d. Interviews.

      e. Rating of selection standards.

      f. Monitoring the selection process.

   3. Upward mobility system: assignment, job progression, promotions, transfer, seniority, training.

      a. Identify the barriers.

      b. Develop affirmative programs to overcome identified barriers.

   4. Wage and salary structure should be reviewed and analyzed to assure nondiscrimination.

   5. Benefits and conditions of employment should also be reviewed and analyzed to assure nondiscrimination.

   6. Layoff, recall, discharge, demotion, and disciplinary action, likewise, should be reviewed and analyzed.

   7. The union contract, if applicable, should be reviewed and analyzed and raised, if necessary, to bring it into compliance with the plan.

G. *Establish Internal Audit and Reporting System to Monitor and Evaluate Progress in Each Aspect of the Program.*

H. *Develop Supportive Company and Community Programs.*

   1. Supervisors should be trained so that they understand the legal responsibilities and organizational commitment to the plan.

   2. Support services.

      a. Personal counseling.

    b. Transportation.
    c. Day care.
    d. Housing.
  3. Job-related evaluation.
  4. Cooperation with job-related community programs.

Summary

The manager as leader has numerous responsibilities in the area of staffing. Hiring, training, judging, remunerating, promoting, and dismissing all fall within the purview of the managerial role. We have discussed each of these and its importance. For purposes of discussion, we have dealt with each area individually; however, there is an interrelationship that exists among them that must be recognized by the manager. As the leader, the manager sets the tone and atmosphere for the organization or a particular unit within a larger organizational context.

REFERENCES

FRENCH, W. L. (1978). *The personnel management process: Human resources administration and development* (4th ed.). Boston: Houghton Mifflin.

GOLDMAN, D. (1981, January). The new competency tests: Matching the right people to the right jobs. *Psychology Today,* pp. 35–46.

SCHRADER, A. W. (1969, Fall). Let's abolish the annual performance review. *Management and Personnel Quarterly,* pp. 20–28.

U.S. EQUAL EMPLOYMENT OPPORTUNITY COMMISSION. (1974). *Affirmative action and equal employment: A guidebook for employees,* Volume 1. Washington, D.C.: U.S. Equal Employment Opportunity Commission.

QUESTIONS FOR DISCUSSION

1. How do the various government regulations mandating equal employment opportunities affect the manager's personal function?
2. How would you determine the qualifications needed to fill a newly created position?
3. Discuss the advantages and disadvantages of the assessment center in the selection of personnel in human service organizations.
4. Discuss the proper role of the manager in maintaining discipline within his or her organization.

SUGGESTED PROJECTS

1. Using volunteers from the class as job candidates, set up and implement a selection system for a first-line supervisor for your agency.
2. Design a performance appraisal system to evaluate the performance of your instructor for this course.

The Manager as Leader
The Function of Motivation

chapter 5

As a leader, the manager influences the actions of others toward the achievement of an expected outcome, yet some employees follow and others do not. To understand why, the manager must consider the desires, wants, needs, and motives of the employees. What is it that employee A wants from his or her work experience? The extent to which the manager understands what employees want from their jobs will, in large measure, determine his or her effectiveness as a leader. The problem is that many managers look at all others through their own "looking glass." That is, they tend to superimpose on the employees the same needs, drives, wants, desires, and motives that the managers have. To be effective, the manager needs to know what "button to push" with each of his or her immediate subordinates. For example, Jane has no interest whatsoever in being promoted to the head nurse's position. She values the bedside contact with the patients. Her need to care for others is the reason she became a nurse. To promote Jane to a supervisory position would significantly compromise the direct patient contact that she finds so meaningful. On the other hand, June is an achiever and would like to be a director of nursing services. She longs for the day when she will become a head nurse. To promote June would meet her needs and desires. The point is that a manager must know his or her employees. That can only occur by communicating with them— listening and interacting. As the manager becomes acquainted with those who work for him or her, the manager can enhance his or her effectiveness as a leader by being responsive to what "turns them on."

That will not be possible in all situations, however. It may be necessary to assign a caseworker in a local welfare office to adult service cases, even though he or she would prefer working with child protective services. Nevertheless, the astute manager would consider transferring the individual as soon as possible. Failure to recognize the employee's preference will inevitably lead to dissatisfaction with the job and will have an impact on morale, with all of the attendant consequences, such as higher rates of absenteeism, more frequent tardiness, poorer quality of work, and lower productivity. Managers would do well to note the advertisement of a midwestern dairy: "Contented cows give good milk." Employees spend a significant amount of each day at work, and the more managers attend to the needs of employees, the more those employees will accomplish for themselves and for the organization. Several years ago, McGregor (1960) took the position that the optimal relationship between individual needs and organizational needs is one in which the needs of the individual are met as he or she works toward meeting the needs of the organization. Again, we stress that the manager must be cognizant of those individual needs.

THEORIES OF MOTIVATION

Maslow (1954) proposed that an individual's needs are arranged in a hierarchy. There are five levels of needs, with the physiological needs being the lowest level of need and self-actualization the highest level. The physiological needs have the highest strength, and once they are met, the safety-security needs become dominant. This process continues through the needs hierarchy, as shown in Figure 5-1. Some examples of each need level are given in Figure 5-2.

Although Maslow's theory was not based on empirical findings, it does provide a conceptual framework in regard to individual employees. An important criticism of the framework is that not all employees have the need to grow and develop, as is indicated in the highest order needs—self-actualization. While Maslow states that there are need deficiencies as you move up the hierarchy, each person's needs must be determined individually. Indeed, highly deficient needs do pose potential dangers for managers. As noted by Gibson et al. (1979), unsatisfied needs can lead to frustration, conflict, and stress (p. 106). The skilled intensive care nurse who is assigned to complete clerical work may have her self-actualization needs blocked by what she considers menial activity. The results may be frustration and stress, which could affect her performance. The point is that the manager needs to be aware of the consequences that may arise from work assignments.

A few years after Maslow proposed the needs hierarchy, Herzberg and his associates (1959) introduced the two-factor theory of motivation. Their research led them to the conclusion that there are job conditions that influence an individual's satisfaction or dissatisfaction. Prior to Herzberg, it was generally assumed that job satisfaction was either high, low, or somewhere in between. However, Herzberg argued that there are factors relevant to the job that lead to dissatisfaction, and that there are other factors that lead to satisfaction. Therefore, as noted in Figure 5-3, there are separate continua for satisfaction and dissatisfaction.

Summarizing the two-factor theory, Herzberg et al. (1959) stated that there are those factors that are extrinsic dimensions of a job and result in

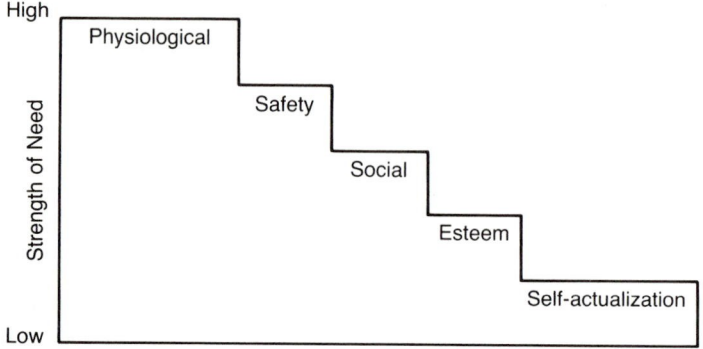

FIGURE 5-1 Maslow's Needs Hierarchy. Data based on Hierarchy of Needs in "A Theory of Human Motivation" in *Motivation and Personality,* 2nd edition, by Abraham H. Maslow. Copyright © 1970 by Abraham H. Maslow. Reprinted by permission of Harper & Row, Publishers, Inc.

dissatisfaction when they are not present. He went on to conclude that if they are present, their impact on motivation is minimal; they serve a maintenance function to reduce the degree of dissatisfaction. Such factors include salary, job security, working conditions, status, organizational procedures, quality of technical supervision, and quality of interpersonal relations among peers, superiors, and subordinates. In other words, these factors are external to the job itself.

There is another set of dimensions, which are intrinsic to the job itself. These conditions directly influence motivation, thereby affecting job performance. They do not prove highly dissatisfying, but they do act as motivators or satisfiers and include achievement, recognition, responsibility, advancement, the work itself, and the possibility of growth.

Although Herzberg's contribution to the study of motivation has been severely criticized, such criticism should not detract from the theory's usefulness to practicing managers. Managers within the human services can be responsive to those dimensions of the work environment that Herzberg identified as motivators. For example, for the local county welfare director to recognize a particular service unit's effort "beyond the call of duty" can go a long way in influencing motivation and subsequent job performance. Further, it is an inexpensive way to reward success.

David McClelland's (1962) contribution to the body of theory on motivation postulates that needs are acquired through an individual's culture. He identified three types of needs: the need for *achievement* (nAch), the need for *affiliation* (nAff), and the need for *power* (nPow). A strong need will lead to behavior that satisfies that particular need. If there is a strong need for achievement, the individual is likely to meet that need by setting challenging goals. He or she will work hard to achieve those goals by using the necessary skills and abilities to accomplish them.

On the other hand, if an individual has a strong need for affiliation, then he or she will be concerned with the quality of interpersonal relationships. To such an individual, social relationships are more important than accomplishing tasks. A person with a high need for affiliation wants to be "liked."

Individuals who have a strong need for power have a marked desire to influence others and to win arguments by exercising power and authority. In this regard, McClelland indicates that there are two orientations. One is negative and is seen in individuals who emphasize dominance and submission; the other is positive and builds upon persuasion and inspirational behavior. McClelland and Burnum (1976) have reported on subsequent

FIGURE 5-2 Examples of Needs. From L. Rue & L. Byars, *Management: Theory and Application* (Homewood, Ill.: Richard D. Irwin, 1977), p. 198.

PHYSIOLOGICAL NEEDS

1. Food and drink
2. Sleep
3. Health
4. Body needs
5. Exercise and rest
6. Sex

SAFETY NEEDS

1. Security and safety
2. Protection
3. Comfort and peace
4. No threats of dangers
5. Orderly and neat surroundings
6. Assistance of long-term economic well-being

SOCIAL NEEDS

1. Acceptance
2. Feeling of belonging
3. Membership in group
4. Love and affection
5. Group participation

ESTEEM NEEDS

1. Recognition and prestige
2. Confidence and leadership
3. Competence and success
4. Strength and intelligence

SELF-ACTUALIZATION NEEDS

1. Self-fulfillment of potential
2. Doing things for the challenge of accomplishment
3. Intellectual curiosity
4. Creativity and aesthetic appreciation
5. Acceptance of reality

research that further amplifies the concept of power and how it is used by managers. They concluded that of the three managerial types studied (affiliation, personal, and institutional), the institutional manager is most effective. Good management is directly affected by the need for power. However, it is important to consider how power is used. The manager who is driven by a need for personal power is self-directed, and, although effective, he or she is not a good institutional builder. Subordinates will identify more strongly with the manager as an individual than with the organization he or she represents. On the other hand, the institutional manager creates an environment in which subordinates identify with the organization and not the person. Over time, the institutional orientation was found to be most effective.

In summary, McClelland believes that needs are learned through environmental experiences; thus, behavior that is rewarded is reinforced and tends to recur more frequently. If the needs of individuals can be determined, then McClelland's contribution can be beneficial in placing individuals in positions where they have the greatest chance to contribute to the organizational mission.

Victor Vroom's (1964) contribution to the body of theory on motivation is the expectancy theory. *Expectancy* is the perceived probability that a given level of effort will result in a specific action. For example, the charge nurse on pediatrics may ask, "If I perform well at this level (effort), will I be likely to be promoted (outcome)?" A corollary question is, What is the strength of an individual's desire for a particular outcome? Vroom calls this *valence*. Performance of the job is a *first-level outcome* and its valence will be determined by an individual's estimate that his or her performance will lead to a series of *second-level outcomes*, such as raises or promotions, and the valence associated with those outcomes. A final component of the expectancy theory is *instrumentality*. Vroom refers to instrumentality as a subjective probability estimate. The following questions illustrate the process that the individual will engage in either consciously or subconsciously:

1. How important are the various second-level outcomes, such as promotions or salary increases? (valence)
2. Will the first-level outcome (high performance) lead to a promotion or salary increase? (instrumentality)
3. Will exerting effort in fact achieve high performance? (expectancy)

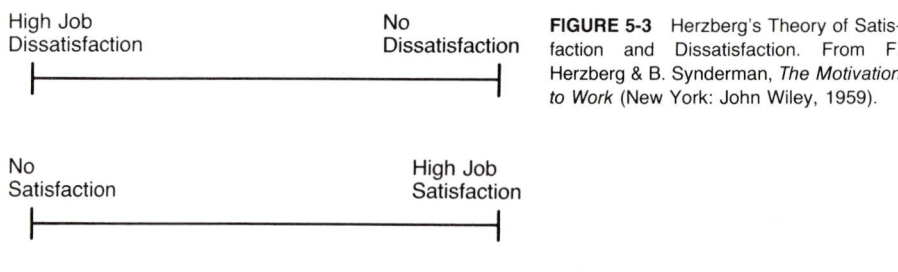

High Job Dissatisfaction — No Dissatisfaction

No Satisfaction — High Job Satisfaction

FIGURE 5-3 Herzberg's Theory of Satisfaction and Dissatisfaction. From F. Herzberg & B. Synderman, *The Motivation to Work* (New York: John Wiley, 1959).

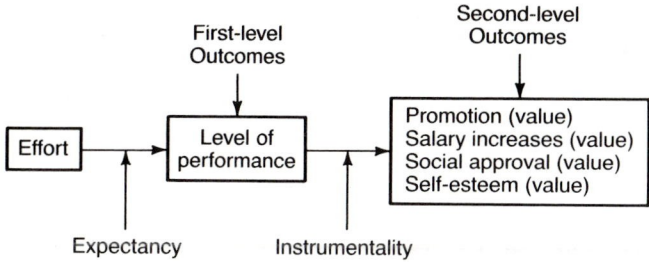

FIGURE 5-4   The Expectancy Theory of Motivation. From J. L. Gibson, J. M. Ivancevich, & J. H. Donnelly, Jr., *Organizations: Behavior, Structure, Processes,* 3rd ed. (Plano, Tex.: Business Publications, Inc., 1979), p. 114.

Figure 5-4 illustrates Vroom's conceptualization of the process of motivation.

Although expectancy theory has its critics, it can be useful for managers. Gibson et al. (1979) noted that in applying the theory, managers should do the following:

1. *Determine* what outcomes are important to each employee. This can be done by asking, observing, and listening.
2. Clearly *identify* what behavior and performances are desired. The subordinate should understand the manager's expectations.
3. Establish levels of performance that are *challenging* yet attainable. If the levels of performance are too high, motivation will be dampened.
4. *Link* important outcomes to desired performance levels. The reward system must be accurate, prompt, and visible. Any system that is inequitable will cause problems. Equity should not be interpreted as equality, where everyone receives the same rewards.
5. Make *sure* that *changes* in outcomes are large enough. In examining the motivational program, a manager should attempt to make sure that changes in outcomes or rewards are large enough to motivate significant behavior. Small changes often result in small increases in effort.

The contributions of Maslow, Herzberg, McClelland, and Vroom provide a backdrop for discussing the relationship between the design of the job and the motivation of employees. Inherent in each of the theories presented is the belief that each individual in the organization is unique. Employees all have different drives, motives, wants, desires, expectations, and life experiences. Their motivation to perform is closely related to the job itself.

THE DESIGN OF THE JOB AND MOTIVATION

In this section we will consider the process by which job tasks and responsibilities are created by the manager. How well this is done will affect the ultimate effectiveness of the organization. There is more to designing jobs than simply identifying the best way to perform a specific job, as argued by Taylor and others (Taylor, 1911). A relatively recent development, known as "quality of work life," has gone beyond the "one best way" approach. The extent to which people satisfy their personal needs in their involvement with the organization will influence their productivity in carrying out their tasks and responsibilities. That does not suggest that the organization's needs are compromised; rather, in designing jobs, managers should consider the relationship between the needs of the organization and the needs of those who work within the organization. McGregor (1960) stated that managers should encourage "the creation of conditions such that the members of the organization can achieve their own goals *best* by directing their efforts toward the success of the enterprise" (p. 49). It has become evident that the more satisfied the employee, the more effective the organization. What the needs of employees are and what obstacles prevent the fulfillment of those needs is the principal concern of job design and redesign strategies.

Job Scope

The application of the principles of division of labor and delegation of authority affects job scope. As jobs within the organization are developed, an important managerial decision is the number of tasks or activities that each job holder will be expected to perform. This is the *range* of a job. Another dimension of job scope is the *depth* of a job, or the amount of discretion each individual has to alter or influence the job. The range of a job is affected by how management divides up the labor, while depth is directly related to the extent of delegation within the organization. It should be noted that with the employment of significant numbers of professionals in human service organizations, the concern for acting autonomously is heightened. Managers should take that into consideration in the design of specific jobs.

Job Relationships

In designing jobs, managers also need to give thought to the extent to which individuals can form meaningful relationships with others and with groups within the organization. As mentioned earlier, the more satisfied and fulfilled an employee is in the job, the more productive he or she will be. Thus, the opportunity to interact with others is an important consideration. Man, as a social animal, needs to have social relationships, although the degree of need varies among individuals. In view of the fact that each of us spends a considerable number of hours in a job, the more we obtain from the job on a personal basis, the more satisfied we will be in our day-to-day activity.

Some of the interpersonal needs employees have will be met through relationships with individuals, but the groups of which they are a part will also have a bearing on the fulfillment of those needs. The more cohesive the group, the more members identify with it and are loyal to it. Frequently, this is affected by how organizations make up units, departments, or bureaus. The more homogeneous the work group, the greater the potential for cohesiveness. If departmentalization is on a functional basis, then those performing similar jobs will be in the same unit or department, creating a more homogeneous group. On the other hand, if departmentalization is by client group, then individuals performing a variety of jobs will be in the same work group, creating a more heterogeneous group. If managers review some of the foregoing discussion, they will see that the problems associated with heterogeneity can be overcome by allowing for greater participation of the group in the decision-making process. The principle of span of control is also important in job relationships. The wider the span of control, the larger the group, the more difficult it is for members of the group to communicate with each other. Communication is an integral factor in the formation of cohesive work groups, be they homogeneous or heterogeneous.

Job Content

Job content refers to the various aspects of the job as perceived by the job holder. The content of a job will be objectively stated in a job description; however, the subjective perceptions of the job holder are of equal importance in any analysis of a specific job.

One approach that has been used to measure perceived job content is the Job Characteristics Index (Sims et al., 1976, p. 197). The following six characteristics are analyzed by the Job Characteristics Index:

1. *Variety*—the degree to which a job requires employees to perform a wide range of operations in their work and/or the degree to which employees must use a variety of equipment and procedures in their work.
2. *Autonomy*—the extent to which employees have a major say in scheduling their work, selecting the equipment they will use, and deciding on procedures to be followed.
3. *Task Identity*—the extent to which employees do an entire or a whole piece of work and can clearly identify with the results of their efforts.
4. *Feedback*—the degree to which employees receive information as they are working, which reveals how well they are doing the job.
5. *Dealing with Others*—the degree to which a job requires employees to deal with other people to complete their work.
6. *Friendship Opportunities*—the degree to which a job allows employees to talk with one another on the job and to establish informal relationships with other employees at work.

With the Job Characteristics Index, job range is measured by the responses to *variety, task identity,* and *feedback;* job depth is assessed by the response to *autonomy;* and job relationships are analyzed by the responses of the employee to *dealing with others* and *friendship opportunities.* Ideally, there should be some common responses among those performing similar jobs.

Another approach used to measure job content is the Job Diagnostic Survey, which includes variety, task identity, autonomy, feedback, and significance (Hackman & Oldman, 1975). This survey adds significance, which is defined as the perceived importance of the work being done to the organization or to others within the organization. It does not measure any characteristics that deal with job relationships. It is argued that the five characteristics of the Job Diagnostic Survey are core dimensions that management can manipulate to increase productivity (Hackman & Oldman, 1975).

Although the two approaches are attempts to measure the employee's perception of a job, it should be kept in mind that one's perception is affected by individual differences and needs. The level of needs satisfaction will have some influence upon the way an individual sees the job.

Approaches to Redesigning Job Range and Job Depth

A major problem confronting many human service organizations is job burnout. Individuals get "fed up" with the job, and this is reflected in high rates of turnover and absenteeism, low productivity, and poor quality of work. Frequently, it is the job itself that fosters the "burned out" syndrome. Is there any way to overcome, control, or prevent burnout? We will consider three approaches: job rotation, job enlargement, and job enrichment.

Job rotation is just what it implies. Employees are rotated through various jobs in an attempt to reduce boredom generated by doing the same thing over and over. Job rotation increases the range of jobs, thus providing more variety. For some employees, being moved around among jobs could be very beneficial; for others, it could be frustrating. If managers are to consider this approach, it will be important for them to know what the employee wants out of the job and what needs could be met through the job. Deciding unilaterally to move people about could prove to be disruptive and dysfunctional to the organization.

Job enlargement refers to increasing the number of tasks to be performed by an employee. Boredom is counteracted by the greater variety provided through the enlargement of the job. Other aspects of job range need to be considered, too, such as providing feedback on the individual's performance, provision of a meaningful work module, proper utilization of the individual's ability, and greater worker control of the job to be completed (Chung & Ross, 1977). Of course, for job enlargement to be effective, the employees must be amenable to it. If they do not have the necessary abilities to handle a more complex array of tasks, it is meaningless to enlarge their jobs. However, as mentioned earlier, managers should know what their employees are able to handle.

The final approach to redesigning a job is job enrichment, which occurs through direct changes in the job itself. With job enrichment, the depth of the job is modified. It provides more freedom to make decisions in areas that affect an employee's job. Job enrichment attempts to have every employee think like a manager in fulfilling the responsibilities of the job.

None of the strategies for redesigning jobs can be successful without the adequate preparation and training of both employees and supervisory personnel. Without proper training, any of the three approaches becomes an empty effort. That is especially true for job enlargement and job enrichment. There must be some significant attitudinal changes among employees and supervisors within the organization. For example, with job enrichment, not all decisions will be left to managerial personnel, and some managers find this quite disconcerting. However, with the proper orientation, any of the approaches can be used to counteract the conditions that lead to burnout and its attendant problems.

THEORIES OF LEADERSHIP

There is no one best way to lead. Although much has been written on the subject of leadership, we will give primary attention to two theories that have a substantial degree of usefulness to the human service manager. We will also review some of the significant contributions that have influenced our selection of the two theoretical approaches.

We would be remiss not to note the contributions of McGregor (1960) and particularly his conceptualization of Theory X and Theory Y. The assumptions that are noted under X and Y will, indeed, influence how a manager deals with people. Figure 5-5 identifies those assumptions, and it

FIGURE 5-5 Assumptions about People. From D. McGregor, *The Human Side of Enterprise* (New York: McGraw-Hill, 1960), pp. 33–34, 47–48. Reprinted by permission of the publisher.

THEORY X

1. The average human being has an inherent dislike of work and will avoid it if he can.
2. Because of their human characteristic of dislike of work, most people must be coerced, controlled, directed, threatened with punishment to get them to put forth adequate effort toward the achievement of organizational objectives.
3. The average human being prefers to be directed, wishes to avoid responsibility, has relatively little ambition, wants security above all.

THEORY Y

1. The expenditure of physical and mental effort in work is as natural as play or rest.
2. External control and the threat of punishment are not the only means for bringing about effort toward organizational objectives. Man will exercise self-direction and self-control in the service of objectives to which he is committed.
3. Commitment to objectives is a function of the rewards associated with their achievement.
4. The average human being learns, under proper conditions, not only to accept but also to seek responsibility.
5. The capacity to exercise a relatively high degree of imagination, ingenuity, and creativity in the solution of organizational problems is widely, not narrowly, distributed in the population.
6. Under the conditions of modern industrial life, the intellectual potential of the average human being is only partially utilized.

can readily be seen how they would affect the manner in which a manager seeks to influence subordinates.

Likert (1961) argued for organizational structures that enhance the involvement of others in the business of managing. Such a participative, or System 4 type, organization, requires individuals in managerial positions who effectively utilize and draw upon the contributions of subordinates. Note the depiction of Likert's (1967) concept in such an organization:

> *Leadership process* includes perceived confidence and trust between superiors and subordinates in all matters. Subordinates feel free to discuss job problems with their superiors who in turn solicit their ideas and opinions.

In his research, Likert (1961) determined the style of supervisory and managerial personnel which he found. They were either *task centered* or *people centered*. It was his conclusion that those who were people centered were more successful and effective in the long run.

Blake and Mouton's (1964) *managerial Grid®* has certainly made a contribution to the study of leadership. They proposed that the *concern for production* and the *concern for people* are compatible through a team management approach. The Grid, as illustrated in Figure 5-6, highlights five types of managers. You will note that each style has significant implications for how managers lead or direct.

At Ohio State University (Fleishman, 1973), a significant body of research on leadership was done, in which two independent factors were isolated: *initiating structure* and *consideration*. These factors are defined as follows:

> *Initiating structure.* The leader organizes and defines the relationship in the work group, well-defined patterns and channels of communication are established, and the manner in which the job is to be done is spelled out.
>
> *Consideration.* Behavior between the leader and the followers is characterized by friendship, mutual trust, respect, warmth, and rapport.

It has been suggested that over time the situation determines how a person will lead. While that might appear to be overly simplistic, we propose that, indeed, it is the case. Tannenbaum and Schmidt (1958) derived from their research that there are three sets of forces that affect leadership: the *forces in the manager*, the *forces in the subordinates*, and the *forces in the situation*. Let us look at these a bit more closely.

The forces in the manager include his or her value system, confidence in subordinates, leadership inclinations, and feelings of security in an uncertain situation. The forces in the subordinates are affected by the extent to which the manager can permit subordinates greater freedom. Greater freedom is possible if the following conditions exist: subordinates have a relatively high need for independence; they have a readiness to assume responsibility for decision making; there is evidence of a relatively high degree of tolerance for ambiguity; subordinates are interested in the problem and see it as important; they possess the necessary knowledge and

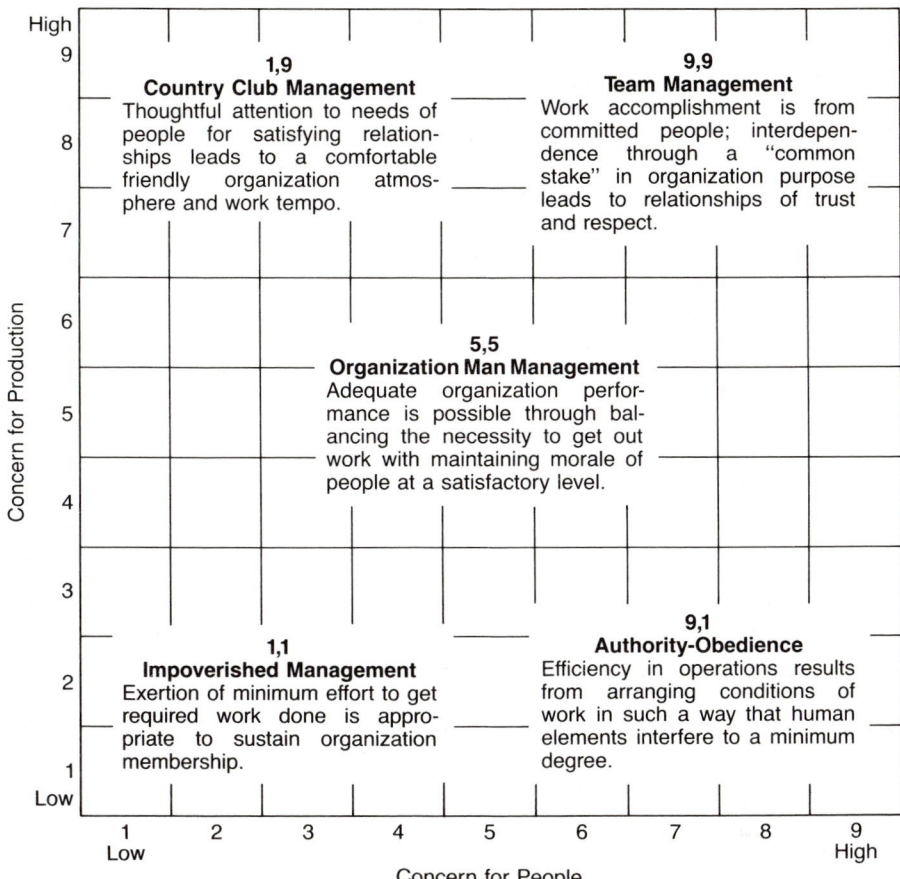

FIGURE 5-6 The Managerial Grid. The Managerial Grid figure from *The Managerial Grid III,* by Robert R. Blake and Jane Srygley Mouton. Houston: Gulf Publishing Company, Copyright © 1985, p. 12. Reproduced by permission.

experiences to deal with the problem; and they have learned to expect to share in decision making. The forces in the situation are affected by the type of organization, the effectiveness of the work group, the nature of the specific problem, and the pressure of time.

Tannenbaum and Schmidt concluded that what they proposed has two implications. First, the successful leader is keenly aware of the forces that are relevant to his or her behavior at any given time. He or she understands himself or herself, the individuals who compose the work group, and the organization and social environment in which he or she operates. Second, to be successful, the leader must be able to behave appropriately. If direction is indicated, then he or she directs; if participative freedom is needed, then the leader provides it. Thus, to be successful, one must maintain a "high batting average" in the assessment of the forces that determine how he or she should behave.

The work of Tannenbaum and Schmidt was augmented by the efforts of Fiedler (1967). Fiedler's contingency model of leadership postulates that the performance of work groups is dependent upon the interaction of leadership style and situational favorableness. The relationship between power and influence is what determines whether one is effective as a leader. In the contingency model, there are three situational factors that influence the leader's effectiveness: leader-worker relations, task structure, and position power. Leader-worker relations refers to the degree of trust, respect, and confidence that followers have in the leader. Task structure refers to the degree to which the job tasks are structured. Position power refers to the power that is inherent in the respective position.

Fiedler indicated that there are two basic styles of leadership: the task-motivated and relationship-motivated. The former satisfies the leader's needs for satisfaction in task accomplishment, while the relationship-motivated style is oriented toward the individual's need to have good interpersonal relations within the group and to have a position of prominence in the group. To determine the dominant style, Fiedler used a unique approach. A Least Preferred Co-Worker (LPC) score is arrived at by asking the individual being assessed to consider all the people with whom he or she has worked and to think of those with whom they could work least effectively, "the least preferred co-worker." The same individual would be asked to describe the person with whom he or she could work most effectively. This would provide a Most Preferred Co-Worker (MPC) score. The two scores are calculated to arrive at the Assumed Similarity Between Opposites (ASO) score. A scale consisting of sixteen items was used for determining both the LPC and the MPC scores and included items such as these:

Frustrating	1	2	3	4	5	6	7	8	Helpful
Tense	1	2	3	4	5	6	7	8	Relaxed
Unpleasant	1	2	3	4	5	6	7	8	Pleasant
Unfriendly	1	2	3	4	5	6	7	8	Friendly
Rejecting	1	2	3	4	5	6	7	8	Accepting

A low ASO score indicates that the most and least preferred co-workers are quite dissimilar, while a high ASO score indicates that there is similarity between the most and least preferred co-worker. Thus, Fiedler classified those with high ASO scores as relationship-motivated leaders and those with low scores as task-motivated leaders.

Fiedler's work is summarized in Figure 5-7 and, as noted, he indicates which style would be most effective.

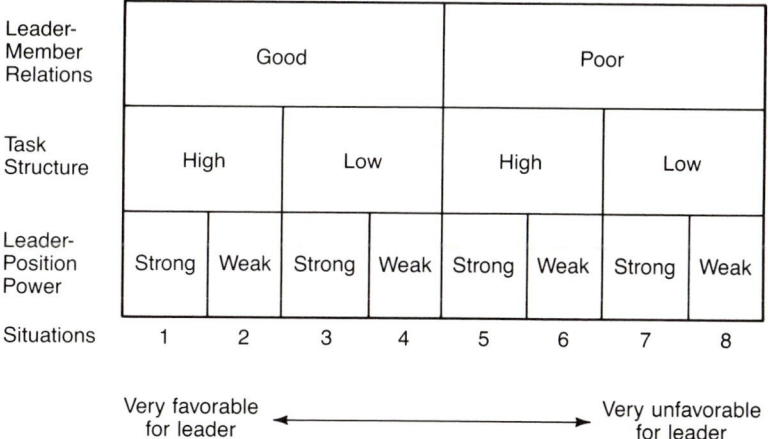

Leader- Member Relations	Good				Poor			
Task Structure	High		Low		High		Low	
Leader- Position Power	Strong	Weak	Strong	Weak	Strong	Weak	Strong	Weak
Situations	1	2	3	4	5	6	7	8

Very favorable   ⟵⟶   Very unfavorable
for leader   for leader

FIGURE 5-7   Relationship of Leadership Style to Situation. From F. E. Fiedler & M. M. Chemers, *Leadership and Effective Management* (Glenview, Ill.: Scott, Foresman, 1974), p. 70.

The foregoing discussion provides the backdrop for the two theories we will highlight. The first of these is the Life Cycle Theory as developed by Hersey and Blanchard (1982). This theory states that as the leader's followers mature, there is less need for structure (task) as well as less need for the leader to be involved with socioemotional support (relationships), as noted in Figure 5-8. Therefore, the maturity of the individuals within the work group should determine the extent to which the leader is involved.

Each of the four leadership styles—telling, selling, participating, and delegating—combines task and relationship behavior. Task behavior deals with the extent to which a leader directs subordinates by telling them what to do, when to do it, where to do it, and how to do it. It involves setting goals for the subordinates as well as defining their roles (Hersey & Blanchard, 1982, p. 152). Relationship behavior, on the other hand, is the extent to which the leader involves himself or herself in two-way communication with those for whom he or she has responsibility. Providing support and encouragement, "stroking," and facilitating behaviors characterize this component of the theory. It requires the leader to actively listen and to support the efforts of subordinates (p. 152).

The concept of worker's maturity grows out of the work done by Argyris (1964) and is a question of degrees. As noted in Figure 5-8, the level of maturity, which is divided into four levels, should influence the leader's style of leadership. The style of leadership is an appropriate mixture of task behavior (direction) and relationship behavior (support).

The relationship between task behavior, relationship behavior, and maturity is shown in Table 5-1.

Let us draw more specifically from Hersey and Blanchard (1982) in further describing each of the leadership styles in Table 5-2.

Implicit in following this approach to leadership is the need to assess the maturity level of the followers and act accordingly. The leader should

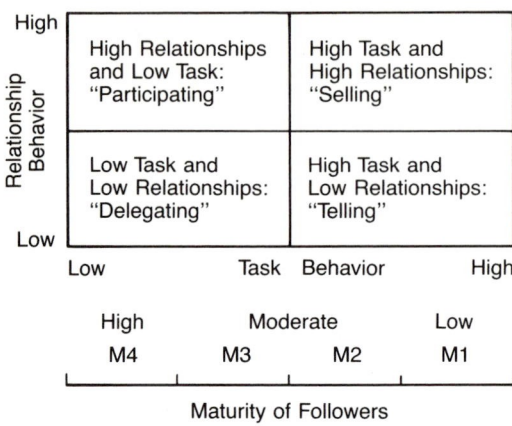

FIGURE 5-8 The Life Cycle Theory. From P. Hersey & K. Blanchard, *Management of Organizational Behavior: Utilizing Human Resources,* 4th edition, © 1982, p. 152. Reprinted by permission of Prentice-Hall, Englewood Cliffs, N.J.

help and encourage followers to mature to the extent that they are able and willing. Such growth is fostered by adjusting the style of leadership as prescribed in Table 5-2. Strong direction of immature followers is appropriate if they are to be productive and contributing members of the organization. However, as the followers mature, there should be a decrease in control as well as in relationship behavior (p. 155). As maturity increases, there is a greater need for autonomy. Yet, if there are slippages in performance, it is appropriate for the leader to back up, reassess the maturity level, and adjust the leadership style. For example if a caseworker is beginning to miss appointments, get behind in the necessary paperwork, and call in "sick" with more frequency, then there has been a slip in performance.

TABLE 5-1. Leadership Styles Appropriate for Various Maturity Levels

MATURITY LEVEL	APPROPRIATE STYLE
M1	S1
Low Maturity:	Telling:
Unable and unwilling or insecure	High task and low relationship behavior
M2	S2
Low to moderate maturity:	Selling:
Unable but willing or confident	High task and high relationship behavior
M3	S3
Moderate to high maturity:	Participating:
Able but unwilling or insecure	High relationship and low task behavior
M4	S4
High Maturity:	Delegating:
Able/competent and willing/confident	Low relationship and low task behavior

Source: P. Hersey and K. Blanchard, *Management of Organizational Behavior: Utilizing Human Resources,* 4th Edition, © 1982, p. 154. Reprinted by permission of Prentice-Hall, Englewood Cliffs, New Jersey.

TABLE 5-2.   Characteristics of the Styles and Leader's Role

STYLE	SUBORDINATE CHARACTERISTICS	LEADER'S ROLE
Telling	Unable and unwilling Lacks competence and confidence Insecure with the task	Directive Clear instructions Defines roles Tells people what, how, when, and where Avoids being viewed as permissive
Selling	Unable but willing Confident but lacks skill Will tend to go along if he or she understands	Directive Reinforcement of willingness and enthusiasm Seeks to get people to "buy into" desired behaviors Offers help and direction
Participating	Able but unwilling Lacks confidence Insecure Reluctance is motivational rather than security problem	Open, two-way communication Actively listens Shares decision making with followers Facilitating
Delegating	Able and willing Confident	Little direction and support Allows followers to carry out plans Limited two-way communication Limited supportive behavior

Source: P. Hersey and K. Blanchard, *Management of Organizational Behavior: Utilizing Human Resources* 4th Edition, pp. 153–154. Adapted by permission of Prentice-Hall, Englewood Cliffs, New Jersey.

In such a situation the leader would need to move back to a selling or even a telling style.

There are several questions that the leader should ask in determining the appropriate style to use:

1. What areas of an individual's or a group's activities do I want to influence?
2. What is the ability or motivation (maturity level) of the individual or the group in each of the selected areas?
3. Which style would be appropriate in each of the areas I want to influence?

It is important to realize that in any job there is a variety of activities that an individual or group performs. Thus, one's style of leadership will vary with the same individual or group, depending upon the activity. For example, Mary is very effective in the area of patient care. Her supervisor knows that there is no need to "look over her shoulder" in that area. However, she is very delinquent in keeping up the entries on patients' charts. In the first area, patient care, the leader can use the delegating style. In the second area, keeping patients' charts current and accurate, the leader needs to be much more directive, or telling.

To use Hersey and Blanchard's approach to leadership effectively, the leader must know those who work for him or her and accurately assess each individual or work group. The attractiveness of Hersey and Blanchard's theory is that it allows for fluid leadership. It is built on the premise that there is no one best way to lead and that a leader must be flexible, dependent upon the situation. While there is a need to be flexible, there is an equally important need to be consistent. The balance can be found through proper assessment and application.

The final theory we will focus upon is that developed by Vroom and Jago (1973). Their approach builds upon the research that has been done in participative decision making. In their model they propose that the situation should determine the degree of participative decision making. They emphasize two criteria of decision effectiveness: quality and acceptance.

Decision quality refers to the objective aspects of a decision that influences subordinate behavior aside from any direct influence on motivation. There are some job-related decisions that do affect performance, such as the size of a caseload, the manner in which a hospital ward will be staffed from 11:00 P.M. to 7 A.M., or the response of the agency to a federal directive. On the other hand, there are decisions that are incidental to performance, such as the color of a telephone in an office, the type of ballpoint pens to be purchased, and what type of economy cars should be purchased for the motor pool. Subordinate participation should be sought when decision quality is important for performance and when the subordinates possess ability and information that the leader does not have.

Decision acceptance refers to the degree of subordinate commitment to a decision. In seeking to determine whether a problem requires subordinate commitment, the leader should ask (1) Will subordinates need initiative and judgment to carry out the decision? and (2) Are subordinates inclined to feel strongly about the decision? If the answer to either question is yes, then the situation has an acceptance requirement. The commitment of subordinates to a decision can be crucial; the more they feel it is "theirs," the more inclined they will be to implement it effectively.

Vroom and Jago designed five decision-making styles: two autocratic styles (AI and AII), two consultative styles (CI and CII), and one group style (GII).

In addition to the five decision-making styles, there are seven diagnostic decision rules. The application of these rules will help determine which decision-making style is appropriate for a particular situation. The diagnostic decision rules are (1) the Leader Information Rule, (2) the Goal Congruence Rule, (3) the Unstructured Problem Rule, (4) the Acceptance Rule, (5) the Conflict Rule, (6) the Fairness Rule, and (7) the Acceptance Priority Rule.

The seven decision rules are used to determine what procedures the leader should not use in a given situation. Rules 1–3 protect decision quality, and rules 4–7 protect decision acceptance.

Although Vroom and Jago's approach to leadership and decision making might appear to be complicated, it is not. A more detailed discussion of its application in the human service organization may be found in Chapter 10.

SUMMARY

We have addressed the role of the leader in the motivation of those who work for him or her. We have addressed the importance of motivation by focusing on selected theorists. The contributions of Hersey and Blanchard as well as Vroom and Jago have been highlighted as practical considerations for the manager. The leader role permeates all that a manager does; thus, it is critically important.

REFERENCES

ARGYRIS, C. (1964). *Integrating the individual and the organization.* New York: John Wiley.

BLAKE, R. R., & MOUTON, J. S. (1964). *The managerial grid.* Houston: Gulf Publishing.

CHUNG, K. H., & ROSS, M. F. (1977, January). Differences in motivational properties between job enlargement and job enrichment. *Academy of Management Review,* pp. 114–115.

FIEDLER, F. E. (1967). *A theory of leadership effectiveness.* New York: McGraw-Hill.

FLEISHMAN, E. A. (1973). Twenty years of consideration and structure. In E. A. Fleishman & J. G. Hunt (Eds.), *Current development in the study of leadership.* Carbondale, Ill.: Southern Illinois University Press.

GIBSON, J. L., IVANCEVICH, J. M., & DONNELLY, J. H., JR. (1979). *Organizations: Behavior, structure, processes* (3rd ed.). Plano, Tex.: Business Publications.

HACKMAN, J. R., & OLDMAN, G. R. (1975). Development of the job diagnostic survey. *Journal of Applied Psychology, 60,* 159–170.

HACKMAN, J. R., & SUTTLE, J. L. (EDS.). (1977). *Improving life at work.* Santa Monica, Calif.: Goodyear.

HERSEY, P., & BLANCHARD, K. (1982). *Management of organizational behavior: Utilizing human resources* (4th ed.). Englewood Cliffs, N.J.: Prentice-Hall.

HERZBERG, F., MAUSNER, B., & SYNDERMAN, B. (1959). *The motivation to work.* New York: John Wiley.

LIKERT, R. (1967). *Human organization: Its management and value.* New York: McGraw-Hill.

LIKERT, R. (1961). *New patterns of management.* New York: McGraw-Hill.

MCCLELLAND, D. C. (1962, July–August). Business drive and national achievement. *Harvard Business Review,* pp. 99–112.

MCCLELLAND, D. C., & BURNHAM, D. (1976, March–April). Power is the great motivator. *Harvard Business Review,* pp. 100–111.

MCGREGOR, D. (1960). *The human side of enterprise.* New York: McGraw-Hill.

MASLOW, A. H. (1954). *Motivation and personality.* New York: Harper & Row.

SIMS, H. P., JR., SZILAGI, A. D., & KELLER, R. T. (1976, June). The measurement of job characteristics. *Academy of Management Journal,* pp. 195–212.

TANNENBAUM, R., & SCHMIDT, W. H. (1958, March–April). How to choose a leadership pattern. *Harvard Business Review,* pp. 95–101.

TAYLOR, F. W. (1911). *Principles of scientific management.* New York: Harper & Brothers.

VROOM, V. H. (1964). *Work and motivation.* New York: John Wiley.

VROOM, V. H., & JAGO, A. G. (1974, October). Decision making as a social process: Normative and descriptive models of leader behavior. *Decision Sciences,* pp. 745–749.

QUESTIONS FOR DISCUSSION

1. "People whose need for power is high should not be employed as managers in human service organizations." Do you agree with that statement? Why or why not?

2. From your experience, which set of assumptions about people (Theory X or Theory Y) has the greater impact on your performance? Why?
3. Which of the leadership theories discussed in the chapter do you feel fit your personality best? Why?
4. Describe the application of expectancy theory to the classroom.

SUGGESTED PROJECT

1. Interview a manager in a local agency. During the interview, determine his or her needs and how he or she attempts to motivate subordinates.

The Manager as Liaison

In the liaison role, the manager focuses on organizational networks. Those networks are composed of a series of contacts that enhance the manager's ability to function in an efficient and effective manner. From the viewpoint of the organization, the liaison role serves a variety of functions. Szilagyi and Wallace (1980) state that individuals in a liaison role

> can facilitate the flow of information between two or more interacting units. The normal flow of information between units usually is focused on formal, time-consuming mechanisms, such as memos and formal meetings. The liaison role provides a more informal mechanism that can reduce the time necessary for accurate information flow. Second, because of frequent interactions, the liaison person is generally well acquainted with the nature of the work of each of the interacting groups. This knowledge can provide such benefits as: (a) the ability to assist in the coordination of various complex activities, (b) ability to provide the interacting units with a better understanding of each other's functions and responsibilities, and (c) providing a continuous way of keeping each interacting unit aware of the current progress of intergroup relationships and day-to-day decision making. (p. 247)

For those benefits to be realized the manager must (1) understand the coordinating function within organizations, (2) possess the tools necessary to carry out the activities associated with the function, and (3) develop the personal characteristics essential to the success of the liaison role. The remainder of this chapter will address those elements.

WHAT IS COORDINATION?

Haimann and Scott (1974) define coordination as the "conscious process of assembling and synchronizing differentiated activities so that they function harmoniously in the attainment of organization objectives" (p. 126). That is, the person in the coordinator role is responsible for bringing together into a smoothly operating whole the many and varied tasks essential for organizational success. The need for such an activity is inherent in the principles of organization design discussed in Chapter 2. The initial division of labor creates separate work-flow patterns, which must be assembled in such a fashion that together they will achieve the desired whole. Similarly, the concepts of delegation, span of control, departmentalization, and so on rely upon proper coordinating activities for their successful implementation. Thus, coordination ensures that all elements of organizational work are related and are linked so that all persons are performing the correct tasks at the correct times in attempting to accomplish organizational goals.

The manager faces three basic coordination relationships in his or her day-to-day activities: vertical, horizontal, and diagonal. The vertical coordinating relationship exists between different levels within the organization; the horizontal, between managers on the same level; and the diagonal, between different levels and/or locations. For example, vertical relationships exist between the Director of Nursing and the charge nurses on the various units of the hospital. Horizontal relationships exist between the head O.R. nurse and the head nurse of the surgical receiving unit. A diagonal relationship exists between the head nurse of each unit and the pharmacy. The impact of these types of relationships upon the operating manager is related directly to the degree of dependency that exists between functions, the uncertainty associated with performing a task, and the perspective of the unit.

The level of dependency between operating units is a result of the extent to which they share resources, responsibilities, and tasks. The greater the degree of self-sufficiency of an individual unit, the lower the level of dependency and, therefore, the lower the need for coordination. Conversely, the lower the level of self-sufficiency, the greater the dependency and the greater the need for coordination. While the degree of dependency is organizationally specific, three general categories may be identified: pooled, sequential, and reciprocal.

Pooled dependency characterizes a relationship in which two or more units within an organization are relatively self-sufficient but each contributes to overall organizational goal achievement. For example, within a state welfare organization, County A and County B each make a unique contribution to the accomplishment of state-level goals; however, each county operates relatively independently of the other. Similarly, within a hospital, the laundry and the pharmacy each perform a set of tasks that enable the hospital to function effectively, yet each performs its services somewhat independently of the other.

When the work flow of one unit is directly linked to the work flow of a second unit, a sequential dependency exists. That is, where the *output* of unit A becomes the *input* of unit B, there exists a direct work-flow dependency that increases the need for coordination. For example, in a local welfare department the finished "product" (output)) of the intake unit becomes the raw data (input) for the eligibility unit. If the intake unit does not complete its work properly or on time, the eligibility unit cannot function. Therefore, coordination must occur to ensure an even flow of work.

Reciprocal dependency exists when there are joint products among two or more units within the organization. For example, in a welfare agency information about the level of services provided by the various program areas (output) becomes the raw data (input) for the quality control unit, which in turn become new input for each of the various program areas. When organizations create centralized services or functions such as data processing, central purchasing, or word processing, those functions will have a reciprocal relationship with the operating departments. Since a joint product results from the reciprocal relationships, a high degree of coordination is required to ensure proper functioning.

Uncertainty in the performance of an organization's or unit's functions is a factor that increases the need for coordination. Uncertainty may result from a number of factors, such as the complexity of the unit task assignments. The coordination problem of a unit assigned to a single task that is repeated day after day will be significantly less than the coordination problem of a unit responsible for a wide range of tasks with intermittent performance requirements. For example, an accounting unit responsible for maintaining accounts will have far fewer problems with coordination than a public relations unit whose tasks may change from hour to hour. In general, the more routine the task and the greater the extent to which the tasks performed by an individual unit are governed by standard operating procedures, the less difficult the coordination problem.

As uncertainty in the performance of a unit's task increases, the need for additional information and a greater number of interactions among units also increases. For example, the emergency unit in a large metropolitan hospital is characterized by a high degree of uncertainty; therefore, both the information requirements and the number of contacts with other units within the hospital tend to be high in relation to general hospital functions.

Finally, the primary focus or perspective of an individual unit will affect the degree of difficulty experienced in coordination. For example, an income maintenance unit focuses upon providing a client immediate relief in the form of dollar payments within a thirty-day period after eligibility determination. In contrast to that short-term perspective, the social service unit focuses upon a more ambiguous set of objectives in dealing with its clients and maintains a much longer-term perspective. Thus, the social service unit will generally be characterized by (1) a greater number of reciprocal dependencies, (2) a large number of interactions with other units, (3) increased information requirements, and (4) more uncertainty in the performance of its functions. This results in a much more complex and difficult coordination problem for the social services unit than for the income maintenance unit.

Table 6-1 provides an illustration of the relationships affecting the need for coordination. The degree of difficulty faced by operating managers in obtaining a high level of performance is determined by the type of dependency, level of uncertainty, and unit perspective. For example,

interacting groups with low interaction requirements (pooled interdependence), low information-flow requirements (low task uncertainty), and lower-

TABLE 6-1. Influence upon the Coordination Activity

UNIT	TYPE OF DEPENDENCY	LEVEL OF UNCERTAINTY	PERSPECTIVE
Planning	Pooled: Public Relations Sequential: Research & Statistics Reciprocal: Finance	High	Long-term
Child Support Enforcement	Pooled: Personnel Sequential: Intake Reciprocal: Court System	Moderate	Intermediate
Eligibility	Pooled: Employee Benefits Sequential: Intake Reciprocal: Payment	Low	Short-term

level needs for integration (minimal differences in time and goal orientation) would encounter the least difficulty in achieving a high level of intergroup performance. Conversely, interacting groups with high interaction requirements (reciprocal interdependence), high information requirements (high task uncertainty), and high required levels for integration (large differences in time and goal orientation) would experience the greatest difficulty in achieving a high level of intergroup performance. (Szilagyi & Wallace, 1980, p. 243)

The discussion of coordination would be incomplete without mentioning the need for external coordination. As we discussed in Chapter 2, human service organizations are dependent upon funding agencies, client groups, other agencies with whom they have entered into joint ventures, and the rule makers who control their delivery of service. Most of those relationships are characterized by a reciprocal dependence with high information requirements and requiring high levels of integration. Thus, within most human service organizations much attention is devoted to managing those relationships.

MANAGING THE COORDINATION FUNCTION

The substance of coordination, as discussed in the previous section, is attempting to obtain the proper action at the correct time from each individual within the organization. The central question to be addressed in this section is, How does the organization achieve coordination? Within organizations the answer to that question may be found in three levels: individual cooperation, organizational direction, and organizational design.

Frequently, within an organization individuals or groups find that voluntary cooperation enhances their performance and simplifies the tasks performed by each. In such instances these individuals or groups are, in fact, engaging in coordinating activities. For example, when a department head discusses a change in work scheduling within his or her unit with other department heads whose work may be affected by the change, even though such discussion is not required, he or she is engaging in a cooperative coordination activity.

All individuals or units within an organization cannot be expected to achieve this cooperative state in all matters and at all times. Indeed, relying upon voluntary efforts is, in many instances, wasteful of organizational resources, so organizations provide direction for their members to ensure coordination of activities. One such method used by organizations is the establishment of standard operating procedures that reduce the required information flows and interactions between groups. All organizations prescribe rules, policies, procedures, and practices that have the effect of standardizing the performance of certain tasks throughout the organization, thereby reducing the level of coordination necessary to perform those tasks. For example, organizations establish travel policies and travel reporting procedures. The reader can readily imagine the confusion that would exist within organizations if each department determined its own travel authorization standards, reimbursement levels, and reporting procedures. To achieve voluntary coordination of travel effort in such a situation would require tremendous effort. That effort is replaced by a single standard operating procedure.

A second level of organizationally directed coordination that is drawn from the principles of organization discussed in Chapter 2 is that of a common superior. Where two or more organizational units are highly integrated and require a coordinated effort, we usually find that they report to a common superior, who is primarily responsible for the coordination of effort between units under his or her direction. This might be called the "kick-it-upstairs" strategy, since it assumes that an individual in a superior position will be able to use the power and authority of the position to resolve problems within his or her sphere of influence. The problems associated with the implementation of this strategy should be obvious when you recall the discussion of span of control.

Where the problems of coordination exceed the ability of the common-superior strategy, organizations are increasingly relying upon the planning process to provide for adequate coordination of organizational tasks. Through the implementation of proper planning procedures, areas requiring coordination with the organization may be identified at the planning stage, and the necessary coordination of tasks may be built into the plan. For example, the implementation of a work release program for prisoners requires efforts by both prison officials and probation staff to ensure that those individuals released, in fact, have suitable employment. Through the planning process necessary activities can be identified and sequenced to give the desired results.

In instances where it is impossible to anticipate all activities or interrelationships, such as in the development of an experimental program, organizations may utilize organizational design strategies such as the project team approach to achieve coordination. Project teams may be temporary to deal with an immediate problem, or they may be permanent to provide long-term coordination for complex programs or projects. In either case, the teams are generally composed of individuals from each of the affected organizational units. Team members maintain a dual responsibility—to the project team and to their home unit. For example, when a state welfare agency was considering a new computerized information system, they put together a project team consisting of representatives from each major program area—finance, personnel, and training. Team members maintained their roles within their home units but were also responsible for the evaluation of various computer systems, analysis of impact upon operations, and the development of a plan for phasing in the new system. Since no individual unit within the state agency could assess all the ramifications of this major change in procedure, the project team was the only means to obtain effective coordination for the new system.

To manage external dependencies,

1. Organizations reduce external demands through: (a) the choice of a domain; (b) the establishment of favorable relationships with external elements; (c) the control of who operates and how they operate in the chosen domain.
2. Organizations minimize the cost of complying with external demands through organizational design. (Kotter, 1979, pp. 88–90)

The choice of domain refers to the mix of services offered by the human service organization. External dependencies may be minimized by selecting services or client groups with which other organizations have little or no involvement. For example, a local welfare agency electing not to expand services to include provision of day-care centers avoids the interagency relationships associated with such a venture. Organizations may also reduce their external dependencies through the establishment of positive relationships with those upon whom they are dependent. The primary reason for the existence of units such as public information departments within human service organizations is to create favorable attitudes among those groups whose support is essential to the organization. Other techniques used by human service organizations to manage the external dependencies include the negotiation of contracts and the establishment of joint ventures, which may have the effect of converting a sequential dependency to a reciprocal dependency, thus giving the agency additional control over the relationship. In addition, human service organizations may attempt to control their domain. For example, they may lobby for legislation or regulations that limit entry or that control the activities of other organizations providing similar services. The extensive licensing and regulation requirements for providing medical treatment and for providing social work practice are examples of this strategy for managing external dependency.

Organizationally, agencies may use boundary-spanning units to deal with external dependencies. For each external dependency identified, the organization may create a separate unit whose responsibility is to interface with the external group. Examples of such units within human service organizations are legislative relations units and public information units. In each of these units the prime objective is to represent the internal organization to an external group upon which the human service organization is dependent.

The boundary-spanning role is a unique aspect of organizational life and, as such, will be given further consideration.

> Two classes of functions are performed by boundary roles: information processing and external representation. Information from external sources comes into an organization through boundary roles, and boundary roles link organizational structure to environmental elements, whether by buffering, moderating, or influencing the environment. (Aldrich & Herber, 1977, p. 218)

An organization or units within an organization are constantly being bombarded with information. If operating managers were required to process all that information, they would quickly be disabled by information overload. The individual in the boundary role, therefore, performs an indispensable service by preventing such overload. The boundary or liaison role person selects relevant information and channels it to the appropriate unit or individual within the organization. In this process he or she condenses and interprets information so that it is in an understandable and usable form when it is communicated to the operating manager for action.

The individual in the boundary role position also represents the organization to external constituencies and monitors the environment. As the organization's representative, the boundary spanner must interpret the position of the organization to the outside groups with whom he or she interfaces. For example, when a state welfare agency changed the level of benefits for AFDC recipients from 80 percent of need to 90 percent of need, it fell upon the legislative liaison to explain the change to members of the legislature in such a way as to gain their support at a time when the legislature was trying to reduce expenditures. The monitoring function involves the active search for changes occurring within the outside environment that may benefit or have an adverse impact upon the legislation. This function involves activities related to the identification of changes in values, procedures, interests, and concerns among those groups with whom the organization must interact. For example, several years ago the USDA modified its procedures with respect to the operation of the food stamp program. States who had advance notice, through their boundary role positions, were able to prepare for the changes and to meet the new guidelines with a minimum of disruption to existing operations.

In summary, the roles of the boundary spanner are to protect the organization from harmful external influences and to acquire and disseminate information necessary to the success of the organization. The performance of these functions can be a rewarding experience for an individual who is equipped with the necessary personality characteristics and skills.

CHARACTERISTICS NECESSARY FOR THE LIAISON ROLE

"Because boundary roles have unique properties relative to more conventional internal roles, effective boundary spanners can be expected to possess different traits, interests, motives, abilities, and experiences than their internal counterparts" (Miles, 1980, p. 343). Perhaps the most essential trait of the successful liaison is a preference for working with people. The tasks already enumerated require a very high level of interaction both with other individuals and in groups; thus, a degree of extroversion is required of the occupant of this role. The role also requires the liaison person to be adaptable and to possess a facility for risk taking. The liaison person will frequently find himself or herself in a position where internal requirements (e.g., policy) are in, or close to being in, conflict with those of the external constituency. He or she must be able to adapt to this uncertain situation and accept the risks involved with the outcome. As one can well imagine, the liaison person must possess a high level of tolerance for stress and have the ability to analyze problems and exercise sound judgment. Typically, therefore, the person selected for the liaison position will be someone with a wide range of experience, interests, and knowledge of the organization. The boundary spanner must have a high level of initiative, since many of the tasks performed will require going well beyond what is "normal" for others within the organization. Finally, the boundary spanner must be loyal to the organization. That is frequently a difficult task, since the information obtained and the contacts made by the liaison person provide him or her with many opportunities to acquire personal power and to use the position for self-interest.

In addition to personality characteristics, the liaison person must possess skills in oral and written communication and in network building. A recent study of successful managers suggests that they, unlike their less successful counterparts, spend a significant amount of time in conversation with others and in building and maintaining networks of cooperative relationships among those who may be able to provide needed information or assistance (Kotter, 1982, p. 156).

In human service organizations an increasing number of managers are finding themselves thrust into the role of directing or participating in interunit/interorganizational tasks or project teams that require them to adopt boundary role behaviors. Thus, the manager should make a concerted effort to acquire the skills associated with team building.

TEAM BUILDING

"Teams are collections of people who must rely on group collaboration if each member is to experience the optimum of success and goal achievement" (Dyer, 1977, p. 4). It is obvious that an open-heart surgery team must exhibit an extremely high degree of collaborative effort if the patient is to survive. While less obvious, it is equally important that members of the work group exhibit a high level of collaboration if their organization is to achieve its goals. Both the open-heart surgery team and the organizational work unit must properly diagnose problems they face, agree upon the strategy to be followed, assign specific tasks to each member, and then implement the agreed-upon procedures. The focus of attention in team building is the work group as a whole, and the activities associated with team building are based on the assumption that the members of the work group can improve their effectiveness through increased cooperative effort.

Team-building efforts are directed toward the diagnosis of needs, the accomplishment of assigned tasks, interpersonal relationships, and processes. Before we discuss these activities, a word of caution is necessary.

> It isn't possible to create a team in every group, even when there is singleness of mission and an absolute need to cooperate. People have different motivations—some are ambitious, devious, and uncooperative, while others are abrasive, self-seeking, and complacent. Some organizations contain many loners too uncomfortable and unskilled at working in groups to ever make the transition to becoming team players. Thus team building is not a viable intervention strategy for every group. (Patten, 1979, p. 12)

The first step in the team-building process is to properly diagnose the situation. The diagnosis is problem oriented and depends upon the development of a precise statement of need. For example, a work group may display dysfunctional conflict behavior; however, immediate establishment of a team development project to resolve interpersonal conflict will be unsuccessful if the real problem lies in inappropriate organizational structure for the work group. The success of the diagnostic step, therefore, depends upon solid data-gathering and analysis techniques.

Initial data may be symptomatic of the need for team development or revitalization. Factors such as declining output, increased complaints or conflict, missed deadlines, increased absenteeism or turnover, budget overspending, low morale, and general ineffectiveness are indicators of problems that may be dealt with effectively through the use of the team concept. Figure 6-1 provides a convenient checklist for determining if team development is called for and for determining the readiness of the organization for the team concept.

Where the symptoms within the work group indicate that the team approach is desirable, additional data gathering is essential to identify the true causes of those symptoms. Any one of several techniques may be used to collect problem-oriented data: standardized questionnaires, individual or group interviews, or open discussion. The method should be comfortable for those from whom the data are to be collected. The vital aspects of this phase are the gathering of sufficient relevant data to permit decision making and the involvement of the work group in all aspects of the data-gathering process.

The work group (team) must also answer some basic questions about itself and its process. For example, decisions must be made about how the team will reach decisions, about agenda building and group process, about how participation from each team member is to be achieved and how differences with the team are to be resolved, and about development of a plan for ensuring that decisions made by the team will be carried out. These matters should be addressed and resolved by the team as a whole early in the development of the team. A typical pattern followed by many

FIGURE 6-1

I. Problem identification: To what extent is there evidence of the following problems in your work unit?

	LOW EVIDENCE		SOME EVIDENCE		HIGH EVIDENCE
1. Loss of production or work-unit output.	1	2	3	4	5
2. Grievances or complaints within the work unit.	1	2	3	4	5
3. Conflicts or hostility between unit members.	1	2	3	4	5
4. Confusion about assignments or unclear relationships between people.	1	2	3	4	5
5. Lack of clear goals, or low commitment to goals.	1	2	3	4	5
6. Apathy or general lack of interest or involvement of unit members.	1	2	3	4	5
7. Lack of innovation, risk taking, imagination, or taking initiative.	1	2	3	4	5
8. Ineffective staff meetings.	1	2	3	4	5
9. Problems in working with the boss.	1	2	3	4	5
10. Poor communications: people afraid to speak up, not listening to each other, or not talking together.	1	2	3	4	5
11. Lack of trust between boss and member or between members.	1	2	3	4	5
12. Decisions made that people do not understand or agree with.	1	2	3	4	5
13. People feel that good work is not recognized or rewarded.	1	2	3	4	5
14. People are not encouraged to work together in better team effort.	1	2	3	4	5

Scoring: Add up the score for the fourteen items. If your score is between 14–28, there is little evidence your unit needs team building. If your score is between 29–42, there is some evidence, but no immediate pressure, unless two or three items are very high. If your score is between 43–56, you should seriously think about planning the team-building program. If your score is over 56, team building should be a top priority item for your work unit.

II. Are you (or your manager) prepared to start a team-building program? Consider the following statements. To what extent do they apply to you or your department?

	LOW		MEDIUM		HIGH
1. You are comfortable in sharing organizational leadership and decision making with subordinates and prefer to work in a participative atmosphere.	1	2	3	4	5
2. You see a high degree of interdependence as necessary among functions and workers in order to achieve your goals.	1	2	3	4	5

FIGURE 6-1 *(cont.)*

	LOW		MEDIUM		HIGH
3. The external environment is highly variable and/or changing rapidly and you need the best thinking of all your staff to plan against these conditions.	1	2	3	4	5
4. You feel you need the input of your staff to plan major changes or develop new operating policies and procedures.	1	2	3	4	5
5. You feel that broad consultation among your people as a group in goals, decisions, and problems is necessary on a continuing basis.	1	2	3	4	5
6. Members of your management team are (or can become) compatible with each other and are able to create a collaborative rather than a competitive environment.	1	2	3	4	5
7. Members of your team are located close enough to meet together as needed.	1	2	3	4	5
8. You feel you need to rely on the ability and willingness of subordinates to resolve critical operating problems directly and in the best interest of the company or organization.	1	2	3	4	5
9. Formal communication channels are not sufficient for the timely exchange of essential information, views, and decisions among your team members.	1	2	3	4	5
10. Organization adaptation requires the use of such devices as project management, task forces, and/or ad hoc problem-solving groups to augment conventional organization structure.	1	2	3	4	5
11. You feel it is important to surface and deal with critical, albeit sensitive, issues that exist in your team.	1	2	3	4	5
12. You are prepared to look at your own role and performance with your team.	1	2	3	4	5
13. You feel there are operating or interpersonal problems that have remained unsolved too long and need the input from all group members.	1	2	3	4	5
14. You need an opportunity to meet with your people and set goals and develop commitment to these goals.	1	2	3	4	5

Scoring: If your total score is between 50–70, you are probably ready to go ahead with the team-building program. If your score is between 35–49, you should probably talk the situation over with your team and others to see what would need to be done to get ready for team building. If your score is between 14–34, you are probably not prepared at the present time to start team building.

(continued)

FIGURE 6-1 (*cont.*)

III. Should you use an outside consultant to help in team building? (Circle appropriate response.)

1. Does the manager feel comfortable in trying out something new and different with the staff? Yes No ?

2. Is the staff used to spending time in an outside location working on different issues of concern to the work unit? Yes No ?

3. Will group members speak up and give honest data? Yes No ?

4. Does your group generally work together without a lot of conflict or apathy? Yes No ?

5. Are you reasonably sure that the boss is not a major source of difficulty? Yes No ?

6. Is there a high commitment by the boss and unit members to achieve more effective team functioning? Yes No ?

7. Is the personal style of the boss and his or her management philosophy consistent with a team approach? Yes No ?

8. Do you feel you know enough about team building to begin a program without help? Yes No ?

9. Would your staff feel confident enough to begin a team-building program without outside help? Yes No ?

Scoring: If you have circled six or more "yes" responses, you probably do not need an outside consultant. If you have four or more "no" responses, you probably do need a consultant. If you have a mixture of yes, no, and ? responses, you should probably invite in a consultant to talk over the situation and make a joint decision.

FIGURE 6-1 Team Building Checklist. From William G. Dyer, *Team Building,* © 1977, Addison-Wesley, Reading, Massachusetts. Pgs. 36–40, Fig. 4.1. Reprinted with permission.

team builders is to spend one or two days meeting with the team in a neutral setting (away from the office) to deal both with the process issues and with initial problem identification. With respect to problem identification, the team ordinarily will identify three types of problems: those beyond the control of the team (e.g., level of funding from legislature); those that will require further investigation or cooperation from other groups and, thus, are beyond immediate consideration (e.g., reorganization); and those that can be immediately addressed (e.g., task arrangement within the team). Following the initial problem identification, the team's first step is to deal with the immediate concerns. Then, it makes an effort to develop a plan for addressing the longer-range problems and to develop mechanisms for coping with those areas that cannot be affected by the team. For each problem area, the team develops an action plan that includes necessary activities and specific team member assignments with completion dates. Subsequent team meetings are devoted to discussion of issues around each problem, progress reports, and evaluation of the team.

An effective team can be recognized from the characteristics of the group process observed. An effective team meeting is characterized by an informal atmosphere, in which each member is free to express feelings and criticisms. The meeting is marked by a great deal of discussion without any one member dominating the group. While there are disagreement and criticism, they are constructive and not in the nature of a personal attack. Decisions are made by general agreement, which requires that all members listen carefully, have a full understanding of team objectives, and contribute freely. Once a decision is reached and specific activities are assigned and accepted, team members work together to achieve the desired results (McGregor, 1960, p. 232). A team that meets these conditions should be a highly productive and effective mechanism within the human service organization.

SUMMARY

This chapter has looked at the liaison role of the manager in the human service organization. When acting as a liaison the manager becomes a catalyst that facilitates goal accomplishment. By bringing together different forces, each with something to contribute to the organization, the manager increases the potential for success. The skills of the liaison role should be continually polished and practiced, since the use of task or project teams will continue to increase in the future.

REFERENCES

ALDRICH, H., & HERKER, D. (1977, April). Boundary spanning roles and organization structure. *Academy of Management Review*, p. 218.

DYER, W. G. (1977). *Team building: Issues and alternatives*. Reading, Mass.: Addison-Wesley.

HAIMANN, T., & SCOTT, W. G. (1974). *Management in the modern organization* (2nd ed.). Boston: Houghton Mifflin.

KOTTER, J. P. (1979, January). Managing external dependence. *Academy of Management Review*, 4 (1), 87–92.

KOTTER, J. P. (1982, November–December). What effective general managers really do. *Harvard Business Review*, 60 (6), 156–167.

McGREGOR, D. (1960). *The human side of the enterprise*. New York: McGraw-Hill.

MILES, R. H. (1980). *Macro organizational behavior*. Santa Monica, Calif.: Goodyear.

PATTEN, T. H., JR. (1979, January–February). Team building part I. Designing the intervation. *Personnel*, p. 12.

SZILAGYI, A. D., JR., & WALLACE, M. J., JR. (1980). *Organizational behavior and performance* (2nd ed.). Santa Monica, Calif.: Goodyear.

QUESTIONS FOR DISCUSSION

1. Why should operating managers in human service organizations be concerned with coordination?

2. "Human service agencies spend too much money that should be going for client services on activities such as legislative relations and public information." Do you agree with that statement? Why or why not?

3. Discuss the advantages and disadvantages to a manager's career of serving in a boundary-spanning position.

SUGGESTED PROJECTS

1. Identify a boundary-spanning role within your organization. List the objectives and the activities you believe would be performed by the manager in this role. After compiling your list, discuss with the manager the actual functions performed. If the two lists are not in agreement, discuss why the differences exist.
2. Divide the class into several groups, all with the same task assignment. Each group should undertake a team-building exercise. At the conclusion of the exercise, each group should discuss ways it could improve team performance.

The Monitor Role

chapter 7

The ultimate measure of successful management is the ability to move the organization consistently toward established goals and objectives. Much of the discussion in this book has described functions and behaviors necessary to achieve those goals and objectives. Successful use of those functions and behaviors, however, is dependent upon the effective exercise of the monitoring activity. The elements needed to implement the other managerial roles are acquired, to a large extent, through the day-to-day monitoring activities discussed in this chapter. In the monitoring role, the manager must (1) develop and maintain effective information systems that accurately describe what is going on within his or her area of responsibility, (2) distill from this great quantity of information those elements that are most critical to successful performance, and (3) periodically evaluate ongoing operations to determine the overall effectiveness of the organization.

THE MONITORING SYSTEM

It is axiomatic that the manager never has enough information about what is really taking place in the organization. On the other hand, managers everywhere complain of information overload. This seeming paradox is the core of the problems faced by the manager acting in the monitor role. While the manager is regularly bombarded with information, that information is frequently fragmented, disorganized, not timely, and unrelated to the specific problem of the day.

Before managers can begin to extricate themselves from this paradox, they must have a clear idea of what must be achieved. Until they know precisely what results they want, they are unable to determine which information will assist them in accomplishing the task. Several essential elements must be considered in the design of a monitoring system.

First, the manager must measure performance against a predetermined set of standards. Organizational and unit plans will have delineated specific areas of accountability for each manager. In addition, each manager will probably have developed some individual goals for his or her unit. For each area of accountability, specific objectives must be established, along with necessary standards of performance. While the development and use of objectives and standards are essential to the monitoring function, many human service managers are very reluctant to undertake those important activities. As Patti states:

> In social welfare organizations, the process of monitoring and controlling organizational activities is complicated by the fact that both service technology and service outcomes are frequently variable and thus difficult to specify and measure. If clients presented similar problems and reacted similarly to the services provided, if desired outcomes could be specifically defined and easily evaluated, and if the agency knew with some certainty that the application of selected procedures would result in predictable outcomes, then the administrative task of monitoring and controlling agency operations would not be too unlike that in many other types of organizations. Clearly, however, these conditions are seldom obtained in social welfare organizations. (Patti, 1983, p. 31)

This uniqueness of purpose or operations can be, and frequently is, advanced by virtually every organizational entity. We argue, recognizing the problems addressed by Patti, that all organizations, including those in the human services, must strive to discover and apply standards for monitoring and controlling activities if they are to be effective. We do not suggest that standards appropriate for a private manufacturing organization be adopted by organizations engaged in providing human services. The standards must always be appropriate to the activity at hand. The monitoring devices useful in an accounting office should certainly not be applied to organizations engaged in direct client service. For example, in an accounting unit the number of transactions handled correctly or the number of reports correctly prepared on time may indicate the effectiveness of the unit; however, in a casework setting, counting the number of clients interviewed or the number of cases closed could lead to a distorted view of effectiveness. Since much work in a human service setting involves confidential exchanges between professionals and clients, the manager may be limited in the choice of monitoring points and techniques and may need to establish a combination of quantitative and qualitative standards. For example, one can argue that effective casework results in the solution of the clients' problems; therefore, the rate of recidivism is an appropriate measure of effectiveness.

Once the manager has developed a suitable set of objectives that reflect the major areas of accountability, the second step is to determine key control points. In any organization or unit, the variety of activities that may be monitored is quite large. While the number of measurable activities is endless, the number of factors critical to success is usually rather small. The manager must ask, "At what point in the flow of work do I find the critical elements that, if properly performed, will lead to effective results?"

Unless the manager takes the time to identify those critical performance elements, he or she may try to monitor all activities and will usually wind up enmeshed in so much detail that he or she is unable to manage at all.

In addition to identifying the elements necessary for success, the manager must ensure that they are monitored in a way that will accurately reflect performance. The delivery of human services involves a complex interaction between clients, agency personnel, and administrative processes. Thus, if the manager focuses on only one area, the feedback received will be distorted and may result in ineffective performance. For example, a manager of a food stamp distribution center established a uniform lunch period (12:00 M.–1:00 P.M.) to discourage employees from taking "excessive lunch time." With all employees leaving and returning as a group, the manager was able to effectively monitor employees' lunch hours. However, clients needing service during that period were left to stand and wait. When designing monitoring techniques, the manager can avoid such an unfortunate consequence by considering total system needs rather than employing isolated devices that apply only to certain situations.

The fundamental purpose of the monitoring role is to identify performance deviation so that corrective action can be taken. Thus, the design of the monitoring activity must provide useful information that points the way to corrective action. Monitoring occurs in the present; therefore, information that is not received at the right time, while it may help prevent a similar occurrence in the future, will not prove useful in correcting today's problems. The focus of the monitoring role is correction; therefore, the monitoring program should be directed toward identifying deviation from plans. The resulting corrective actions should be designed to get the activity "back on track," not to affix blame or impose punishment. That is an important point, since much of the resistance to the monitoring function within organizations has its roots in the fear that deviations, once discovered, will be followed by some type of penalty. To alleviate that fear, the manager must take care to assure all those involved that monitoring is a positive force, whose ultimate purpose is to improve the effectiveness of the organization.

In summary, the fundamental role of the monitoring system is to assist the manager and, therefore, the organization to accomplish established goals. To be effective, the system developed must incorporate the following basic principles: (1) measure activities against predetermined standards of organizational performance; (2) recover useful information about each of the areas of accountability; (3) focus on correction of deviations from planned performance rather than on identifying individual mistakes; and (4) focus on critical elements of performance.

THE INFORMATION RETRIEVAL SYSTEM

In Chapter 8, the discussion of the disseminator role of the manager will focus on the importance of the manager in the communication channel of the organization. In this chapter, we are concerned with the development of the information network as it relates to the monitoring function. The communication functions involved in the monitor and disseminator roles are inseparable, since the quality of what is disseminated is dependent upon the quality of what is collected. Thus, the manager in the human service organization must continually strive to improve the quality of the information retrieval system. According to Mintzberg (1973), there are five broad categories of information received by the manager: internal operations, external events, analyses, ideas and trends, and pressures (pp. 68–69).

Periodically, every manager receives formal, organizationally generated reports related to the operations he or she supervises. They may take the form of budget statements, quality control reports, caseload levels, or demographic profiles of target client groups. These formal, organizational reports are continuously supplemented by the manager's observation of the activities taking place within the organization and by verbal reports from subordinates. In short, the combination of formal and informal internal reporting provides the manager with information about the level of activity.

From the external environment, the manager receives a wide variety of information useful in monitoring the organization. For example, the manager receives journals and newsletters related to the field of activity, program managers exchange formal and informal information, and managers receive information by meeting with client groups. In short, the manager obtains external information useful in seeing current activities in perspective with the larger environment.

From time to time, the manager will initiate or receive unsolicited special analyses related to particular problems in or opportunities for the organizational unit. For example, the director of a food stamp program may form a task force to analyze the effects of mail versus the effects of direct distribution, or a manager may engage an outside consultant to analyze the current level of employee morale. The purpose is to assist the manager in preparing to cope with elements likely to have substantial impact upon operations.

The manager must continue to scan the environment for trends and new ideas in order to avoid organizational obsolescence and ensure that his or her program maintains its vitality. For example, the manager attends professional conferences or training programs to obtain the latest information related to service delivery.

Finally, the manager obtains information from special-interest lobbying groups, from subordinates seeking to pursue their pet program ideas, and from political leaders seeking special attention for their particular interests. Such information is vital to the manager in maintaining an appropriate balance for unit activities.

Each source of information available to or sought out by the manager has implications for the effective monitoring of operations. The problem confronting every manager, however, is how to keep the information system simple enough and current enough to be useful. While much remains unknown about how individual managers accomplish that objective, research gives us a general idea. First, effective managers deliberately create complex information networks "with many talented people in them and with strong ties to and among their subordinates" (Kotter, 1982, p. 163). Figure 7-1 reproduces Kotter's view of a typical manager's information network. It should be noted that the network includes a large number of participants selected to encompass the full range of the manager's accountabilities. Second, the information received from the information network is brought to bear on a carefully developed network of interrelated problems.

One distinctive characteristic of top managers is that their thinking deals not with isolated and discrete items but with portfolios of problems, issues, and

FIGURE 7-1 A Typical General Manager's Network. Reprinted by permission of the Harvard Business Review. An exhibit from "What Effective General Managers Really Do" by John P. Kotter, November/December, 1982. Copyright © 1982 by the President and Fellows of Harvard College; all rights reserved.

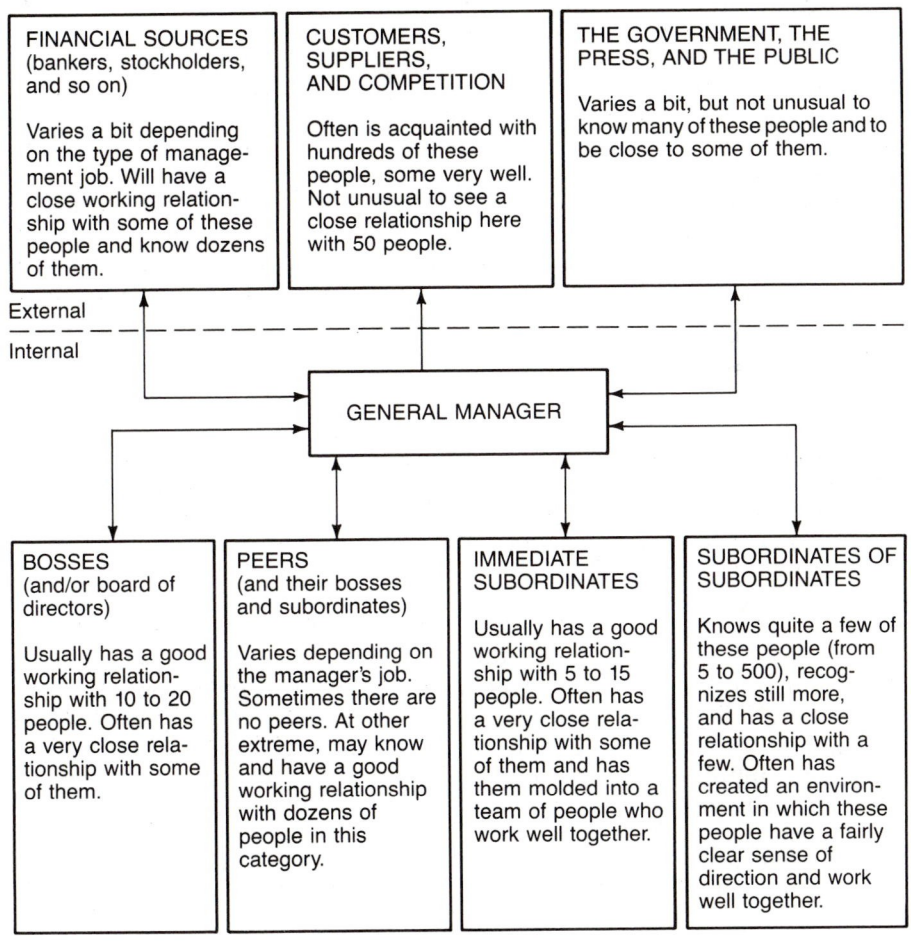

> opportunities in which (1) many problems exist simultaneously, (2) these problems compete for some part of his or her immediate concern, and (3) the issues are interrelated. The cognitive tasks in problem management are to find and define good problems, to "map" these into a network, and to manage their dynamically shifting priorities. (Isenberg, 1984, p. 86)

Such activities require smoothly functioning information retrieval systems.

MANAGEMENT INFORMATION SYSTEMS

The term *management information system* (MIS) conjures up the specter of endless bureaucratic reports that have neither meaning nor use to many human service workers and managers. Each of us can cite many horror stories of reports that required hours to complete and that, after submission, were never heard of again. Similarly, each of us regularly receives reports that either are entirely inaccurate or have little or no bearing on our particular activity. The foregoing discussion, however, makes it clear that the systematic acquisition and evaluation of timely, accurate, and useful information are essential components of the effective management of organizations. Lacking such information, the manager is likely to make poor, if not disastrous, decisions related to programs under his or her direction. Given the demonstrable need for an effective MIS system, why have human service organizations experienced such difficulty with it?

First, the rapid introduction of computer-assisted information systems and the tremendous expansion of the capabilities of computers have had some unfortunate consequences. In many instances, top management has refused to support the systems and, in some cases, has been openly hostile toward them.

> Many of these managers were initially professionals who carry with them the culture and attitudes of the profession, including the strong resistance to quantitative measures of their organization's activities. They argue, sometimes persuasively, that professional work is too complex and diffuse in its impact to be easily accounted for and that naive attempts to account for its outcome might undermine the credibility and integrity of the work itself. (Herzlinger, 1977, p. 84)

Of course, the only way a computer-assisted information system will meet the organization's overall needs is if top management is fully committed to the system and participates actively in all stages of its development.

Second, the desire to develop a single system that addresses all of the information and analysis needs of the organization, coupled with the availability of computers with tremendous capacity, has led to unfortunate outcomes in many organizations.

> Computer graveyards are most often found in large hospitals and welfare departments. They have mammoth data-processing requirements that supposedly can be met by buying large computers and "integrated" management

information packages. The systems will somehow solve all the organization's information needs, from record keeping to planning and control reports. Since the human mechanisms for obtaining and "inputting" the data are weak, however, an integrated system never quite succeeds. Moreover, the technical problems of programming and operating such a system are sometimes beyond the capability of the organization and its system contractor. (Herzlinger, 1977, p. 84).

The resulting complexity and centralization of the system fail to support the differing data needs of the users.

The lack of technical expertise within many human service organizations has led to the creation of specialized units of "computer experts" who are responsible for the system. These experts frequently "approach problems differently, use different languages, and have different goals" (Kirtisch & Weisbord, 1977, p. 6) from those of the personnel who will will be using the output from the system. The orientation of these "computer people" is usually toward the hardware and unique applications, while the "users" are generally oriented toward clients and the solution of their individual problems. The resulting communication problem leads to frustration for both groups and to the very real possibility that the system will be ineffective.

In spite of the problems that may be encountered, a properly developed and operated management information system remains the best solution to the tremendous data needs of managers in human service organizations.

Among the potential advantages it affords are: access to reasonably comprehensive and systematic data about various aspects of program operations, an improved capability to objectively assess program performance, somewhat greater flexibility in retrieving and analyzing information requested by external organizations, and an enhanced opportunity for rationalizing program decisions. (Patti, 1983, p. 182)

First, management must conduct a thorough value analysis of the present information system. Each link in the information chain must be looked at from the perspective of timeliness, reliability, and usefulness. Particular emphasis should be placed upon the currently used reports within the organization. Is the information requested still necessary? Is the information required for external reporting purposes? Is the same information being collected in several different formats? Is the information needed for decision making? Is the information being channeled to those who will need it? Questions like those may reveal problems such as duplication of effort and ineffective reporting. The lack of such analysis may lead to results like those in the following example.

A state services planning unit decided to develop and implement a comprehensive intake information system as a component of the existing management information system. The program was developed at the state level to provide aggregate data necessary for the planning unit to determine future service needs. A consolidated intake form was created to provide a comprehensive picture of client eligibility for all services. Since the data were placed in the computer at the local level, the central planning group was able to recover information related to the statewide level of activity for all services. After several months of operation, the system began to experience difficulties. Data were being entered inaccurately or not at all, many complaints were being received from local program directors about the time necessary to comply, and there was a general questioning of the need for the system. An investigation determined that the local programs were receiving little useful feedback and that they were simply duplicating the information for local use. The system was redesigned, requiring approximately eighteen months, to give local offices on-line capability that allowed them to quickly recover the specific information they required about clients. Since the system now met the needs of the local offices, it rapidly became successful. Had the state office performed a good value analysis before undertaking the project, much time and expense could have been saved.

That example brings up a second requirement for a good management information system: Those who are going to be responsible for the maintenance and use of the system should be involved in its development and implementation. The ultimate purpose of a management information system is to assist in the decision-making process; therefore, priorities must be established for information needs. Establishing priorities requires input from all segments of the organization. If the system users are full partners in its development, many problems can be overcome. Obviously, not every future user of the system will be involved in its development, so care must be exercised in selection of the developmental team. Those selected should possess the knowledge and the authority to be effective members of the team.

> It is common to see teams where users are at too low a level in their own departments to contribute the required information or to make needed decisions. At best they constantly refer to others who have the information or the authority, acting as liaison between the computer specialist and their department. This is neither effective nor as efficient as it could be if the department were adequately represented. At worst, the user again goes along, abdicating this function to the computer specialist. The outcome is always less than full participation, and unsatisfactory results are almost inevitable. (Kirtisch & Weisbord, 1977, p. 9)

After current information flows have been analyzed, information requirements identified, and priorities established, a system that will meet the organization's needs must be developed and implemented. Such a system should be as simple as possible and user friendly. Most human service personnel are not going to become computer specialists, so the system should avoid the use of complicated person-computer interactions. Insofar as possible, the user should be able to communicate with the computer using simple and familiar terminology. The system should be as flexible as possible. With the rapid sophistication of minicomputers and microcomputers, information networks are now possible that will allow individuals to access data, individual or aggregate, for analysis on-line. In short, both the equipment and the system should allow for maximum usability. In the development of the system, the organization should give maximum consideration to its effective implementation. That is, the instructions (documentation) to users should be meticulously written and tested. The documentation not only must be clearly written and complete but also must provide the user with programmatic justification for each element in the process. Finally, during the development stage, attention should be given to the proper training of those who will operate and use the system.

In summary, an effective management information system is essential to effectively monitor operations. Such a system, however, is filled with potential problems if it is not properly designed and implemented. The manager, to avoid as many problems as possible, must (1) understand the workings of the current information system, (2) determine information needs and priorities, (3) ensure maximum organizational input into the development of the system, and (4) ensure that the system is understood by organizational personnel.

THE EVALUATION OF OPERATIONS

Periodically, the manager must turn his or her attention from the day-to-day activities and conduct to overall evaluation of the organizations in the unit's programs. The term *program evaluation* is typically used to refer to all procedures used to determine the extent to which a program of services is meeting (or has met) its previously established goals and objectives. An effective system of program evaluation must, therefore, be concerned with objectives (what the manager wants the program to accomplish), resources (personnel, funds, materials that can be utilized in seeking to accomplish objectives), and outcomes (products resulting from performance). That suggests some general tasks and criteria for program evaluation: planning, goal identification, baseline assessment, follow-up assessment, and analysis of results (Christian & Hannah, 1983, p. 152). Such an evaluation system focuses on program effectiveness (outcomes) rather than on level of activity.

A large number of human service organizations create special units charged with this responsibility. Others employ outside consultants to conduct extensive internal and external program evaluations. While it is beyond the scope of this book to present details of the methods of those specialists, it is essential that the manager understand his or her role in program evaluation. Because there are specialists to perform the mechanics, that does not mean that each program manager may forget about the activity. Without this periodic appraisal of his or her own program effectiveness, the manager will be unable to determine the true worth of the activities that consume each day.

Throughout this book, a system of management called Management by Objectives has been mentioned as a useful tool for the human service manager. Because of its versatility, it is also an excellent mechanism through which the manager can evaluate the effectiveness of programs. Management by Objectives (MBO) is a "process that systematically links objectives, plans, monitoring, and evaluation, and a system that facilitates and integrates planning, decision making, staff development, and a host of other organizational activities" (Raia, 1974, p. 11). The overall usefulness of MBO derives from the philosophy and the process.

Management by Objectives is both a philosophy and a system of management that focuses on results achieved. Philosophically, MBO is a planning system that incorporates participative management. It is "a process whereby the superior and subordinate managers of an organization jointly identify its common goals, define each individual's major areas of responsibility in terms of the results expected, and use these measures as guides for operating the unit and assessing the contribution of each of its members" (Odiorne, 1979, p. 53). The manager desiring to implement an MBO system, whether organizationwide or within a single unit, must (1) understand the organization's basic purposes, directions, and mission; (2) accurately identify areas of responsibility throughout the organization and establish objectives that will lead to goal attainment; and (3) control progress toward objectives through periodic meetings and reports.

Organizational statements of purpose and mission are typically very broad and somewhat vague generalizations of expected outcomes. The first task of the manager desiring to use an MBO system, therefore, is to translate those statements into specific results and outcomes expected. At this stage, the manager must be careful to specify results rather than activities engaged in. For example, "increase the number of patients seen per week" is an activity statement related to the results area of "patient schedule." Thus, the activity may be performed at one level of the organization, while the responsibility for the patient treatment schedule may reside elsewhere. While this distinction may seem minor, it is of the utmost importance that activities not be confused with results. The delineation of results areas is also useful in determining who should be responsible for what results in the organization.

The expected results areas must next be assigned to specific positions throughout the organization. In many human service organizations, this classification of responsibilities is long overdue. Frequently, there exists little agreement between employees' perceptions of job responsibilities and those of the organization. In the MBO system, those differences are resolved through a joint determination and written agreements of what is involved in the job, together with a mechanism for communicating what is being done, when it is being done, and how well it is being done. These discussions get at the substance of the job (results) rather than the form (activities) of the job. Here we are asking each individual to identify his or her unique contribution to the organization. In short, each person in the system comes to an understanding of why his or her job was created to begin with.

Once each individual understands the results expected, the next step is to establish objectives that will enable those results to be accomplished. Objectives, like results areas, must be clearly and precisely stated. What, then, makes up a good statement of objectives? First, the objective must be specific. If the statement is too general or includes multiple subjects, the accomplishment of the objective may be self-defining. For example, "to improve client relations" is an objective that can be achieved through almost any action because we do not know the form of relations (multiple subjects) or the extent of the change sought (specific).

A second characteristic of a good objective is its measurability. In the objective statement, an attempt should be made to specify the deadline for the completion of something, the quantity of something, the cost of doing something, or an observable outcome. For some objectives, a straight count (e.g., number of patients seen) may be appropriate, while others may be measured best with percentages (e.g., percent under budget). Many of the most important objectives in human service organizations, particularly in direct service, do not lend themselves to direct measurement, but even here a good objective statement will delineate the prerequisites of meeting the objective. For example, a juvenile probation officer may use "the absence of delinquent acts" as a measure of direct service objective. The point is that if no time frame or measure is provided, the manager will be unable to tell if the objective has been met or not.

Finally, an objective must be challenging. Objectives that are either too high or too low will result in poor performance. The performance required to meet the objective should conform to the ability of the person to whom it is assigned.

Once objectives have been established for each of the results areas, an action plan must be developed. The action plan focuses upon the activities necessary to accomplish the objectives. Action plans also serve to coordinate objectives of various units to ensure consistency and continuity of effort. Measurement and control are facilitated by the action plan, since key activities and performance milestones are essential ingredients of such plans. Many organizations utilize devices such as the PERT process or performance budgets as a basis for the action plan. The plan, however, must be the basis for ongoing review and reports to assess the success of the organization operating an MBO system.

In summary, Mondy et al. (1983) conclude that if the following guidelines are adhered to by organizations, MBO may be more effective:

1. Secure top management support and commitment.
2. Specify the overall objectives of the program and communicate them throughout the organization.
3. Emphasize MBO as an overall philosophy or system of management rather than just a performance appraisal technique.
4. Allocate adequate time and resources to instruct each person in the organization in the nature and philosophy of the system.
5. Recognize that all goals must be realistic and attainable and that they must contribute to the overall purpose of the organization.
6. Be willing to modify the goals as changes in the environment dictate. Continuous review is a must.

7. Be sure to clarify responsibility and authority relationships so that everyone understands what's expected in the MBO system.

8. Insist that goals be written and stated in measurable terms to be attained within a specified period of time.

9. Make the goal setting process a joint activity between superiors and subordinates.

10. Recognize that MBO will not solve all managerial problems. (p. 133)

SUMMARY

In this chapter we have examined some issues related to the manager's responsibility for monitoring the activities under his or her direction. "Getting a particular employee or operating unit to perform its task is only part of the challenge in achieving organizational success" (Webber et al., 1985, p. 318). In the monitoring role, the manager seeks to answer the questions "Are we performing the correct tasks?" and "Are we performing the tasks correctly?" To perform this dual function, the manager must have a clear understanding of the results necessary to achieve organizational goals. Second, the manager must build an information network and retrieval system that will continuously provide data related to the major performance criteria. Finally, the manager must periodically evaluate his or her area of responsibility against the goals established for effectiveness.

REFERENCES

CHRISTIAN, W. P., & HANNAH, G. T. (1983). *Effective management in human services.* Englewood Cliffs, N.J.: Prentice-Hall.

HERZLINGER, R. (1977, January–February). Why data systems in nonprofit organizations fail. *Harvard Business Review.*

ISENBERG, D. J. (1984, November–December). How managers think. *Harvard Business Review.*

KIRTISCH, R. S., & WEISBORD, M. R. (1977, Spring). Getting computer people and users to understand each other. *Advanced Management Journal,* pp. 5–14.

KOTTER, J. P. (1982, November–December). What effective managers really do. *Harvard Business Review,* pp. 156–167.

MINTZBERG, H. (1973). *The nature of managerial work.* New York: Harper & Row.

MONDY, R. W., HOLMES, R. E., & FLIPPO, E. (1983). *Management: Concepts and practices* (2nd ed.). Boston: Allyn & Bacon.

ODIORNE, G. S. (1979). *MBO II: A system of managerial leadership for the 80's.* Belmont, Calif.: Fearon.

PATTI, R. J. (1983). *Social welfare administration: Managing social programs in a developmental context.* Englewood Cliffs, N.J.: Prentice-Hall.

RAIA, A. P. (1974). *Managing by objectives.* Glenview, Ill.: Scott, Foresman.

WEBBER, R. A., MORGAN, M. A., & BROWNE, P. C. (1985). *Management: Basic elements of managing organizations* (3rd ed.). Homewood, Ill.: Richard D. Irwin.

QUESTIONS FOR DISCUSSION

1. Discuss the monitoring function as a process for helping the manager accomplish organizational goals.

2. Using the concepts developed in this chapter, develop and discuss a set of monitoring criteria for a clinical caseworker.
3. How would you go about establishing an MBO system for the professors in your school?
4. Under what conditions would Management by Objectives not be a suitable system within an organization?
5. Some human service managers contend that a computer-assisted management information system violates professional standards of practice. Do you agree or disagree? Why?

SUGGESTED PROJECTS

1. Using the MIS concepts discussed in this chapter, analyze one component of your organization's system (e.g., report form). If you find that it does not meet the effectiveness criteria, redesign the component.
2. Design a plan for an MIS system that utilizes the microcomputer for your department.

The Manager as Disseminator

This chapter will focus on the manager's role as the *disseminator* of information. The information that is transmitted is primarily that which comes from the external environment into the organization and that which is sent from one subordinate to another (Mintzberg, 1973). In many instances the human service organization sits in a "fishbowl," and the importance of adequately handling information cannot be overemphasized. Whether or not the manager effectively fulfills this role will determine the extent to which the relationship to the external environment is viewed as responsive or unresponsive to the pressures and demands placed upon the organization. Further, the effective handling of information within the internal environment will affect the extent to which the organization functions in a coordinated manner. This places a tremendous responsibility on the manager. Throughout the text we have repeatedly made reference to the importance of communication, and it is vital to the manager's *disseminator* role.

INFORMATION FROM THE EXTERNAL ENVIRONMENT

The human service manager sits in a position that is very visible and that is, to some extent, vulnerable to changes that occur external to the day-to-day operations of the organization. Therefore, he or she has to be responsive to whatever is occurring that may have an impact on the image and effectiveness of the organization's mission and purpose. As Mintzberg (1973) notes, the information that the manager receives is either factual information or value information. What does he or she do with it? For example, if the Director of Nursing Services learns through the "grapevine" that the intensive care unit on the pediatric ward may be phased out, he or she needs to share the information with the relevant subordinates. At this juncture it is only rumor or gossip, but it is important that some thought be given to the possibility. Hospitals are going through some very difficult times, largely because of policy decisions being made by the federal government. The impact of decreased funding reimbursements to hospitals for Medicaid and Medicare patients has been devastating to some hospitals. An intensive care unit is an expensive operation and may be a luxury that can no longer be afforded. Yet, at the same time the hospital cannot afford to lose the confidence of the public in its care of very sick children. If the intensive care unit were to be phased out, there would be a need to assimilate the patients into the ward, but with no loss of nursing care. What we are suggesting is that the manager, in this instance the Director of Nursing Services, should discuss the matter with key personnel and consider with them the strategic decisions that might need to be made.

Now, when information such as the kind just illustrated comes into the organization, the manager must decide whether or not to share the information. One thing to keep in mind is that if the manager is hearing such gossip or rumor, it is quite likely that subordinates are as well. In general, it is better to deal with this type of situation frankly than to let information circulate uncontrolled. Keep in mind that serious damage can be done to the morale of those who would be affected, and when morale starts to deteriorate, poor performance follows. The manager must weigh the potential consequences of his or her decision.

When the human service manager receives information of a factual nature, he or she must determine whether it is correct or incorrect. If it is correct, then it should be sent on to the appropriate individual. If it is incorrect, it should be investigated as to why it is incorrect and should be corrected before it is sent on. However, there are instances where incorrect information needs to be sent on so that subordinates can make the necessary corrections. For example, let's suppose that the local public welfare office receives a report from the state office saying that the number of child abuse cases handled at the local level is not accurate. The county director should direct the supervisor of the protective service unit to go back and check the records and make the corrections, which the director will then send back to the state office. In this example the supervisor is in the best position to have the right information and should be given the responsibility to make the information accurate.

In other instances the manager may receive incorrect factual information that he or she must deal with before it gets out of hand. Frequently, that type of information comes in the form of rumor or gossip, but not always. The director of a state agency receives a phone call from a member of the board accusing the staff of making a decision to fund a program on the basis of political considerations. Although this is not correct, the director must handle the matter with the staff as well as with other members of the board. Failure to address the accusation might well erode the position of the director and, of equal importance, the confidence in and the integrity of the agency. If confronted with such a situation, the manager should get the facts and communicate them to the appropriate individuals. What we are suggesting is that in such situations the manager should act aggressively. He or she should not react defensively, because that would only lend credibility to the unfounded accusation.

As noted earlier, information that comes to the manager is of either a factual or a value nature. Factual information is much easier to deal with, primarily because it is either correct or incorrect, and this can easily be determined. Value information is a bit more difficult because it "deals with preferences—someone's arbitrary belief of what 'ought' to be" (Mintzberg, 1973, p. 72). Values are merely what is thought to be important in the minds of those who seek to exercise power over decision making, yet they are important because they guide subordinates in their decision-making responsibilities (Mintzberg, 1973, pp. 72–73).

Let's take a closer look at the importance of values. A value can be defined as "an enduring belief that a specific mode of conduct or end-state of existence is personally or socially preferable to an opposite or converse mode of conduct or end-state of existence" (Rokeach, 1973, p. 5). There-fore, whether consciously or subconsciously, one's values become a stan-dard for the individual's actions (Gibson et al., 1985, p. 72). When value information comes to the manager, he or she weighs that information not only from his or her personal perspective but also from the organizational perspective. Thus, what is done with it, how it is handled, and where it goes will be influenced by the manager's perception of the consequence of the information according to his or her own value system and the organiza-tion's value system. Needless to say, that puts the manager in a rather powerful position in regard to information that is received. It ought to be apparent that the manager's values have a profound effect on the decisions that are made. Consider the following:

> In *establishing objectives,* value judgments are necessary regarding the selection of opportunities and the assignment of priorities.
>
> In *developing alternatives,* it is necessary to make value judgments about the various possibilities. When *choosing an alternative,* the values of the decision maker influence which alternative is chosen.
>
> When *implementing the decision,* value judgments are necessary in choosing the means for implementation. In the *evaluation and control* phase, value judg-ments cannot be avoided when taking corrective action. (Harrison, 1975, p. 42)

Similarly, when value information comes to the manager, he or she has to consider the influence that the sender of the information has either in the external environment or in the organization's internal environment. If a report comes to the chief probation officer from the chief justice of the supreme court, then that should be viewed as influential and must be handled accordingly. On a daily basis, the manager will receive information from a variety of sources, often from those who are seeking some measure of control. A grievance from the union steward should not be taken lightly, and the concerns registered in the grievance should be handled with the appropriate subordinates.

It is likely that value conflicts will arise. A value conflict occurs when the information received is not consistent with the manager's value system or the organization's value system and it often creates a dilemma for the manager. For example, suppose that the local county welfare director receives a letter of complaint from the Klu Klux Klan. The complaint might be valid, but the director's value orientation might be diametrically opposed to that of the Klan. If the director yields, will that be viewed as giving in? Yet, if the changes are not handled, will that lead to adverse public reaction that could damage the agency? When placed in such a situation, the manager must weigh the advantages and disadvantages of any action and then make the decision on the basis of that evaluation. Yes, mistakes will be made, but the manager has to use his or her best judgment. The individual's values as well as the values embraced by the organization have an effect on the decision to be made.

INFORMATION INTERNAL TO THE ORGANIZATION

Throughout the organization the manager will have subordinates who will share information. Again, the information might be either factual or value information. As we have said before, the manager has to act on the information that is received. By virtue of the formal authority that comes with the manager's position, he or she will receive information from the internal environment. The manager should disseminate that information according to the established hierarchy of the organization. A director of nursing services will have a number of supervisory nurses who report to him or her and will be given information that has to be shared among the supervisors. The information should be given to the appropriate individual(s) within the organization. As was the case with the information received from the external environment, factual information is usually easier to handle—either it is accurate or it is not. We suggest that the manager deal with incorrect internal information in the same manner as was discussed previously. The importance of the information is not minimized in any way because it comes from within the organization.

Value information that comes to the manager from within the organization creates some of the same dilemmas that have already been discussed. The manager must be aware of his or her own value orientation and keep in perspective the extent to which it should influence how information coming from subordinates is handled. This is especially important in avoiding the imposition of one's values on others. For example, if a supervisor in a local welfare department has strong anti-abortion views, that could affect the supervisor-supervisee relationship in the unit. If it is an agency's policy that unwed pregnant recipients of AFDC should be given information about various options to deal with pregnancy, including abortion, then that policy should be supported. The director of the local department may or may not agree with the policy; it still must be followed, irrespective of personal values. Similarly, let's suppose that the county director receives information about the personal behavior of one of his or her staff members—specifically, that one of the female social workers is living with a man to whom she is not legally married. Further, let's assume that the director has very strong, religiously based beliefs that such behavior is wrong and sinful. Yet, the social worker is exceptionally competent and her work performance is above that of any other worker in the office. While the director may not agree with the personal life-style of the worker, the evaluation of her performance should be based on how she does her job, not on how she lives. On occasion, there is a fine line between a staff member's personal behavior and its affect on the organization. If the personal life of the staff member begins to compromise the agency's reputation or integrity, then the manager has the responsibility to deal with the employee about the problem.

Included in the functions embraced by the disseminator role is the responsibility of interpreting the community to the professional staff. The organizational impact of personal behavior should be influenced by the community's mores. If the local office is in a small, rural, southern area of the country, the behavioral demands on the staff might be much different from the demands on the staff of an office in a large, urban, northern area. The manager has to be sensitive to where he or she is and must handle situations according to that reality.

In handling information, the manager is often confronted with the *dilemma of delegation* (Mintzberg, 1973, p. 74). What to delegate? When to delegate? That dilemma is compounded by what the manager knows by virtue of his or her position and the extent to which he or she shares the relevant information with the subordinate who has the responsibility to handle a delegated task. Much of what the manager knows is in his or her memory system; thus, the failure to share the relevant information can be all too common. No individual in a managerial position can do everything—the manager must delegate. In the process of delegation, the manager has a duty to provide the subordinate with the information necessary for a well-founded decision. Without that information, the subordinate will make poor decisions—not because the subordinate is unequal to the task, but because he or she lacks sufficient information. Every manager must strive to keep this from occurring.

EFFECTIVE COMMUNICATION

Throughout the text we have emphasized the importance of communication. An effective communication network is the glue that holds any organization together. In his classic book, Chester Barnard (1938) emphasized the importance of communication in achieving cooperative effort from those within the organization. Much has been written and even more said about the need to communicate. The lack of communication has been given as a reason why marriages fail as well as why organizations do not function effectively and efficiently. Indeed, communication is essential, and anyone who is going to be successful as a manager must recognize that fact.

Communication can be defined as the "transmission of information and understanding through the use of common symbols" (Gibson et al.,

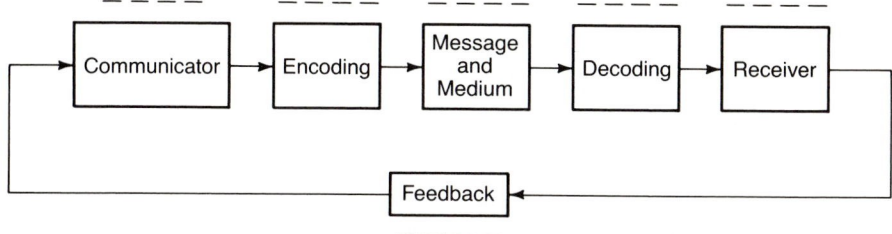

FIGURE 8-1 The Communication Process. From J. L. Gibson, J. M. Ivancevich, & J. H. Donnelly, Jr., *Organizations: Behavior, Structure, Processes,* 5th ed. (Plano, Tex.: Business Publications, Inc., 1985), p. 533.

1985, p. 533). The common symbols can be either verbal or nonverbal. Simply put, the communication process contains five elements: who (communicator) says what (message) in what way (medium) to whom (receiver) with what effect (feedback) (Gibson et al., 1985, p. 533). As illustrated in Figure 8-1, the act of communication comprises several elements.

The *communicator* is anyone within the organization who has something to communicate and must do that by translating what he or she wants to communicate into a set of symbols, a language; thus, what is to be communicated is *encoded.* As the encoding process takes place, the result is the *message* to be sent. That can be done either verbally or nonverbally. The message is carried out by a *medium*—face-to-face, telephone, memo, computer, policy statement, and so on. The message must then be *decoded* by the *receiver* and interpreted. If the process stops at this point, it is incomplete. There should always be feedback, which lets the communicator know if the receiver properly interpreted the message. Failure to provide for feedback will often lead to misinterpretation of the message. At any step in the process it is possible for the intended message to get distorted; in communication theory, that distortion is referred to as *noise* (Gibson et al., 1985, p. 535). Illustrations of noise might be the sending of multiple messages, misinterpretation of words, inadequate time, distractions, and value judgments.

In the process of communication, the manager should strive to be receiver oriented. Will the message be understood? Will it be interpreted correctly? This underlines again the importance of providing for feedback, which will let the manager know if the message is understood as intended. Yet, for a variety of reasons, barriers to communication do occur. Figure 8-2 illustrates the things that can lead to communication gaps and foster breakdowns in the communication process.

As a manager, you must recognize that no two people are the same. Each person comes from a different field of experience. The experiences that an individual has had will affect the process of communication. The factors identified as contributors to communication gaps are catalogued within the fields of experience of both the sender of the message and the receiver. The manager can work toward the improvement of communication by being aware of the factors that lead to breakdowns. He or she needs

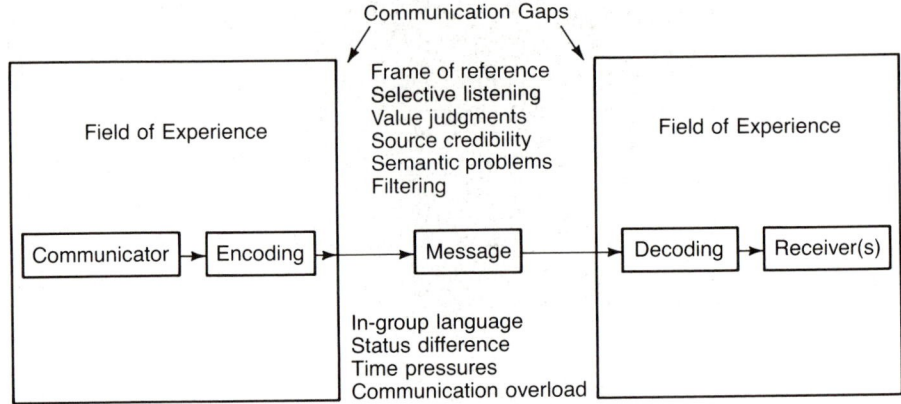

FIGURE 8-2   Barriers to Effective Communication. From J. L. Gibson, J. M. Ivancevich, & J. H. Donnelly, Jr., *Organizations: Behavior, Structure, Processes,* 5th ed. (Plano, Tex.: Business Publications, Inc., 1985), p. 547.

to be aware that the perceptions that people have come from their frames of reference. He or she also needs to be aware that people tend to hear what they want to hear (*selective listening*), that the receiver of the message will interpret it by making his or her own *value judgments,* and that the *credibility of the source* of the message will influence how it is received. The manager must also be aware that words mean different things to different people, which creates *semantic problems,* that *in-group language* and jargon can confound communication, and that information can be *filtered* as it is manipulated through the organization. Some individuals may attempt to make the annual report look better than it really is by playing down the negative aspects. The *status differences* that are found in organizations can also lead to distortion. If someone lower in the hierarchy makes a verbal contribution to a discussion, those higher up might say, "Oh, what does he know, he's only a line worker!" The *pressures of time* and *communication overload* can also lead to a breakdown. "I just don't have time to give you all the details" can lead to the receiver going in a direction that was not intended. Similarly, too much information coming all at once can create problems. As the available technology has made communication of large amounts of information possible, it has also had a tendency to lead to information overload. Managers can control that overload. The guiding principle should be not to get and not to give more information than is necessary.

Being aware of the potential gaps in communication is one thing; doing something about them is another. What can the manager do? Managers must work toward being understood, but they must also work to better understand. There is a conscious decision to be made. The manager must continually strive not only to improve his or her messages but also to listen to what is communicated to him or her. Let's look at some suggestions for improving communications (Gibson et al., 1985, pp. 549–556).

1. Follow up: Attempt to determine if the intended meaning was received; assume you are misunderstood.

2. Regulate information flow: Regulate the quality and quantity of information to ensure an optimum flow; do not give too much or too little.

3. Utilize feedback: Provide for mechanisms that indicate whether the message was received properly and in its intended form; use face-to-face feedback when possible.

4. Empathize: Put yourself in the "shoes" of the receiver; have a feeling for how the receiver will receive the message.

5. Repeat: Do not be afraid to repeat information, especially when it is of a technical or critical nature.

6. Encourage mutual trust: Create an atmosphere of mutual trust and confidence within the organization.

7. Use time effectively: Recognize that receivers receive many messages, not just yours; use retreats or time away from the office to deal with major areas of concern.

8. Simplify language: Avoid trying to impress the receiver with your vocabulary or technical knowledge. Will the receiver understand what I'm saying?—that is the guideline to follow.

9. Listen effectively: Listen with understanding; want to listen. Davis stated the following Ten Commandments for Good Listening—stop talking, put the speaker at ease, show the speaker you want to listen, remove distractions, empathize with the speaker, be patient, hold your temper, go easy on argument and criticism, ask questions, and stop talking. (Davis, 1972, p. 394)

10. Use the grapevine: The grapevine exists in all organizations. You cannot do away with it, so use it.

The manager is a communicator. How well he or she communicates will depend on the effort made to continually improve. The manager must recognize that for the organization to be effective, people within it must be able to communicate effectively. Communication must be allowed to flow upward, downward, horizontally, and diagonally. It is only as that happens that good, understandable communication will be achieved and the performance of the organization will be enhanced.

Much of what we have been discussing has been verbal communication. Communication can also be nonverbal. The manager needs to recognize that nonverbal communication can be as important as what is said or written. Posture, eye contact, gestures, facial expressions, physical contact, and distance can communicate a great deal to the receiver. For example, if the manager never makes eye contact with the subordinate when praising his or her performance, the subordinate may question the manager's sincerity.

SUMMARY

In this chapter we have discussed the *disseminator* role of the manager. The manager receives information from outside the organization as well from within the organization. Decisions must be made as to how the information will be handled. If it is factual information, it is relatively easy to handle. If it is value information, it is somewhat more difficult. We have discussed several approaches that can be taken in dealing with such information. Finally, we have discussed the importance of communication in the handling of information. We have identified barriers to effective communication and have suggested some approaches to improving communication.

REFERENCES

BARNARD, C. I. (1938). *The function of the executive.* Cambridge, Mass.: Harvard University Press.
DAVIS, K. (1972). *Human behavior at work.* New York: McGraw-Hill.
GIBSON, J. L., IVANCEVICH, J. M., & DONNELLY, J. H., JR. (1985). *Organizations: Behavior, structure, processes* (5th ed.). Plano, Tex.: Business Publications.
HARRISON, E. F. (1975). *The managerial decision-making process.* Boston: Houghton Mifflin.
MINTZBERG, H. (1973). *The nature of managerial work.* New York: Harper & Row.
ROKEACH, M. (1973). *The nature of human values.* New York: The Free Press.

QUESTIONS FOR DISCUSSION

1. Describe a communication problem in your organization using the concepts developed in this chapter.
2. Discuss how you would deal with the problem discussed in question 1.
3. Develop a list of criteria you would use to determine whether you should share with subordinates organizational information you have received.
4. Discuss and give specific examples of the common barriers to effective communication outlined in this chapter.

SUGGESTED PROJECTS

1. Keep a diary of situations you have encountered that are examples of communication barriers. Using the concepts of this chapter, develop a list of tactics you could have used to convert those situations into effective communications.
2. Develop a profile of the channel of communication, both upward and downward, for your college.

The Manager as Entrepreneur

chapter 9

"If you want things to be different, something has to change." In fulfilling the role of *entrepreneur,* the manager is frequently questioning, looking, and assessing how the organization is functioning. He or she must be constantly considering new ways to deal with problems, issues, and concerns. Human service organizations are dynamic entities, and that is what makes the management of them a challenging and, we hope, rewarding activity. Failure to change and be responsive to the environment fosters a stagnant and static climate that will be frustrating and nonproductive. Mintzberg's (1973) concept of the entrepreneur is one of managing controlled change. That is, it is not change for the sake of change, nor is it haphazard modification and adaptation. This chapter will focus on the role of entrepreneur and will introduce some approaches to change that human service managers should find useful.

THE CONTEXT OF CHANGE

A few years ago the authors were responsible for the development and implementation of a nationwide training program for managers and supervisors in human service organizations. That activity brought us into frequent contact with personnel from organizations throughout the country. Often, we would comment that the one constant we found from state to state was the phenomenon of change. Inevitably, state human service organizations were going through reorganization, getting ready for it, or trying to adapt to a recent reorganizational change. When a new manager comes into an organization or is promoted into a higher-level position, he or she believes there are newer and "better" ways to conduct the activity of the organization. Yet, we would issue a warning: Do not move too hastily.

Employees' typical inclination is to view any change in leadership with some suspicion and apprehension. There is an air of uncertainty and ambiguity, which will only be heightened if hasty, ill-conceived changes are made. Certainly, any organization or unit therein ought to take on the "flavor" of the leader, but we suggest that this be accomplished through careful and thoughtful planning.

PLANNING AS A FUNCTION OF CHANGE

Planning is essential to the effectiveness and efficiency of any organization. The function of planning should be viewed as a systematic approach for getting from point A to point B—the plan describes and delineates how that will be accomplished. Planning serves as a bridge, as depicted in Figure 9-1.

In order to determine where an organization is at the present time, the manager should draw upon the variety of resources available. *Talk* to people, *listen* to them, *consider* their suggestions, *weigh* the alternative approaches, *communicate* decisions, *elicit* reactions, and *act* on the best available information.

The function of planning is continuous; it is not a one-time activity. In this regard, Koontz and O'Donnell (1976) refer to the concept of *navigational change*. Once a plan is developed, it is not etched in stone, but as circumstances dictate, the manager leads the organization through various adaptations and modifications. The question may be raised, Then why plan? A plan is a blueprint; it provides the boundaries and the direction, but although the main course remains constant, deviations will always be required. Let's suppose that a director of nursing services is asked to develop a five-year staffing plan. It might be supposed that on the basis of current hospital capacity, proposed construction modifications, and current staff composition it would be a simple matter to put together such a plan. Yet, there are matters within the environment that are beyond the director's control. They include the availability of trained staff to hire, the retention of current staff (i.e., no one retires prematurely, resigns, or dies), the construction schedule (i.e., it meets the published deadline), the security of the director's job (i.e., he or she is not relieved of the directorship). Let's just look at one of those aspects. The nursing schools in the area have been graduating a given number of nurses each year; the director assumes the same will hold true for the future. However, the legislature refuses to

FIGURE 9-1 The Plan as a Bridge

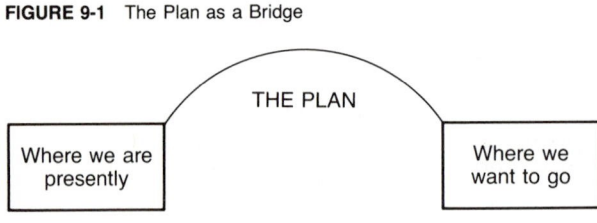

fund the school that has been producing 40 percent of the graduates. Of those who do graduate, 25 percent do not pass the compulsory state examinations. What happens to the plan? Chaos? Not necessarily. If the director has given thought to various alternatives and contingencies, the situation will not be so chaotic. Indeed, adjustments in the previously stated projections will have to be made, but the director can navigate around them if he or she has given thought during the planning stages to such unintended consequences. Contingency plans are nothing more than anticipating the "what ifs" that can put the best of plans into the proverbial tailspin.

> Any good plan has built-in contingencies and alternatives. One real payoff in planning comes from the search and identification of contingencies. The search process causes the planners to consider events and evaluate their potential impact on the organization. If and when such events occur, the organization is in a much better position to take proper actions. (Rue & Byars, 1986, p. 150)

An effective way for the manager to determine alternative approaches is to communicate with a variety of individuals within the organization, especially with those who will be responsible for implementing the plan. To impose a plan on those who will be responsible for carrying it out is to court disaster. Employees can either consciously or unconsciously sabotage any expected activity. The astute manager is aware of that possibility and seeks to find ways to control it.

To illustrate this point, consider the experience of a large human service agency that sought to implement a statewide management information system. Pilot projects had been carried out in several counties, and on the basis of that experience, the system was put into place. A substantial amount of planning had gone into the development of the system, yet the management staff failed to gather reactions from a broad spectrum of workers who would be responsible for filling out the required forms. The forms were sent out, meetings were held to explain the system, and then it all came unglued. Workers were uncertain as to the need for the system because they did not see what it was going to do for them. They were annoyed with the increased paperwork, and once the forms were sent in, the workers never heard anything more about them. So, they began to put down numbers indiscriminately. The figures going into the state office bore no resemblance to the reality of the caseloads and care activity. Consciously, the workers wanted to "show them," and they did.

In the preceding illustration, the development of an information system was a noble effort, and it could be shown how it would enhance the data gathering of the agency and ultimately how that could have a positive effect on the activity of the line workers throughout the state. The breakdown came in how the system was developed. Sufficient attention was not given to the reactions of those who would be filling out the forms. Certainly, the management team could insist that the workers do the job correctly, but such insistence does not guarantee compliance. They would have saved a significant amount of time, money, and effort had they paid more attention to reactions and suggestions. Further, involvement of workers at the beginning has the potential of strengthening commitment to and identification with the intended change. Managers must realize that they need those throughout the organization to pull together as a team. It is not uncommon for managers who have been away from the line of activity for several years to forget "what it's like down there," so soliciting opinions and reactions is a valuable exercise.

To be effective, planning must be held together by effective, two-way communication. Likert (1967), in describing the System 4 organization, indicates that it is characterized by a communication network that goes up, down, and sideways. In such an organization, the manager demonstrates a keen appreciation for what is communicated both verbally and nonverbally. We have dealt more specifically with the process of communication in Chapter 8, but here we emphasize the need for it in the planning process.

The very act of managing others to achieve the organizational mission requires planning. A suggested approach to planning is that developed by Rue and Byars (1986) and is illustrated in Figure 9-2.

The process shown in Figure 9-2 is not a set of mutually exclusive events. Rather, it should be viewed as a set of overlapping and interacting components (Rue & Byars, 1986). The first step in the process is to complete a *self-audit* to determine "where are we now?" As stated previously, before an organization can have any idea of where it wants to go, it must first have some idea of where it is. The setting of objectives that are the benchmarks of the plan will be influenced by the outcome of the self-audit. The following checklist is adapted from Rue and Byars (1986).

1. What is our present financial situation?
2. What condition are our facilities and equipment in?
3. What is the availability of qualified personnel?
4. Is the current organizational structure appropriate?
5. What are the organization's major policies and strategies?
6. How do we "stack up" against similar organizations?
7. What are the productive and nonproductive units within the organization?
8. What is the quality of the service that we provide?

Once the self-audit is completed, the second step is to *survey the environment,* those factors external to the organization. They are factors over which the manager has no control and include:

1. The potential impact of population growth and mobility
2. The economic conditions that could affect the intended outcomes
3. The political environment, both local and national
4. The government regulations that should be reviewed
5. The availability of potential resources, both public and private
6. An assessment of any competing organizations.

To illustrate the importance of studying the environment, let's suppose that Sunshine Hospital, located in a Sunbelt state, is considering set-

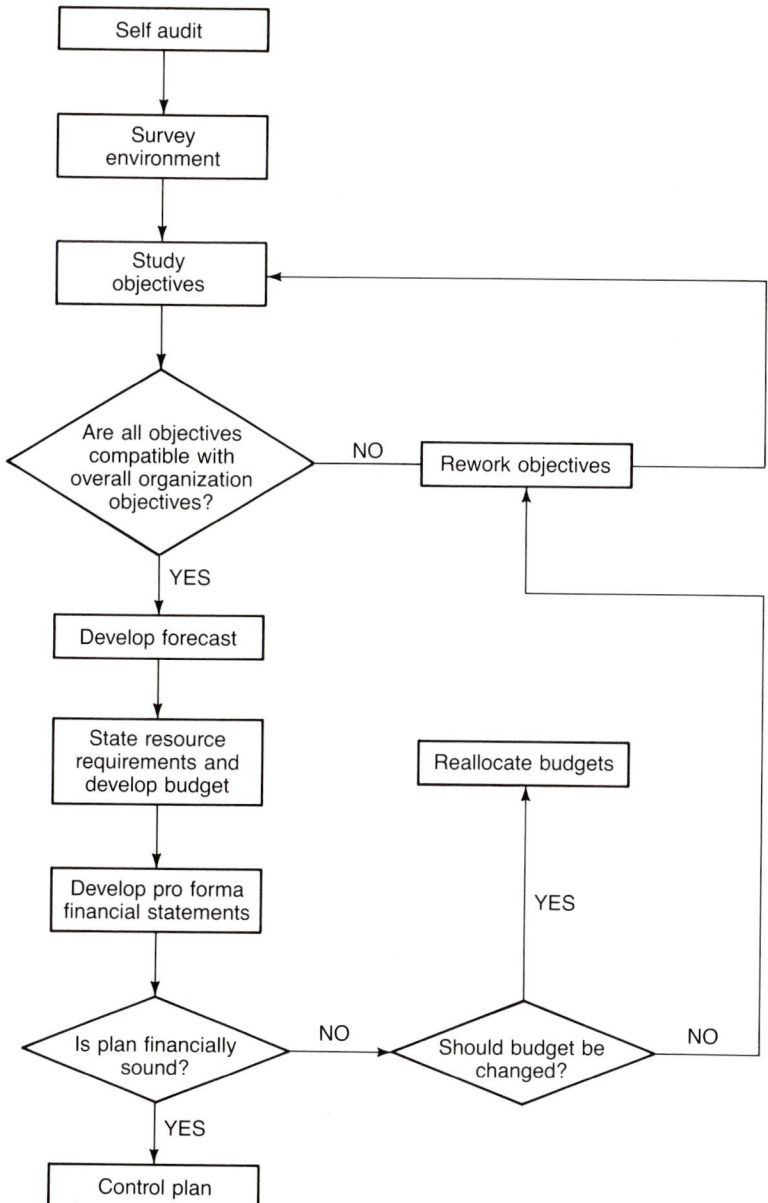

FIGURE 9-2 The Planning Process. From L. Rue & L. Byars, *Management: Theory and Application,* 4th ed., (1986), p. 158. © Richard D. Irwim, Inc., 1977, 1980, 1983, and 1986.

ting up a nursing home for geriatric patients. What should management be concerned about in the survey of the environment? First, it is known that the elderly population of the Sunbelt states is increasing. Each year, more people retire to those areas, so the availability of older people is going to increase. Further, it is becoming more apparent that many older people have not adequately prepared for their later years. With increasing inflation, those on fixed incomes will have fewer "real dollars" to live on. The probability of the shrinking buying power of the dollar will, no doubt, be a factor that the hospital will have to take into consideration. Likewise, the political environment at all levels will be forced to face the increasing number of older citizens. In recent years, it was evident that the Reagan administration had to reconsider its intent to slow down Social Security cost-of-living increases. The older population is a vocal and increasingly well organized pressure group that politicians will not be able to ignore. Additionally, relevant government regulations should be reviewed, such as those dealing with Social Security, Medicare, Medicaid, various building codes, and staffing regulations. It may be that the cost of modifying an existing structure is too great to bring it up to code specifications, and the project will have to be abandoned. A determination of potential funding sources should be undertaken. Are there any public monies available, for example, from the Community Development Act, or are there potential private sources, such as foundations or wealthy individuals in the community? The prevailing social attitudes and values should be weighed. Granted that there is a growing concern and appreciation for the elderly, but is that reflected locally? Can support be expected from the local community? Finally, an assessment should be made of existing facilities that provide a similar service. Will the Sunshine Hospital's nursing home be any different? If so, how? To complete such an inventory will provide management with a good "feel" for the environment.

The first two steps, the *self-audit* and the *survey of the environment,* lay the foundation for the next step of the planning process: *setting objectives.* An objective, by definition, "is simply a statement of results to be achieved" (Morrisey, 1976, p. 66). The objectives identify measurable accomplishments which the plan is seeking to complete. They are benchmarks or milestones that let the manager know how things are progressing.

The involvement of staff in setting objectives can be a significant motivational factor. Giving them a part in the process allows them to develop a sense of ownership, which minimizes the "we and they" syndrome and results in commitment to the successful accomplishment of the objective. Commitment is the antithesis of compliance, and one or the other will frequently be present. Involvement is the hallmark of a popular approach to management, Management by Objectives (MBO). MBO is discussed more fully in Chapter 7. MBO has been the subject of much criticism, especially from the not-for-profit sector. However, we suggest that much of the criticism has been unwarranted and premature. To effectively use MBO, an organization must recognize that it takes time for individuals throughout the organization to learn to adapt to the approach. Any organization that seeks to use MBO should be prepared to allow from three to five years for it to become an effective management tool. To abort the system earlier than that can be foolish and quite costly. MBO can work if given the chance. Critical to its success is management's willingness to "ride out" the developmental period.

To put the setting of objectives into its proper perspective, it should be noted that it is a process that operationalizes in measurable terms the purpose (mission) of the organization and the goals that have been identified. Figure 9-3 illustrates this process.

It should be recognized that while it is possible to establish objectives for many aspects of the activity of human service organizations, it is also probable that there will be subjective dimensions that are not measurable. Yet, we strongly suggest that the manager make the effort, to the extent practical, to work toward the development of measurable statements. For example, let's suppose that a manager has as an objective the improvement of communication among his or her employees. While that is a subjective expectation, it is possible to state various measurable activities that could lead to the desired improvement; for example, holding weekly staff meetings, meeting individually with employees, visiting the work area (Morrisey, 1976, pp. 75–76). Additionally, in seeking to identify measurable objectives, the manager must be careful not to use the excuse that quality cannot be measured. He or she should search for indicators of quality. Such indicators might be the number of cases closed, the amount of decrease in the number of patient complaints about the nursing service, the number of clients who are successfully employed following a job retraining program. We recognize that it is not a simple matter to identify measurable objectives for subjective aspects of the organization's mission, but we emphasize the need to work toward that end.

The setting of objectives does not occur in a vacuum. Any objective statement must fit into the total organizational scheme. Top management has the responsibility to prescribe the limits within which each unit in the organization sets unit objectives. However, each unit's objectives must go in the same overall direction in which management wants to move the organization.

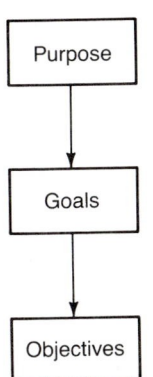

FIGURE 9-3   The Perspective of Objective Setting

As noted earlier, an objective is "simply a statement of results to be achieved" (Morrisey, 1976, p. 66). An objective should contain four major elements:

1. An action or accomplishment verb
2. A simple measurable key result
3. A date or time period within which the result is to be accomplished
4. The maximum investment, in terms of money, work hours, or both, which will lead to the objective's being achieved (Morrisey, 1976, p. 66)

Consider the following objectives, which illustrate those elements:

1. To develop and implement phase I of a new management information system for the total organization, effective April 1, at a cost not to exceed 120 work hours.
2. To reduce the error rate to an average of 3 percent by September 31, at a cost not to exceed 80 work hours.
3. To develop and implement a quantitative employee appraisal system for head nurses, effective January 1, at a cost not to exceed 90 work hours.
4. To send five supervisors to management training during the first quarter at a cost not to exceed $2,000.

Once the objectives have been stated, it is necessary for the manager to determine if they are consistent and compatible with the organization's objectives. If there is any inconsistency, it must be resolved before any additional steps can be taken. Needless to say, it is important that the organizational purpose or mission, overall goals, and objectives be known throughout the organization. If, for example, the hospital's administration is interested in increasing the income productivity of the emergency room, then that should be communicated to the director of nursing. It would certainly have programmatic and staffing implications for the nursing staff. If there is any inconsistency, the objectives need to be reworked. Following the reworking, the issue of compatibility must be addressed. If there is evident compatibility, then the next step, *forecasting,* can be carried out by the manager.

Forecasting is simply anticipating the future. What can be expected to influence the organization in the foreseeable future? Granted, there are some intangibles that can never be anticipated. For example, if the state legislature passes a new law that has direct impact, it can drastically alter a plan. Further, a shift in the political climate, an unforeseen economic recession, and a major scandal are but a few of the intangibles that can alter a sound and thoughtful forecast. Yet, there are some indications as to what will happen in the next five years. For example, it is apparent that the population throughout the country is getting older. That fact has numerous implications for the human services. More medical services will be needed for the elderly, and it would be prudent for hospitals to anticipate that need. At the same time, more people will be drawing Social Security and the attendant medical benefits from Medicare and Medicaid. Undoubtedly, hospitals should give attention to that trend. Similarly, the public welfare system will be affected by the shift in population from one area of the country to another. What we are suggesting is that population shifts and trends can be indicators for the human services in setting priorities for their programs. Not only is the population getting older, but also there will, no doubt, be continued migration to the Sunbelt states. The proportion of elderly will continue to increase in those areas as individuals seek a more favorable climate.

We have mentioned that the political climate should not go unheeded. In recent years, there has been a conservative shift throughout the country. Such a shift does affect the human services. An example is the recent decision of the administration in Washington to "clamp down" on recipients of disability assistance through Social Security. If that shift continues, it will require managers to do more with less. The astute manager will recognize that and will anticipate required changes in the services provided. Rather than sitting back and waiting, he or she will plan accordingly. A wise manager does not reflect on the past; he or she plans and works toward adapting for the future while functioning in the present.

Without question, there is frequently a direct relationship between the political climate and the economic climate. Economic cycles have an obvious effect on the human services. A manager must recognize that fact and plan within a realistic context. A downturn in the economy will have a direct impact on human service organizations. As unemployment rises, the revenues coming into a given governmental unit will decrease. A southern state responded to such a condition by initiating proration. The state agencies had their budgets prorated by 10 percent, even 15 percent. Thus, although funds were appropriated by the legislature, the total appropriation was cut by those percentages. To effectively respond to that, human service managers were required to function with less at a time when the demand for services was on the increase because of the economic conditions. The point we are emphasizing is that managerial personnel must be responsive to the economic realities that affect their respective agencies.

The manager must also pay attention to changing societal values. As values change, so do demands for specific kinds of services. For example, as the use of contraceptives and abortion has become more accepted, the availability of adoptable children has decreased drastically. Some agencies have had to expand and modify their service delivery systems just to survive. The phenomenon of organ transplants has brought with it many unanswered ethical and moral questions that hospital personnel must wrestle with and resolve. Placing children in single-parent families is a relatively recent development that has had an impact on foster placement and adoptions. Additional examples could be provided, but it should be evident that such changes must be recognized and anticipated in the planning process.

In the planning process, it is necessary and important to engage in forecasting. One approach is the use of the survey: Experts—those "in the know"—can be surveyed as to their predictions for the future. It is simple to use, but the result is opinion, not fact. There is a technique that is a bit more systematic than simply sending out a survey. The technique referred to is the Delphi Technique (Delbecq, 1975), and it seeks to achieve a consensus. In the context in which we are using it, it would seek a consensus on the direction of the human services within the next five years. Through several iterations, usually three, the forecast becomes more refined and accurate. Essentially, the approach entails the following procedures:

1. A panel of experts is chosen. "Expert" should be defined as anyone with relevant input. The number on the panel can vary, and an initial commitment is elicited before the first questionnaire is issued.

2. The initial questionnaire is designed. The number of questions should be limited, as should the amount of space for responses. The object at this point is to obtain specific and concise input.

3. After receipt of responses to the first questionnaire, a second questionnaire is developed. It is critical to accurately reflect the responses from the initial questionnaire and to develop the second questionnaire in a format that will begin to provide statistical convergence. The questions might be constructed in the format of a Likert-type scale in which respondents are asked to indicate the extent to which they agree or disagree with a specific statement. Another approach might be to have the respondents rank-order a series of statements.

4. After receipt of the responses from the second questionnaire, a third questionnaire is prepared. Primarily, an attempt is made to provide opportunity for the panel of experts to select a response that has emerged as the dominant choice. Thus, consensus is achieved. For example, the third questionnaire might indicate the statements that received the highest ranking or approval and ask the respondents to indicate their extent of agreement.

5. A final report is distributed to members of the panel. Such a report generally contains a ranking of statements by priority, as well as the amount of dissension for each statement.

Other methods for forecasting can include obtaining a representative sample of direct service providers and eliciting from them contributions, ideas, trends, and expectations about service in their particular area of expertise. Often, they are in the best position to know. Surveying clients, patients, and patients' family members can also provide additional information that can be quite helpful and, in some instances, quite revealing.

A final suggested technique for forecasting is the nominal group technique (Delbecq, 1975). It uses a structured meeting as a mechanism for obtaining high-quality information from groups familiar with a particular area. The communication within the group is written except at specific times. The written responses are limited and are shared with all members. The specific steps in using the approach are:

1. Individuals are selected to participate. The criteria for selection can include expertise, experience, or ideas about the issue or area being considered.

2. The issue or area is presented to those selected to participate. The role of the members to help define the issue or area of interest is made explicit.

3. The total group is divided into groups of five to eight persons. Each group is presented with an exploratory question. Participants identify facts and resources needed to deal with the question. This identification process is done in writing and without discussion.

4. Each group selects a recorder, who will list verbatim all of the ideas generated by members of the group. There continues to be no discussion at this stage.

5. Following the complete listing of all ideas, the group recorder will conduct a clarification, elaboration, and evaluation discussion of the ideas. These ideas are to be discussed sequentially. No ideas are to be eliminated.

6. Each participant then ranks the ten most important ideas on the list. There is no interaction among members in doing this. Each group makes its decision based on the outcome of the members' individual votes.

7. Each nominal group's ranking is shared with the total group. Discussion can be held on these voting patterns with a final secret vote by participants.

The use of modern technology can be quite beneficial in forecasting. There are existing computer programs that are designed to do this, and they should be used when appropriate. If an organization has access to a computer and the staff competent to use the existing technology, then the manager can seek such assistance in the process of forecasting.

Once the forecasts and objectives have been developed, they must be converted into actual resource requirements (Rue & Byars, p. 56). Several questions need to be answered: What are the staffing requirements? What staff will be needed and in what number? What equipment will be needed? What type of facility will be required? Are there any special materials that must be purchased? In short, what are the cost expectations attached to the plan? We will discuss the budgeting process in Chapter 11, but we mention it here because every plan must be translated into cost requirements.

Closely aligned with the preceding step in the planning process is the development of *pro forma* financial statements. In reference to action to be taken (the plan), what are the expected revenues and expenditures? Can the course of action pay for itself, or will it have to be carried by other facets of the total system? That cannot be answered without considering the inflow and outgo of financial resources. Is the plan financially sound and feasible? If that question cannot be answered yes, then the proposed budget must be reworked until it can be determined that the plan is sound and financially feasible. It may well be that at this point some major readjustments will be required; however, if a plan cannot be supported financially, it will not accomplish the outcomes expected.

The final step in the process is to have a *control plan.* Plans should be reviewed periodically to determine if there have been any major deviations. Changes that affect the direction of the plan can occur outside of the organization. On the other hand, situations can arise within the organization that require a reallocation of resources and priorities. What the manager is doing is relating the plan to reality, and that should be done in every plan. If an MBO system is being utilized, that provides a very helpful vehicle for such reviews. We strongly recommend that reviews be done on at least a quarterly basis.

Planning is a vital part of the *entrepreneurial* role. Planning should not be viewed as a waste of time, nor should it be viewed as an end product. The manager is constantly looking for ways to improve, to redesign, to reallocate, or to change, and planning must be an integral part of that activity.

CHANGE AND THE ORGANIZATION AS A SYSTEM

It is important for the human service manager to view the organization as a system. That is, he or she cannot operate in a vacuum. There must be a recognition that if change is initiated in one area of the organization, it has an effect throughout the organization. For example, if there is an adjustment in the compensation schedule in one area, it can have serious dysfunctional implications in other areas. Recently, a sizable state agency serving juvenile offenders began its own school system and in doing so raised the teachers' salaries to a competitive level. While the salaries were raised for the teachers, the concern was the effects such increases would have in other areas. Indeed, the manager can take the position that compensation will be based on "whatever the traffic will bear," that compensation will be commensurate with what it takes to get the best available personnel. Yet, there are definite disadvantages to this approach, especially to morale throughout the total organization. The guiding principle should reflect a sense of equity. We do not mean to belabor this point, but we do believe that if the organization is sound from a systems perspective, serious dysfunction can be anticipated, controlled, and handled.

As we consider the human service organization as a system, perhaps Figure 9-4 will be helpful (Steiner, 1977, p. 17).

The input includes the assigned resources of money, time, people, technology, and equipment.

Indeed, in any human service organization money is vital and critical. It is with money that services are performed, people are paid, equipment is purchased, and "the rent is paid." There are individuals within some systems who have the knowledge and skill to utilize the technology. In other systems such knowledge and skill must be purchased from outside the organization. In any event, the technology is beneficial only if it is used, and used appropriately. That may require that personnel be trained to effectively incorporate the available technology into the operation of the organization.

As the inputs come into the organization, they must be converted, and that is accomplished through the process mechanisms. The administrative functions of planning, decision making, directing, controlling, coordinating, and evaluating are supported by the organizational structure and the management systems and procedures. In making the organization an effective operating unit, the structure of the organization is an important factor. It defines how managers and others should interact in reference to the budget, personnel, and information. It is in this phase that the inputs are converted to lead to organizational output.

The output is the end product. The delivery standards indicate the type of service to be delivered, the acceptable quality and quantity of the service, and an acceptable cost for the service to be delivered. The program definition adds specificity to the activity of the organization by detailing the priorities, objectives, elements, activities, and how all of those will be evaluated.

What we are suggesting is that there is a process that must be recog-

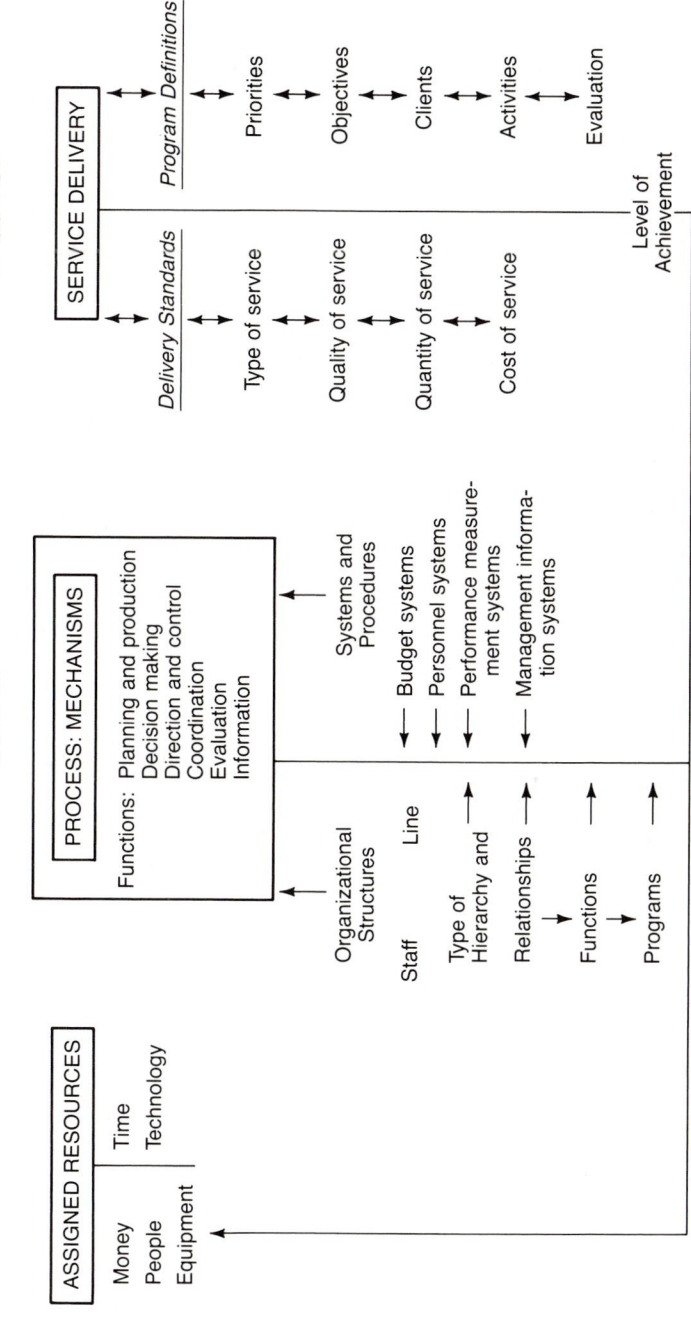

FIGURE 9-4 The Production Process. From R. Steiner, *The Human Service Organization: From Survival to Achievement* (Beverly Hills, Calif.: Sage Publications, Inc., 1977), p. 17.

nized by the manager. We have briefly discussed that process from a system orientation because we believe that you cannot view change from any other perspective and be successful as a manager. Failure to do so can lead to confusion and can compromise the effectiveness and efficiency of the organization.

EFFECTIVE MANAGEMENT OF CHANGE

Recognizing that change does not occur within a vacuum, the manager has to consider how he or she can effectively introduce change and manage the process of change. Change within the organization does not just happen. It may be induced by internal forces as well as by forces external to the organization. The effective manager constantly surveys the environment to consider ideas and creative ways to improve. That requires the manager to have his or her "ear to the ground." In Chapter 8 we dealt with the importance of communication, but its significance cannot be minimized at this point. As the manager, you need to listen to what is being said by those within the organization and by those outside it. As you listen, you will begin to gather information that can help you in deciding how a particular problem, concern, or opportunity might be handled. Peters and Waterman (1982) discuss the importance of "Managing by Wandering Around." That is, be visible both to those who work in the organization and to those external to it.

How the manager deals with change is vitally important. It is necessary to keep in mind that there might be some resistance to change. As illustrated in Table 9-1, there are things that the manager can do to mini-

TABLE 9-1. Acceptability of Change

Change is more acceptable when it is understood than when it is not.

Change is more acceptable when it does not threaten security than when it does.

Change is more acceptable when those affected have helped to create it than when it has been externally imposed.

Change is more acceptable when it results from an application of previously established principles than when it is dictated by personal order.

Change is more acceptable when it follows a series of successful changes than when it follows a series of failures.

Change is more acceptable when it is incorporated after previous change has been assimilated than when it is incorporated during the confusion of other organizational changes.

Change is more acceptable if it has been planned than if it is experimental.

Change is more acceptable to people new on the job than to people old on the job.

Change is more acceptable to people who share in the benefits of the change than to those who do not.

Change is more acceptable if the organization has been trained to accept change.

Source: R. M. Besse, "Company Planning Must Be Planned," pp. 62–63. Reprinted with the permission of *Dun's Business Month* (formerly *Dun's Review*). April 1957, Copyright 1957, Dun & Bradstreet Publications Corporation.

mize resistance. If the manager takes to heart what has been suggested, dissatisfaction and concern can be managed. Much of what is suggested revolves around a basic understanding of people and acting upon that understanding. To effectively control resistance, the manager must, among other things, keep the employees informed and involve them in the change process.

In assessing various patterns of organizational change, Griener (1967) found that the most successful pattern was one he identified as a *shared* approach to change. The shared approach involved people throughout the organization in handling the problem situation and proposing solutions. They were an integral part of the process. Contrasted with that approach was the *unilateral* approach and the *delegated* approach. The former introduces change in an authoritative manner, while the latter gives to subordinates complete responsibility in defining the problem and acting on it. The manager should provide some boundaries within which the group will act and not leave them to flounder. Enough is known about human behavior to indicate that the more people within the work place are involved in decisions, the more committed they are to the decision. Workers want to believe that they have some control over what happens, especially when decisions affect them. The *shared* approach allows for that involvement, and it has proven to be the most successful way to deal with organizational change.

Likert and Likert (1976) further emphasize the need for group participation in the resolution of conflict. We mention that here because conflict often accompanies change. When something difficult is being considered, the proposed change will undoubtedly affect individuals within the organization. Beer (1980, pp. 102–103) identifies four areas in which members of the organization may experience losses due to change:

1. *Loss of competence.* As old ways of doing business are discarded, individuals may have to learn new skills and develop different attitudes and new behaviors; thus, their sense of competence may be threatened.

2. *Loss of relationships.* New patterns of interaction may accompany change as individuals are reassigned or new settings for decision making are created. Developing new relationships and the loss of old relationships may be a cost of change.

3. *Loss of power.* Change typically means a shift in power and influence. Some gain, while others lose.

4. *Loss of extrinsic rewards.* Change may find some within the organization gaining in compensation and perquisites, while others may have rewards taken away.

As people within the organization experience change, the manager should recognize their perceived concerns as well as their real concerns. As we mentioned in another chapter, an employee's motivation to perform can be affected by any number of things, including change. Workers become very comfortable with a set of routines and job expectations, and any change that affects those areas can have an adverse effect on motivation. Anticipating that, the manager can listen, encourage, support, counsel, and educate his or her staff to offset frustration, anxiety, and apprehension.

Thus, the loss of motivation will be less. Similarly, it is important for top management to work with mid-level managers on the same concerns. Frequently, it is the mid-level managers who have the direct contact with the line staff, so they *must* support the change and provide the necessary supports to make it successful.

The interrelationship between planning and change is apparent throughout the previous discussion. Change does not just happen, or, if it does, the chances of it being successful are minimal. Change should be a thoughtful, systematic, and planned process. Individuals throughout the organization need to know *what* is to happen, *when* it will happen, *how* it will happen, and *who* will be involved. Further, specific responsibilities for specific aspects of the change need to be developed into a plan for action, and all of those ingredients—the who, what, when, and where components—must be built into the plan. The more thought that is given to the proposed change, the more likely it is that it will succeed. Also, keep in mind that the manager must give consideration to the impact of change in other parts of the system. That will require communicating with other parts of the organization to clarify what effects there might be and then developing the corresponding plans throughout the organization that will support the change. For example, if a manager of a mental health center desires to set up a flexible work schedule for employees, he or she needs to consider the impact it might have on compensation, job descriptions, supervisory responsibility, monitoring systems, and staff. Failure to give thought to those areas could lead to catastrophic results.

SUMMARY

In this chapter we have addressed the *entrepreneurial* role of the manager. We have dealt with planning and change as it occurs within the organization. We have also discussed the need to view the organization as a system. The manager is in a position to look at problems and make plans to deal with them. Change will occur and the more thought that is given to it and to all of its ramifications, the greater the probability of its success.

REFERENCES

Beer, M. (1980). *Organization change and development: A systems view.* Glenview, Ill.: Scott, Foresman.

Besse, R. M. (1957, April). Company planning must be planned. *Dun's Business Month* (formerly *Dun's Review*), pp. 62–63.

Delbecq, A. (1975). *Group techniques for program planning: A guide to nominal group and delphi processes.* Glenview, Ill.: Scott, Foresman.

Griener, L. E. (1967, May–June). Patterns of organization change. *Harvard Business Review,* pp. 119–130.

Koontz, H., & O'Donnell, C. (1976). *Management: A systems and contingency analysis of managerial functions* (6th ed.). New York: McGraw-Hill.

Likert, R. (1967). *Human organization: Its management and value.* New York: McGraw-Hill.

Likert, R., & Likert, J. G. (1976). *New ways of managing conflict.* New York: McGraw-Hill.

MINTZBERG, H. (1973). *The nature of managerial work.* New York: Harper & Row.

MORRISEY, G. (1976). *Management by objectives and results in the public sector.* Reading, Mass.: Addison-Wesley.

PETERS, T., & WATERMAN, R. H. (1982). *In search of excellence.* New York: Harper & Row.

RUE, L., & BYARS, L. L. (1986). *Management: Theory and application* (4th ed.). Homewood, Ill.: Richard D. Irwin.

STEINER, R. (1977). *Managing the human service organization: From survival to achievement.* Beverly Hills, Calif.: Sage Publications, Inc.

QUESTIONS FOR DISCUSSION

1. "Management planning is inconsistent with the basic goals of a human service organization—meeting the needs of individual clients." Do you agree or disagree with that statement? Justify your position.
2. How can human service organizations improve the planning process?
3. Describe how you would implement a change of staffing patterns among human service workers.
4. How would you overcome resistance to change in a human service organization?

SUGGESTED PROJECTS

1. Have the class decide upon a "new program" for your organization. Using the concepts discussed in this chapter, develop a comprehensive plan for implementing the program.
2. Develop a plan for introducing major curriculum changes in your college's degree program.

The Role of the Disturbance Handler

chapter 10

Conventional management wisdom holds that through effective performance of the functions of planning, organizing, directing, and controlling, the manager eliminates conflicts. For example, in the discussion of organizational structure, we found that tasks are assigned, departments created, and authority and responsibility delegated for the purpose, at least partially, of eliminating conflict throughout the organization. Indeed, conflict and crises were considered to be examples of poor management and harmful to the organization.

Mintzberg, on the other hand, specifies the activity of disturbance handler as one of the basic roles of the manager. In this role the manager deals with unforeseen situations or events over which he or she has little or no control. For example, when two caseworkers disagree about whether a battered child should be removed from the home, the supervisor must intervene. Mintzberg (1973) notes that "every manager must spend a good part of his time reacting very quickly to high-pressure disturbance situations" (p. 84).

The basic tool used by the manager in the performance of the disturbance handler role is decision making. Decision making is part of every facet of the manager's activity. Indeed, the effectiveness or ineffectiveness of managers is largely dependent upon the quality of their decisions. While the skills necessary for planning, organizing, leading, and controlling are essential to the manager, it is the ability to effectuate sound decisions that is critical to the effectiveness of the plans, organization, and leadership as control functions. So critical is this aspect of the manager's responsibility that many management scholars believe that "management is decision making."

In this chapter we will first discuss the techniques involved in managerial decision making. Next we will deal with the nature of organizational conflict by examining the decisive role of the manager in managing such conflict.

MANAGERIAL DECISION MAKING

In its simplest form, the process of managerial decision making may be thought of as making a conscious choice among possible courses of action. That simplistic view, however, directs one's attention to the final step rather than to the multistep process that is decision making. Further, that view masks the significance of differences that exist with respect to the basic situations requiring decisions and between the various levels of management.

In Chapter 2 the work of Talcott Parsons was cited in discussing the role of the organizational participants—technical, managerial, and institutional. That scheme is also useful in the understanding of decision making within an organization. The types of decisions made by each of those subgroups are typically quite different in nature and impact.

Technical decisions are those related to the basic work elements and rely heavily upon the technical knowledge of the decision maker. For example, a supervisor in a facility for the mentally retarded may have to decide if a resident exhibiting behavior problems should be sent on an outing into the community. In making that decision, the supervisor is likely to rely upon such factors as previous experiences with the resident (how frequent the behavior problems are and how long they last), the ability and experience of the accompanying staff (their ability to handle such situations), and the effect of the resident's behavior upon other residents.

Often, problems in this technical category may be considered routine in that they have been dealt with previously and may occur repeatedly; thus, the decision is the application of a standardized response. Within an organization many "decisions" are of this nature, requiring the application of a standard operating procedure or routine solution. Other examples include rescheduling work when employees are absent, ordering materials and supplies, and reimbursing employees for travel expenses. The establishment of routine responses to recurring situations reduces the time the supervisor must spend dealing with such decisions and standardizes the response to particular situations throughout the organization.

Managerial decisions support the work activity and are primarily directed toward the integration and coordination of the work activities within the organization. As was discussed in the chapter dealing with organization structure, there has been a tendency for increased specialization and differentiation of functions within organizations. That makes more complex the task of ensuring that all parts of the organization are performing properly and achieving the goals established for the organization. Thus, much of the decision making of middle-level managers deals with interface activities, such as the proper sequencing of work so the effort of one unit will not be held up because of the failure of a second unit, upon whom the first unit depends. In short, the managerial decisions within an organization relate to having the "right things, in the right places, at the right times" so that all parts of the organization will function in an integrated fashion.

Institutional decisions relate to the fundamental nature of the organization. They deal with issues such as expansion or contraction of services, capital investments, funding, and the relationship of the organization to the larger environment. These decisions generally have a more profound impact upon the organization and its members and are more long-term than managerial decisions. For example, if a state department of corrections should decide to abandon a single statewide penal institution in favor of several smaller regional institutions, the result will affect every aspect of the organization. New facilities will have to be constructed, funding acquired, staff transferred, and administrative procedures revamped.

Figure 10-1 shows the relationship between managerial levels within the organization and the three types of decision situations. It should be pointed out, however, that within an organization, such a scheme for decision making is not this likely to be clearly identifiable. Neither are decisions evenly distributed among the three levels of managerial leadership. The first-line supervisor may make hundreds of routine decisions during the course of a workday, while the chief executive may take months or even years to reach a single decision. Regardless of the type of decision or the managerial level, the decision maker should engage in an identifiable process for reaching and implementing a decision.

FIGURE 10-1   The Relationship between Levels of Management and Situational Decisions in an Institution for the Mentally Retarded

MANAGEMENT LEVEL	TECHNICAL	MANAGERIAL	INSTITUTIONAL
Supervisory	Should John go on the field trip? Which staff should be assigned to which residents?		
Managerial		Should professionals (R.N., social worker, etc.) be organized according to discipline or function? What administrative link should be established between group homes and institutions?	
Institutional			Should we move away from institutional care toward group home care? Should we contract out laundry and food service?

THE PROCESS OF DECISION MAKING

The decision-making process comprises four distinct phases or steps. An individual decision may require only minutes to complete this process, or many months may pass before a final decision is reached. Time available and the consequences or impact of a decision will largely determine the attention given to each of the four steps in the process. For example, a physician faced with a choking person does not have time to call in consultants or weigh all possible alternatives to treat the patient. On the other hand, a state corrections department may spend a great deal of time on each of the steps in the decision process before implementing a work release program. Similarly, a decision about the expenditure of $100 will not have the same consequences to the organization as the implementation of a new program costing $5 million per year. The manager, therefore, must exercise discretion in the application of the decision-making process to particular problems facing him or her.

Step I: Stating the Problem

An essential, yet often overlooked, starting point for the decision process is the statement of the problem. Many managers are tempted to jump from an indication or a symptom of a problem to a decision, with only a hazy notion of the true problem. The first indication of a situation requiring a decision is frequently but a symptom of a more basic problem requiring attention. For example, excessive absences by employees may be symptomatic of more fundamental issues, such as inadequate compensation or job dissatisfaction. The manager who simply addresses the problem of absenteeism is not likely to come to a decision that will correct the situation.

The initial step in problem formulation is to gather facts. What information related to the problem is needed? What needed information is available? Can additional information be developed? Those sample questions indicate that at this stage of the decision process an absolute analytic approach and a questioning attitude are required. In addition to accumulating pertinent facts or information related to the problem, the decision maker must look at the environmental context and determine the realistic boundaries for an acceptable solution. For example, the administrator of a small day-care center whose total capital expenditure budget is $2,000 and whose clients are having difficulty with transportation should not spend time collecting and analyzing information related to the purchase of a $20,000 van to provide transport.

A useful technique to ensure an accurate and complete statement of any problem is to develop a written problem statement. Reducing one's thoughts to writing forces a more precise and logical statement. Further, since by writing it down the manager is creating a documentation that can be referred to in the future, the manager is more likely to take great care to ensure that proposed solutions are consistent with organizational objectives. Elbing (1978) summarizes the steps involved in producing a clear written formulation of a problem in the following way:

1. The problem should be stated explicitly. Avoid general statements about vague feelings of concern.
2. A working diagnosis should be included. This contains a description of the symptoms observed, the nature of the suspected problems, and what the underlying causes are thought to be.
3. The problem should be stated in specific behavioral terms. Individuals are generally unable to change general conditions, but they can alter specific behavior. Telling subordinates that they lack motivation leaves them to interpret what is meant by "motivation." Telling them that they report to work late too often does not.
4. The problem statement should specify how this problem relates to the organization as a whole and to its various parts. Although the primary responsibility for a particular problem may be found in one department, other departments may also play a role. While the marketing department may bear the primary responsibility for low sales, improper quality control by the production department might be an important contributing factor. (p. 110)

In summary, the manager must make every effort to state the problem in terms that are specific, that include the assumptions being made about the problem, that establish the behavior objectives for acceptable solutions, and that are stated in an organizational context.

Step II: Generating Alternatives

Seldom does any given problem have a single solution. Thus, the second step in the decision-making process is the generation of alternatives. At this stage, the manager is faced with the choice of "going it alone" or involving subordinates, other managers, or both in the process.

The manager electing to act individually will be relying primarily upon past experience. The greater the depth and breadth of the manager's experience, the more likely the resulting decision is to be satisfactory. This perhaps is the most widely used method employed by managers in the development of alternative solutions. Faced with a situation requiring action, the manager searches his or her memory for circumstances similar to those of the present problem. Those past problems and their solutions are compared to the present occurrence, and, where similarities exist, a similar course of action is adopted. Of course, the manager adjusts the decision to fit the present situation.

When the manager lacks the depth or breadth of experience necessary to generate alternatives or have confidence in an unilateral decision, he or she may choose a participative process. Even an experienced manager may want to involve others within the organization in certain decisions. Two of the problems faced by every manager are, When is participation by others in decision making necessary, and How much participation is necessary?

Vroom and Jago (1973) have developed a taxonomy useful in determining the appropriate management decision-making style. Their model relates possible decision styles to the attributes of the problem to be solved. The five types of management decision styles are categorized as follows:

AI. You solve the problem or make the decision yourself, using the information available to you at this time.

AII. You obtain the necessary information from your subordinate(s), then decide on the solution to the problem yourself. You may or may not tell your subordinates what the problem is in getting the information from them. The role played by your subordinates in making the decision is clearly one of providing the necessary information to you, rather than generating or evaluating alternative solutions.

CI. You share the problems with relevant subordinates individually, getting their ideas and suggestions without bringing them together as a group. Then you make the decision, which may or may not reflect your subordinates' influence.

CII. You share the problem with your subordinates as a group, obtaining their ideas and suggestions. Then you make the decision, which may or may not reflect your subordinates' influence.

GII. You share a problem with your subordinates as a group. Together you generate and evaluate alternatives and attempt to reach agreement (consensus) on a solution. Your role is much like that of chairman. You do not try to influence the group to adopt "your" solution, and you are willing to accept and implement any solution that has the support of the entire group.

In addition to the five decision styles, there are seven diagnosis decision rules. The application of these rules will help determine which decision-making style is appropriate for a particular situation. The diagnosis decision rules are:

1. *The Leader Information Rule*
   Quality of the decision is important.
   Leader does not possess enough information or expertise to solve the problem alone.
   Eliminate AI.

2. *Goal Congruence Rule*
   Quality of the decision is important.
   Subordinates are not likely to pursue organizational goals in the efforts to solve the problem.
   Eliminate GII.

3. *Unstructured Problem Rule*
   Quality of the decision is important.
   Leader does not possess the necessary information or expertise to solve the problem alone.
   Problem is unstructured.
   Thus, need to provide for interaction among subordinates who are knowledgeable about the problem.
   Eliminate AI, AII, and CI.

4. *The Acceptance Rule*
   Acceptance by subordinates is critical.
   Not certain an autocratic decision will be accepted.
   Eliminate AI and AII.

5. *The Conflict Rule*
   Acceptance by subordinates is critical.
   Not certain an autocratic decision will be accepted.

Disagreement among subordinates is likely.
Thus, need to provide those in disagreement with full knowledge of the problem.
Eliminate AI, AII, and CI.

6. *The Fairness Rule*
    Quality of the decision is unimportant.
    Acceptance is critical.
    Autocratic decision not certain to be accepted.
    Thus, need to generate acceptance by allowing subordinates to interact and negotiate a fair method for resolving differences with full responsibility for determining what is fair.
    Eliminate AI, AII, CI, and CII.

7. *The Acceptance Priority Rule*
    Acceptance is critical.
    Autocratic decision not certain to be accepted.
    Subordinates are motivated to pursue organizational goals.
    Thus, need to provide for equal partnership in decision making, which will lead to greater acceptance without risking quality.
    Eliminate AI, AII, CI, and CII.

The seven decision rules are used to determine what procedures the leader should not use in a given situation. Rules 1–3 protect decision quality and rules 4–7 protect decision acceptance. In Figure 10-2 the seven decision rules are illustrated by the use of a decision tree. You move from left to right along the tree by asking the following questions:

1. Does the problem possess a quality requirement?
2. Do I have sufficient information to make a high-quality decision?
3. Is the problem structured?
4. Is acceptance of the decision by subordinates important for effective implementation?
5. If I were to make the decision by myself, am I reasonably certain that it would be accepted by my subordinates?
6. Do subordinates share the organizational goals to be attained in solving the problem?
7. Is conflict among subordinates likely in preferred solutions?

A brief example may clarify the use of the flowchart. You are the manager of an office with one clerical person and six professionals. A problem has developed with the answering of the telephone when the secretary is at lunch and on break. Your problem is how to obtain coverage during those periods. To question 1 (quality of decision) you answer "NO," since each of the professionals is competent to handle this duty. Answering no to question 1, you ask the next relevant question, 4 (acceptance), to which you answer "YES" since the professionals are likely to resist this duty. The next step, then, is question 5 (if you decide, will they accept), to which you also answer "NO," which will lead you to the use of decision style GII: share problem with group and implement the group decision.

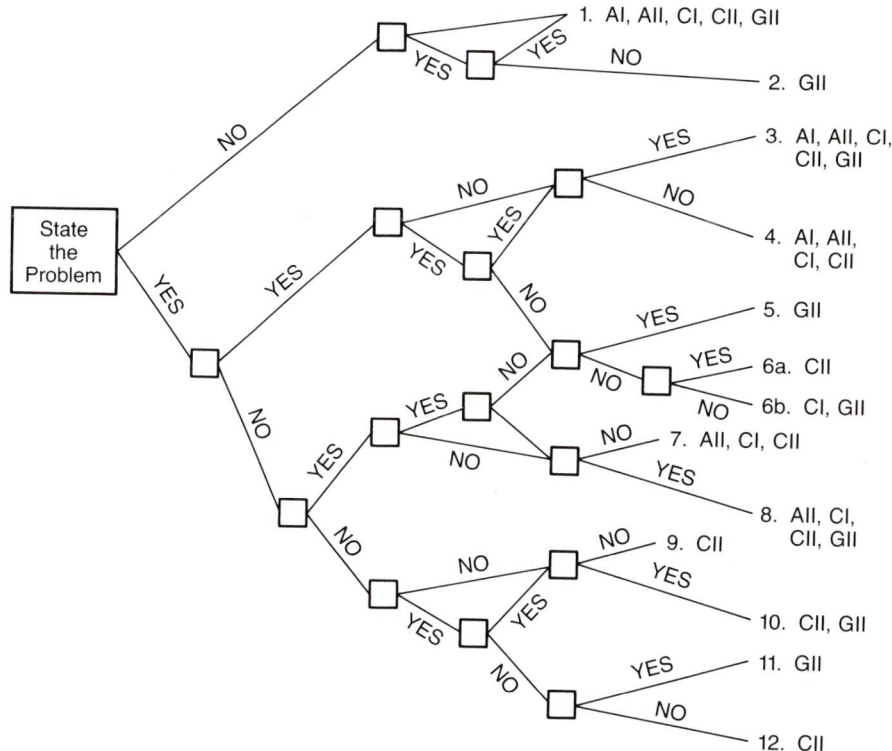

FIGURE 10-2 Decision Process. Adapted from V. H. Vroom & A. G. Jago, "Decision Making as a Social Process: Normative and Descriptive Models of Leader Behavior, *Decision Sciences,* October 1974, pp. 745–749. Published by the Decision Sciences Institute (formerly the American Institute for Decision Sciences).

Step III: Analyzing Alternative Solutions

The analysis of alternatives, the third step in the decision-making process, requires a consideration of each alternative with respect to its efficiency and effectiveness. The manager must rigorously examine each alternative, asking such questions as: Will this alternative prevent this situation from occurring again in the future? Is this alternative consistent with organizational goals? Are the outcomes expected from this alternative consistent with the objectives established in the statement of the problem? Is this alternative within the guidelines established for a satisfactory solution? What are the risks associated with this alternative? In responding to such questions, the manager must be careful to maintain an open and objective viewpoint with respect to each alternative under analysis. There is a great temptation to become "locked in" to a particular alternative early in the process. That may cause the manager to overestimate the value of one alternative, while underestimating the value of other possible solutions.

For each alternative that meets the criteria for an acceptable solution, a list of advantages and disadvantages should be developed. This element in the process is crucial because through the identification of relative advantages and disadvantages the manager will discover potential problems that may affect the implementation of the alternative selected. In short, it provides a convenient starting point for planning the implementation of the decision.

Step IV: Implementing the Decision

Some managers believe that once they have made a decision the task is complete. Nothing is further from the truth, for every decision must be accompanied by a well-thought-out plan for implementation and execution. The effective manager will develop an action plan for the successful implementation of each decision. The action plan should, in as much detail as possible, specify the activities that must be carried out, when each of those activities must be accomplished, who within the organization will be responsible for each activity, and what standard of performance is expected for each activity. It should also establish a feedback mechanism to inform the decision maker of the progress in implementing the decision. Next, the manager must communicate the details of the decision as specifically as is necessary to ensure the understanding and cooperation of subordinates. Finally, the manager must continue to monitor the activities assigned or delegated to be certain that the desired results are being obtained. Since delegation is such a key element in this sequence, it will be explained further.

DELEGATION OF AUTHORITY

It should be apparent that managers in the higher levels of the organization cannot make all the decisions; they must rely upon others throughout the organization. A manager is analogous to an orchestra conductor. The conductor does not play all of the instruments but relies upon the individuals in the orchestra to come together to produce a harmonious quality in the piece being played. This is equivalent to collective management. The manager works through others to accomplish the ultimate response for which the organization exists.

Koontz and O'Donnell (1976) have identified the following principles of delegation, which should be followed for delegation to be effective:

1. *Principle of delegation by results expected.* Authority delegated to an individual manager should be adequate to assure the ability to accomplish results expected.

2. *Principle of functional definition.* The more a position or a department has clear definitions of results expected, activities to be undertaken, organization authority delegated, and authority and informational relationships with other positions understood, the more adequately the individuals responsible can contribute toward accomplishing organizational objectives.

3. *Scalar principle.* The more clear the line of authority from the top manager in an organization to every subordinate position, the more effective the responsible decision making and the organization communication.

4. *Authority-level principle.* Maintenance of intended delegation requires that decisions within the authority competence of individuals be made by them and not be referred upward in the organization structure.
5. *Principle of unity of command.* The more nearly complete the reporting relationship of an individual to a single superior, the less the problem of conflict in instructions and the greater the feeling of personal responsibility for results.
6. *Principle of absoluteness of responsibility.* The responsibility of subordinates to their superiors for performance is absolute once they have accepted an assignment and the right to carry it out, and superiors cannot escape responsibility for the organizational activities of their subordinates.
7. *Principle of parity of authority and responsibility.* The responsibility for actions cannot be greater than that implied by authority delegated, nor should it be. (pp. 378–381)

Indeed, there is a risk in delegation. The risk is that subordinates will make mistakes. "The better a man is, the more mistakes he will make—for the more new things he will try" (Drucker, 1974, p. 457). If managers are not willing to delegate, then individuals within the organization will be retarded in their growth and development. Further, the manager's willingness to let others make decisions will be influenced by his or her own security. The more secure a manager is with himself or herself, the more comfortable he or she is with delegation. Each manager must realize that the greatest resource available to him or her is the people within the organization. Managers in human service organizations should show the same consideration for their employees that they do for the clients or patients the organization serves. To do less is to compromise on the potential that rests within the organization.

An additional component of delegation is trust. Delegation implies trust between superior and subordinates. Trust is developed through the experiences that the manager has with delegation. As mentioned earlier, subordinates will make mistakes, but learning from mistakes can make them effective and productive contributors to the organization's ultimate purpose. A manager's reluctance to delegate, for whatever reason, inevitably leads to frustration among the members of the work unit and can also lead to organizational stagnation.

In summary, decision making is a primary responsibility of every manager. In carrying out that responsibility, the manager must follow a logical and sequential process to ensure that his or her decisions are both efficient and effective in accomplishing the goals of the organization.

MANAGING ORGANIZATIONAL CONFLICT

The decision process in organizations is a potential source of conflict between individuals within the organization, between an individual and the work unit, between work units, or between the organization and its environment. Decisions affect what is done within the organization, who performs which activities, and when those activities are performed. Each represents a potential conflict, since individuals or units may view the results of the decision as detrimental to their preferred position. Likert defines conflict as "the active striving for one's own preferred outcome which, if attained, precludes the attainment by others of their own preferred outcome, thereby producing hostility" (Likert & Likert, 1976, p. 7). From this definition it is obvious that the potential for conflict exists within every organization and that organizational life contains a variety of sources that may lead to conflict.

When properly managed, conflict within an organization may provide some important benefits to the organization. It provides the manager with information about the functioning of the organization. Similarly, managed conflict may act as a stimulant and may result in innovation. Some level of conflict within the organization may actually increase the ability of the organization to meet its goals. Conflict becomes dysfunctional when it leads to destructive competition, which expends organizational energies and resources in a fashion not directed toward desired organizational outcomes.

INDIVIDUAL VERSUS JOB CONFLICT

Individuals within human service organizations may experience conflict either from their relationship to the job itself (role stress) or from their relationship with other people within the organization. Person-job conflict, or role stress, may arise from the assignment of an individual to a job that is beyond his or her abilities. For example, an experienced and effective caseworker who is promoted to casework supervisor may be able to perform only a limited number of the functions required of the new role, thus producing conflict. At the opposite extreme, the assignment of an individual to a job that utilizes a minimal amount of his or her overall skills may result in role stress. For example, when a social worker with a graduate degree is assigned a highly programmed clerical job, the result will very likely be low morale and low job satisfaction.

Inconsistent and contradictory information is also a source of job-related conflict for individuals within organizations. The organizational demand on a particular position may call for simultaneous work behaviors, which the individual may consider impossible to carry out. For example, a nurse may be instructed to provide superior patient care and, at the same time, be instructed to spend more time on the record-keeping function. To the nurse, those demands seem conflicting. A related source of conflict is conflicting or inconsistent demands from different people within the organization. Multiple lines of authority within the organization may have differing expectations about the performance of a particular job, thus placing the job holder in a conflict. For example, the budget officer may expect a reduction in expenditures, and the program director may expect expenditure of all budgeted funds. Since both of those individuals may have something to say about performance evaluation, the employee experiences substantial role conflict.

There are several ways that individuals may respond to conflict between themselves and their job demands. The most obvious response is withdrawal, that is, resignation from the job, or even from the organization, which is probably undesirable for the organization. Rather than withdraw completely, the individual may withdraw selectively (increased absenteeism). When faced with conflicting demands from two or more persons in superior positions, the individual may follow the direction of the one perceived to be the more powerful or the one with the greater position authority. Another possible response for an individual experiencing job conflict is to change his or her expectations. The nurse who seeks superior patient care, when blocked by administrative routine, may decide that patient care is not so important after all and may concentrate on administrative duties. Yet another response is to establish rules of procedure, that is, deal with conflicting demands on an alternating basis. The final, and perhaps the healthiest, response is to attempt to reconcile conflicting demands. That may take the form of confronting the source (superiors or peers) of the conflicting demands to resolve the conflict or of negotiating a new or modified set of role expectations.

STRATEGIES
FOR MANAGING ORGANIZATIONAL CONFLICT

Not all conflict in organizations is an individual-job conflict. Even when individuals experience none of the stress discussed in the previous section, there may still be organizational conflict.

Litterer (1966) identifies four areas of potential conflict that, unless properly managed, may lead to destructive competition. First, destructive conflict may develop when two or more units within the organization have incompatible goals. For example, each time the fraud and abuse section of the welfare department discovers a case of "welfare fraud" (the goal of that unit), the discovery reflects negatively upon the unit that originally extended the benefits. Second, even where goals are compatible, conflict may occur over the appropriate methods for reaching the goals. Within a child welfare unit, for example, there may be agreement about the ultimate goals but significant disagreement about whether the appropriate approach is foster care or institutional care. A third general source of conflict within organizations is the disruption of existing status patterns. For example, the increased status of the hospital administrator may be perceived by the medical staff as having decreased their position in the hospital hierarchy and thus may lead to a conflict. Finally, conflict may develop as a result of the individual's or unit's viewpoint about the organization. The intake clerk, who must face clients in need on a day-to-day basis, is likely to hold a very different view of the organization from that of the director of the agency, who must respond to a wide variety of organizational pressures.

Strategies for managing those types of conflict may be either structural or process oriented. These two types of strategies differ in the degree to which they promote or reduce the interaction of the parties or units involved in the conflict. The structural approach minimizes direct contact, while the process approach increases direct contact and depends upon the parties involved to resolve the conflict.

The structural approaches to conflict management rely upon the basic principles of organizational design and coordination (discussed in detail in Chapter 2). Each relies upon some modification of the work-flow system to eliminate a conflict-producing situation. Problems of the individual-job relationship may be addressed through modification of job descriptions or the establishment of standard operating procedures. Thus, the individual faced with conflicting instructions may rely upon basic documentation to resolve the conflict ("That task is not in my job description"). Conflict between individuals within a unit may be resolved by appeal to higher authority. The higher authority hears the issues in conflict and renders a judgment, which must be "accepted" as the solution by the conflicting parties.

Some structural approaches act to separate the conflicting parties by creating a buffer zone between them. For example, a hospital pharmacy may not be able to satisfy the medication needs of each ward on time, thereby creating conflict. One buffering approach would be to establish medication inventories on each ward, which would reduce dependence on the pharmacy and thus reduce the conflict. A similar buffering strategy is to create duplicate resources. For example, an organization may maintain a centralized copying service, which causes delays and produces conflict between the copy service and other departments. Allowing each department to have its own small copying machine will reduce dependence and narrow the area of conflict. Both of those strategies, while commonly used, are expensive and may produce undesirable suboptimization for the organization. A final approach to the buffer strategy is the use of a boundary-spanning or liaison position (discussed in more detail in Chapter 6). The role of this position is to provide lateral communications and coordination between conflicting parties. For example, the role of the press representative within an agency is to act as a buffer between operating units and the media.

Structural approaches to conflict management also include consolidation strategies. In its simplest form, such an approach calls for the merger of conflicting departments into a single, unified unit. For example, conflict may arise between an intake unit and an eligibility unit because of the work-flow dependency between the two units. Consolidation into a single intake-eligibility department provides for more effective coordination and utilization of resources. Further, by placing the control of resources in a single unit, the potential for conflict is reduced.

The process strategies, as we noted earlier, attempt to resolve conflict by increasing the interaction between the units or individuals in conflict. Consultation is an often-used management tactic for resolving conflict within the organization. Here, the manager takes a passive role, providing information and technical assistance, relying upon increased understanding of the problem area to bring the parties to a solution. Mediation, a related tactic, again relies upon the skills of the manager to prompt conflict resolution. As a mediator, the manager is more active, suggesting common goals, suggesting alternatives, and bringing the conflicting parties together for face-to-face discussions. The manager, acting in the mediator role, must exercise care *not* to dictate a solution, but must let the conflicting parties work out their own solution. Direct negotiation (discussed in detail in Chapter 12) provides for conflict resolution directly between the parties.

In recent years confrontation has become increasingly popular as a mechanism for resolving conflict. Constructive confrontation, according to Schultz and Johnson (1971), includes "(1) clarifying the issues with parties; (2) expressing feelings descriptively; (3) expressing facts and fantasies; and (4) resolution and agreement" (p. 48). Within organizations the use of either the team approach or the Matrix organization structure facilitates constructive confrontation as a strategy for resolving organizational conflict by establishing a common work structure, joint decision processes, and common goals for organizational members.

In summary, the manager must ensure that conflict within the organization is managed in a way that stimulates goal achievement instead of destructive competition. The techniques we have outlined should be practiced at every opportunity to perfect this critical disturbance handler role.

CONCLUSION

This chapter has dealt with the role of the manager as a disturbance handler in a human service organization. The ability to make high-quality decisions and the ability to constructively manage conflict are essential skills for the successful manager.

REFERENCES

ELBING, A. (1978). *Behavioral decisions in organization.* Glenview, Ill.: Scott, Foresman.

DRUCKER, P. F. (1974). *Management: Tasks, responsibilities, practices.* New York: Harper & Row.

KOONTZ, H., & O'CONNELL, C. (1976). *Management: A systems and contingency analysis of managerial functions* (6th ed.). New York: McGraw-Hill.

LIKERT, R., & LIKERT, J. (1976). *New ways of managing conflict.* New York: McGraw-Hill.

LITTERER, J. A. (1966). Conflict in organization: A re-examination. *Academy of Management Journal, 9,* 178–186.

MINTZBERG, H. (1973). *The nature of managerial work.* New York: Harper & Row.

SCHULTZ, R., & JOHNSON, A. C. (1971, Summer). Conflict in hospitals. *Hospital Administration,* pp. 36–50.

VROOM, V. H., & JAGO, A. G. (1974, October). Decision making as a social process: Normative and descriptive models of leader behavior. *Decision Sciences,* pp. 745–749.

QUESTIONS FOR DISCUSSION

1. "Management may be defined as decision making." Discuss.
2. The instructor has asked you to make a decision for the class on whether to assign a term paper or give a comprehensive final examination. Using the Vroom-Jago model, describe how you would make this decision.
3. As an operating manager, would you prefer to work for a supervisor who used individual decision making or for one who used group decision making? Why?

4. Each time you begin studying for an examination, you are making a decision about how to use your time. Analyze how you approach this decision.

5. Discuss the functions of organizational conflict within a human service organization.

6. From the discussion of the management of conflict, what considerations should the manager give this phenomenon when making staffing decisions?

7. Discuss the usefulness of the various conflict management strategies to a manager in a human service organization.

SUGGESTED PROJECTS

1. Interview an administrator about the types of conflict experienced by his or her organization. During the interview, try to identify the source of conflict within the organization.

2. Write a report to the administrator suggesting specific measures you would take to better manage conflict within the organization. Justify each measure you suggest.

The Role of the Resource Allocator

chapter 11

In the resource allocator role, the manager determines the shape and direction of the organization. The vast majority of decisions made by the manager result in a resource allocation of one kind or another. Through as simple an act as deciding not to talk to a subordinate about a project, the manager may convey to the subordinate that time and effort should not be directed toward the project. This chapter will concentrate on two major resource areas: finances and time. By the way the manager schedules personal time, he or she is telling others what is considered important. The way the manager addresses the question of budgeting and financial management also establishes for others within the organization which activities, projects, and programs are important.

FINANCIAL MANAGEMENT

The allocation of financial resources presents the manager with a tremendous challenge. The decisions made in this area provide the shape and substance for the programs of the agency. Both the quantity and the quality of an agency's service delivery are affected by this process. That is particularly true during periods of declining resources, for during those periods the manager will be making decisions that will change the course of the operations of his or her area of responsibility. Thus, decisions must be made with care and with full knowledge of their long-run effects.

Because this process is tedious, time-consuming, and difficult, some managers try to avoid it by applying simplified decision rules. For example, faced with either an increase or a decrease in funds, some managers simply spread the increase or decrease evenly across existing programs. This process, especially when dealing with decreases, leads to waste and increasing mediocrity.

The effective manager accepts the challenge of resource allocation and works to carry out the goals of the agency through effective resource allocation. This requires the establishment of priorities, careful analysis of programs, and continuous monitoring of resources. The discussion in this section deals with the basic elements involved in allocating scarce resources among a variety of worthwhile projects and programs and presents tools and techniques useful in the management of financial resources.

BUDGETING

Budgeting in its simplest form is the projection of revenues and the projection of expenditures. This "two cigar box method," however, fails to recognize the proactive role of the manager in resource allocation. Without specific information about the nature of expenditures within categories and programs, the manager is unable to evaluate the effectiveness of his or her area of responsibility. Within human service organizations the budgeting function involves a budget development process that results in one of several types of budget documents. The discussion that follows will introduce the reader to a logical process for the development of a budget and provide a basic introduction to the line-item, program, and performance budgets, the planning-programming-budgeting system, and Zero-base budgeting.

The Budget Process

The budget of any organization provides a financial plan that details how the organization intends to disburse the revenue it expects to receive. The budget plan differs from the types of plans discussed previously in that it deals specifically with money. That is, the budget specifies "how much" and "for what" money is to be spent for a specific period of time. The development of such a document may be broken down into several distinct but related steps.

A critical first step that is too often overlooked in the development of the financial plan is the establishment of clear goals and objectives. Such statements detail the purpose for which the agency makes expenditures, thus directing attention to the results expected rather than to the activity expected. Since the budget process should be a tool for greater organizational effectiveness, the more attention given to the development of sound goals and the specific objectives leading to goal attainment, the more useful the budget. The central questions to be asked are, What needs are we going to address? (goals) and How are we going to address those needs? (objectives).

The statement of goals and objectives provides the basis for the development of an action plan, the second step in the budgeting process. This involves the development of alternative methods for meeting the objectives and the enumeration of resources essential to success. For example, an agency serving the mentally retarded may have as one of its goals "the improvement of public understanding of mental retardation." An objective supporting this goal may be "the production and airing of one TV commercial per month to explain the physical characteristics of retardation." The action plan would then detail alternatives (contract with an advertising agency, use agency public information staff, and so on) and cite the resources required for each alternative (personnel, equipment, supplies, and so on).

The third element in the process is the estimation of costs associated with each alternative. Each alternative is composed of a set of activities, each representing a necessary expenditure to the agency, which must be projected. Projection of those costs (personnel, travel, supplies, and so on) provides the documentation necessary to evaluate the various alternatives and to justify budget requests to funding sources.

The fourth step in budget development is to estimate expected revenues. This requires not only a knowledge of potential funding sources but also an ability to forecast their priorities and abilities. The interested manager will need to have, at minimum, knowledge of the allocation methods used by potential funding sources, their projections of expected revenues, existing commitments, their goals, and the level of demand being made for funds.

Projected expenditures must next be compared to and reconciled with expected revenues. The key question at this stage is, What affordable alternative(s) will best meet the goals and objectives? Since it is very likely that expected expenditures will exceed projected revenues, the manager will have to decide upon priorities among the list of goals and objectives. The incorporation of results-oriented statements at the initial stage of the budgeting process should ease this otherwise painful process. Which goals and objectives contribute most to the accomplishment of the mission of the agency? What alternatives are the most efficient and effective?

The final step in the budget development process is to put the decisions made into the proper format. Whatever the format, the manager should be certain to include in the budget all resources needed to carry out the programs requested. This is essential, since the budget is not only a financial plan but also a mechanism for control through the comparison of actual and projected expenditures. While each organization will have its own specifications for budget format, one system or a combination of the line-item, program, performance, program-planning, or zero-base budgeting systems is most commonly used in human service organizations.

Line-Item Budgets

The line-item budget categorizes the various costs by the object of the expenditure. Table 11-1 illustrates the simplest form of the line-item budget. The line-item budget facilitates accounting for both revenues and expenditures in a systematic fashion. This budget type maximizes the control of expenditures, since it provides a continuous record of how the

**TABLE 11-1. Get Well Hospital
Administrative Budget—October 1, 19— to September 30, 19—**

Personnel:		
Professional	$84,512	
Clerical	33,667	
Support	19,281	$137,460
Employee benefits (30% of salaries and wages)	$41,238	41,238
Total personnel		$178,698
Operating funds:		
Staff travel	$18,981	
Liability insurance	5,378	
Equipment (office)	2,500	
Communications (postage, telephone, etc.)	3,100	
Office supplies	2,900	32,859
Total administrative costs		$211,557

money is being spent. It allows the manager to determine, at any time during the period, whether or not monies are being spent within the intended categories. Further, this method quickly identifies problems with the level of expenditures. For example, if the manager responsible for administering the budget in Table 11-1 discovers on January 1 that $18,000 in travel funds have already been expended, he or she may have to reevaluate travel policies for the remainder of the year. This example also points out one of the major disadvantages of the line-item budget: It reduces the flexibility of the manager to administer financial resources. Thus, an agency or department faced with favorable changes during the budget period does not have authority to make the necessary adjustments called for by the situation.

Program Budgets

The program budget is organized on the basis of function. The budget format is directed toward the goals of the organization. Table 11-2 presents a brief example of the program budget.

**TABLE 11-2. Any-Town Police Department
Operating Budget—October 1, 19— to
September 30, 19—**

PROGRAM	EXPENDITURES
Administration	$ 79,000
Traffic	34,000
Homicide	21,000
Vice	16,000
Burglary	65,000
Total	$215,000

The program budget clearly identifies the goals of the organization and provides information about the priorities placed upon each program as reflected by the funds committed. Thus, the police department of Table 11-2 clearly attaches more financial importance to the role of the burglary program than to traffic, homicide, or vice. This type of budgeting overcomes the disadvantage of the line-item budget, noted previously, by providing the manager the flexibility to adjust funds from one category to another within the program. While this type of budget increases the line manager's flexibility, it has the disadvantage, from an organizational viewpoint, of reducing controls over purchases made by those people.

Performance Budget

The primary difficulty with both the line-item budget and the program budget is that they do not indicate *why* a specific expenditure was made. The performance budget is developed to provide a basis for measuring performance as well as determining costs. Starling (1982) highlights the distinction with this illustration:

> As the end result of line-item budgeting, government should be able to tell the public that an agency spent, say $19,872,403.91, with so much going to salaries and wages and fringe benefits, so much spent on various materials and supplies, and so much paid out under each of numerous contracts. As a result of performance budgeting, on the other hand, government should be able to tell the public how much public service was delivered for this $19,872,403.91. (pp. 242–253)

Table 11-3 provides a sample performance budget that also combines the line-item and program concepts.

As can be seen from the sample budget, both program funding level and categories of expense are presented, as well as the measures of performance. Thus, the manager can determine the total to be expended within the program, the amount of time to be expended on specific items (personnel, travel, and so on), and the number of services to be purchased.

The major problem encountered in performance budgeting is the determination of the appropriate measures of output and level of service. The measures used in the sample budget in Table 11-3 relate to the efficiency of the program and are useful in comparing the costs of different alternatives for delivering the training specified. A real question, however, is how much will be learned and what will be the impact on the agency, or how effective will the program be in helping meet the goals of the organization?

Planning, Programming, Budgeting System (PPBS) and Zero-base Budgets

PPBS and Zero-base are systems of budgeting that speak directly to the question of effectiveness. Lohman (1980) describes PPBS as

TABLE 11-3.   Sample Performance Budget
October 1, 19— to September 30, 19—

Staff Development and Training	
Personnel:	
Professional (6 full-time)	$120,000
Clerical (3 full-time)	27,000
Consultants (75 days)	18,750
Employee benefits (30% full-time salaries and wages)	44,100
Total personnel	$209,850
Operating Funds:	
Staff travel (75 trips @ $250/trip)	$ 18,750
Instructional supplies ($15/trainee)	33,750
Office supplies	7,500
Equipment (maintenance and acquisition)	2,250
Total Operating Funds	$ 62,250
Total	$272,100
Performance Measures	
Training events	150
Number of trainees (15 per session)	2,250
Cost per training event	$1,814
Cost per trainee per year	$120.93

perhaps the penultimate rational model of budget-making—beginning with the definition of the objectives of all operating programs, and proceeding through the analysis of alternative strategies, the adoption of preferred strategies, and the creation of management information systems for monitoring the performance of implemented strategies. (p. 144)

The systems approach forces those making budgets and those making program plans to coordinate their activities.

PPBS begins with a statement of goals and objectives, followed by an analysis of current programs together with possible alternatives, with the objective of developing improvements in existing programs. Once desirable programs are developed, the next step is to delineate the characteristics of those programs (staff, client population, supplies, equipment, and so on). United Way of America provides a convenient set of criteria for the analysis of possible program alternatives:

1. Feasibility: Is the alternative economically, socially, and/or politically feasible at this time?
2. Timing: Is this the "right time" for this type of program?
3. Legality: Are there legal barriers?
4. Benefits: What benefits would the potential recipients of the services receive?
5. Effectiveness and Efficiency: How effective is the alternative in achieving the desired impact and how efficient is the use of resources?
6. Appropriate Manpower Availability: Can current agency staff handle the alternatives, will they need special training, and are the necessary types of personnel in the agency not currently available?

7. Capital and Operating Costs: How does the alternative program(s) compare in terms of initial and continuing financial requirements?
8. Other Funding Possibilities: Is the alternative likely to produce partial funding from other sources (public and/or private)? (Ehlers, 1976, p. 323)

Following the analysis of alternatives, budget requests are developed for review. This review involves a comparison of specific program funding requests with goals to determine the extent of funding to be granted. As a final step, the budget request must be reconciled with the level of funding, which may require modification in the original program plan.

Zero-base budgeting (ZBB), in essence, is a variation of PPBS. "The essence of the zero-based approach is a combination of the linkage of planning and budget decisions found in PPB (this time, in what are called 'decision packages') with an essentially incremental decision model that serially and marginally makes decisions on decision packages" (Lohman, 1980, p. 145). The key question in the system is, How does productivity change? Many managers make the implicit assumption that productivity will increase or decrease in direct proportion to a change in funding levels. For example, one may assume that if the number of personnel in a program is doubled, the amount of service provided will also double. That may or may not be the case. The ZBB procedure calls for the budget maker to return to a base of zero and to develop and reanalyze alternatives with a view to increasing efficiency with the next budget. By forcing a reexamination of each facet of agency programs and through the development of decision units subject to higher-level review, ZBB provides a more realistic picture of the relationship between inputs and outputs in the budgeting process.

FINANCIAL MANAGEMENT

Whatever the budgeting process used by an agency, the manager must be equipped to live within the funds allocated. Management of the funds allocated requires continuous monitoring throughout the budget period to ensure that the purposes for which funds were allocated are being met.

In budget-based organizations, a basic assumption of the process is that expenditures made will match funds allocated at the end of the budget period. Indeed, failure on the part of agencies, in the form of either surpluses or deficits, to meet that test of equality may have adverse consequences. Thus, the manager should be able to project, as early as possible, the potential for surpluses or deficits. A useful tool for this type of projection is break-even analysis.

The manger seeking to use break-even analysis will need to first identify fixed and variable costs in the agency. A fixed cost is one that does not change with the level of service, such as rent on the building. A variable cost is a cost that is dependent upon the level of service, such as the direct staff time per unit of service or materials used per unit of service delivered. Total cost is equal to fixed costs plus variable costs. Figure 11-1 shows the

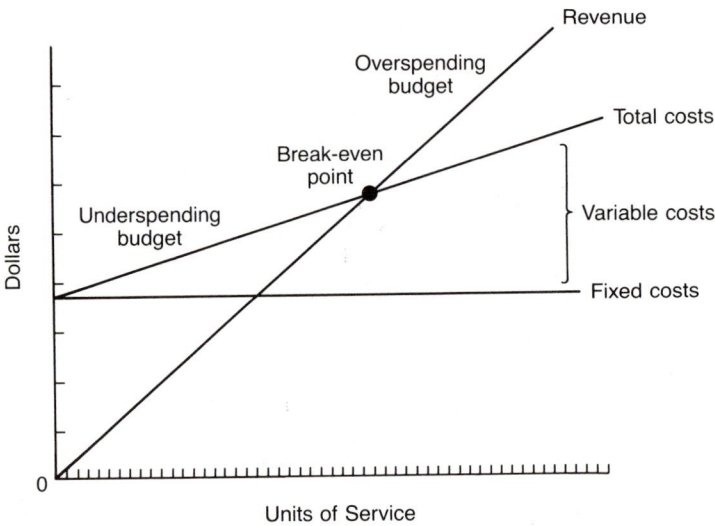

FIGURE 11-1   Break-Even Chart.

relationship between costs, revenue, and actual service delivery.

Using this type of diagram, the manager will be able to annualize the current level of service delivery and project the potential for surplus or deficit. For example, if a manager who calculates that 10,000 units of service will allow the agency to break even with the funds allocated finds that current service is being provided at an annual rate of 11,000 units, he or she may make adjustments to avoid the imbalance.

To ascertain the types of changes possible, the manager will have to rely on other budget-based data. One such source is an analysis of budget variances. Table 11-4 provides a sample format of this type of analysis.

From this type of experience table, the manager can see how each category of expenditure is comparing to the budgeted amount and to last year, as well as those categories that are over and under budget projections. Such comparison will allow the manager to concentrate upon specific budget items for control or for reallocation. For example, the figures in the table reveal a $10,575 surplus during the first six months of the fiscal year. An analysis of the variances indicates that the bulk of this surplus is the result of a vacant staff position and an additional secretary. Since the secretary is to be retained and the vacant position is to be filled next month, the net surplus at the end of the year is projected at $6,700. With this information, the manager is able to decide upon the reallocation of these funds well in advance of the "year-end crunch," the typical time for "adjusting the budget" in human service organizations.

For the manager with multiple program responsibilities, this simple variance analysis may not provide sufficient information to (1) monitor the expenditures of the various programs, (2) make interprogram com-

TABLE 11-4. Statement of Variances
For the Month of March and the 6 Months Ending March 31, 19—

MONTH				BUDGET CATEGORY	YEAR TO DATE (6 MONTHS)			
THIS YEAR'S ACTUAL	THIS YEAR'S BUDGET	LAST YEAR	THIS YEAR'S VARIANCE		THIS YEAR'S ACTUAL	THIS YEAR'S BUDGET	LAST YEAR	THIS YEAR'S VARIANCE
12,000	13,000	11,900	1,000	Professional staff	67,000	78,000	71,400	11,000
3,000	2,500	2,700	(500)	Clerical staff	16,700	15,000	16,200	(1,700)
4,500	4,100	4,000	(400)	Employee benefits	23,800	24,600	24,000	800
600	800	700	200	Maintenance	4,200	4,800	4,200	600
200	125	200	75	Supplies	875	750	750	(125)

parisons, or (3) understand the trend of expenditures among several programs. A technique useful for doing those three things is ratio analysis. Ratio analysis simply establishes the proportional relationship between two variables. For example, administrative cost divided by total service dollars yields the proportion of administrative cost to total service costs, allowing the manager to identify critical program dimensions. Key questions addressed by ratio analysis are, How are the relationships between variables changing over time? How do these relationships compare between programs? Are there changes in these relationships that need immediate attention?

The primary task for the manager who wishes to use ratio analysis is to develop meaningful relationships. Since any two variables will yield a ratio, the manager must decide upon the key decision points within the program or agency. For example, the cost of telephone service to numbers of clients served is a ratio; however, since the cost of telephone service is probably not sensitive to the number of clients, that relationship is not

FIGURE 11-2   Diagram of Operating Budget Process. From R. L. Benke, Jr., "Utilizing Operating Budgets for Maximum Effectiveness," *Managerial Planning,* September–October 1976, p. 34.

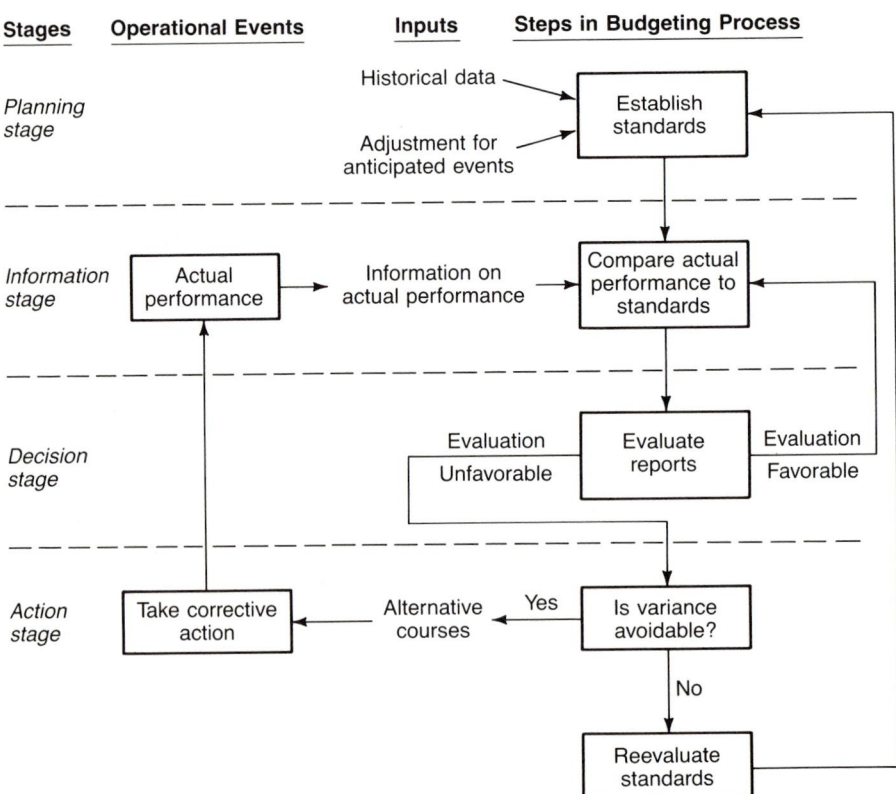

likely to be meaningful for the manager. On the other hand, the cost of clerical time to numbers of clients served is likely to be a ratio of importance to the budget manager. A second factor involved in the use of ratio analysis is the establishment of baseline data or standards. A ratio of $1 administrative cost to $15 service delivery has no meaning unless placed into context. A good starting point in the development of standards is an examination of historical financial data to determine the past relationships and the pattern of change.

In summary, the purpose of budgeting and financial management is the control of expenditures to ensure the accomplishment of agency goals and objectives. To accomplish that purpose, every manager must understand and use the process as an integrated system. Figure 11-2 provides a summary and an operating plan for this purpose. For the manager who follows these steps, the task of financial planning and control will be greatly simplified.

TIME MANAGEMENT

The second category of resources the manager must allocate is time—both personal and staff. The adage "time is money" is all too often forgotten by operating managers. The proper management of time requires planning and rational allocation. Conscious decisions must be made as to how both your time and that of your staff will be utilized. The following discussion is intended to provide a framework for those decisions.

Allocating Time

The effective management of time requires, first of all, an understanding of how we are presently using our time. Second, the effective manager develops a plan for the use of available time. Finally, the manager must make decisions about use of time that are consistent with the plan.

The first step in the process requires an analysis of the present use of time. A convenient starting point for that analysis is the development of a time log. A time log is simply a running record of how time is spent over a period of time. Table 11-5 is an example of a format for a time log.

An examination of the activities in Table 11-5 reveals two major time components: organization-required and discretionary. The time required by the organization may be further divided into boss-required (attendance at the weekly staff meeting, which may not be omitted without the threat of penalty) and routine-required (discussion of the budget request, which must be given attention if the goals of the organization are to be met). Discretionary time includes both personal time and time spent on those projects the manager desires to devote himself or herself to. The object of good time management is to increase this discretionary time component so as to better deal with the organization time component and to have more time available for manager-initiated projects.

With the time log in hand, the manager is ready to analyze activities and develop a plan for the more effective use of time. The first step in this

TABLE 11-5. Time Log
Date: Tuesday, April 11, 19—

TIME SPENT		TIME USE	WITH WHOM	PURPOSE
START	END			
9:00 A.M.	9:20 A.M.	Discussion	Jane and Bill	Budget request
9:20 A.M.	9:26 A.M.	Telephone	Dan	Approve vacation time
9:26 A.M.	10:05 A.M.	Coffee break	——	——
10:05 A.M.	11:38 A.M.	Weekly staff meeting	Boss	Discuss upcoming public hearings
11:38 A.M.	12:00 noon	Telephone (3 calls)	Sam, Jane, Doug	Sam: personal
				Jane: update on budget
				Doug: progress report by area
12:00 noon	1:15 P.M.	Lunch	Boss and Dan	——
1:15 P.M.	1:30 P.M.	Wait for Doug	——	——

planning process is the development of goals and objectives. This phase involves the identification of the manager's goals for the organization, of personal career goals, and of life goals. Break down these goals statements into time periods, such as "Accomplish in the next six months," "Accomplish in the next five years," and so on. Further, to each goal, assign a priority (1, 2, 3, . . .) that corresponds to the importance of that goal for the manager. Finally, for each goal, list the activities that will contribute to goal accomplishment, and compare these activities with the present use of time. Do present activities coincide with the list of activities consistent with goal accomplishment?

If the answer to that question is no, you need a strategy for correcting this situation. The key questions to ask are, What activities are stealing time? What can I do to prevent this theft? While the list of responses to those questions will vary among managers, there are several categories of typical time stealers, such as the failure to delegate, interruptions, crises, attending to others' priorities first, meetings, unorganized work space, waiting, and travel time.

When a manager performs work that should be performed by a subordinate, he or she is stealing his or her own time. When deciding upon an activity, the manager should always ask, "How can I best use my time?" By failing to delegate, the manager not only is using personal time unwisely but also is failing to develop subordinates. The principles discussed here should guide the manager to more effective time management.

Interruptions are an inevitable part of the manager's life. Even though interruptions cannot be eliminated, the manager can take several steps to control the time stolen by phone calls or by subordinates' or peers' dropping in with problems to discuss. First, analyze the interruptions: Who is responsible for most of them? Are the matters priority items? Could any of them have waited? If the interruptions are time-stealing activities, the manager can take steps to gain control over them: (1) Set up several periods throughout the week devoted to "seeing others." (2) Set up periodic staff meetings to handle topics of typical interruptions. (3) Block out time each day when you are unavailable ("closed-door policy"). (4) Have telephone calls screened to make certain that no one else can handle the situation. (5) If possible, return all telephone calls at one time. (6) When handling an interruption, telephone or personal, get to the point quickly. (7) End the interruption when the purpose has been accomplished.

Many operating managers thrive on their ability to handle crises, so they seize upon any problem as a means to demonstrate that ability. While crises, in the true sense of the term, will occur within even the best-managed organizations, rush "projects" and "crises" are frequently time stealers. Faced with those situations, the manager must examine priorities and ask the question "Should time be spent solving a short-term situation, or should the time be spent working toward more important long-term goals?" Often, time spent planning will avoid the short-term crises that steal time.

The demands upon the manager's time by others within the organization pose a dilemma for most operating managers. The effective manager recognizes that he or she cannot do everything that everyone else wants done. The question is when to say "No." While there are no hard-and-fast rules for deciding when to say no, the manager should consider whether the request represents a high priority to the organization, the importance of the person making the request, and what activities will be left undone if the request is granted.

Meetings may be either time stealers or valuable tools to conserve time. When an important change or decision is being considered requiring communication, input, or coordination of several people, a meeting may be the most time effective tool to accomplish the task. Meetings for the sake of meetings, however, can steal large blocks of time. To make meetings more effective, several points should be considered: (1) Clearly define the purpose of the meeting, (2) include only the people necessary to accomplish the purpose, (3) always prepare and distribute a written agenda in advance so the attendees can be prepared, (4) specify in advance a starting time and an ending time, and then adhere to those times, (5) keep the discussion limited to the topic, and (6) following the meeting distribute minutes listing decisions made and follow-up steps required.

The failure to properly organize both the work space and the work time often results in lost time. Properly locating the office furniture, having a place for everything and keeping it there, and maintaining a reasonably orderly desk space will ease the manager's time problems. Similarly, scheduling of work time will ensure effective use of time available. For example, plan activities (thinking through problems, dictation, and so on) that can be accomplished while traveling to and from other activities or that can be done while waiting for an appointment. An excellent tool for scheduling work time is the "to do list." Each day make a list of all items that need attention. Next, examine the list to see which items can be delegated, and then establish priorities (A's, B's, C's) for the remaining items. Schedule the "A" priority items first and tackle them first. Set deadlines for completing each task. If an "A" priority cannot be completed in one day, set a target for completing a part of the task. Next, schedule routine items and previous commitments. Finally, schedule time for interruptions and uncommitted time.

Using the points outlined will improve the manager's ability to gain control of personal time and will help him or her to use subordinates' time more effectively. Time is one of the scarcest and costliest resources within the organization and must be allocated wisely if the organization is to achieve its goals.

CONCLUSION

This chapter has stressed the importance of the resource allocation role of the manager in a human service organization. This role is likely to become increasingly important in the future as public pressure for increased accountability increases, since resource allocation is a principal mechanism for establishing and measuring accountability. The human service managers of the future must master the techniques of resource allocation if they are to be successful.

REFERENCES

LOHMANN, R. A. (1980). *Breaking even: Financial management in human service organizations.* Philadelphia: Temple University Press.

STARLING, G. (1982). *Managing the public sector.* Homewood, Ill.: Dorsey.

UNITED WAY OF AMERICA (1976). *A "PPBS" approach to budgeting human service programs for United Way.* Alexandria, Va.: United Way of America. Quoted in W. H. Ehlers et al. (1976). *Administration for the human services: An introductory programmed text.* New York: Harper & Row.

QUESTIONS FOR DISCUSSION

1. Discuss the adequacy of the budgeting process in a human service organization with which you are familiar. In your discussion relate the elements of the process to the requirements enumerated in this chapter.
2. As an operating manager, which of the types of budgets discussed in the chapter would you prefer to work with? Why?
3. What are the advantages and disadvantages of the Zero-base and Program-Planning Budgeting Systems?
4. As the manager of a service delivery unit, you have a budget of $250,000. You are assigned fixed costs of $100,000, and the variable cost is $100 per client. At what number of clients served will you break even?
5. Discuss in detail some strategies the manager could use to increase the time available to him or her for planning.

SUGGESTED PROJECTS

1. Keep a time log for a two-week period. At the conclusion of the two weeks, analyze how you spent your time and develop a plan for improving your use of time.
2. Assume that your class is an operating unit in a human service organization. Develop a performance budget for the next twelve months using the budget process discussed in this chapter.

The Manager as Negotiator

chapter 12

Negotiation is an essential skill for all managers, although they may not label their activities as negotiations. Managers prepare, present, discuss, and reach agreement on a wide range of topics: budgets, staffing, programs, cooperative work relationships with other agencies and departments, job responsibilities—the list is endless. Those activities make the manager a negotiator. The role of managers in this process flows from their central position within the organization. As Mintzberg (1973) describes it,

> The manager participates because as figurehead his presence adds credibility to the proceedings and as spokesman he represents his organization's information and value system to outsiders. But most important, as resource allocator the manager has the authority to commit organizational resources. (p. 91)

Sayles (1964) explains the necessity for managerial negotiations:

> Because of the division of labor imposed on the modern organization, the manager rarely controls all the resources needed to do whatever has been assigned. . . . Further, there are people, other than his own boss, who depend upon him and who have the job of keeping watch over him. All these conditions require the development and maintenance of particular patterns of relationships. They are not optional, extra, or necessary as good human relations; they are an integral part of the administrative task. (p. 58)

Thus, the success or failure of a project or program may depend upon skill in managing negotiating relationships.

NEGOTIATING RELATIONSHIPS

The negotiating relationships faced by the manager may be separated into three distinct types. First, the manager is responsible for obtaining resources, approvals, and support from superiors, creating an "upward" negotiating relationship. In these situations care must be taken to establish and maintain a positive attitude towards oneself and the issue under discussion. That is critical when dealing with superiors, since the ability to force the superior into agreement is restricted. Consider this exchange between a Bureau Chief of a State Welfare Department and the Commissioner of Human Services in a large eastern state:

BUREAU CHIEF: Jane, my department desperately needs this program and it's only three million dollars.

COMMISSIONER: Bill, where am I going to get three million dollars?

BUREAU CHIEF: Why, from the legislature, of course.

COMMISSIONER: Look, Bill, we have been discussing this proposal for four hours and you still don't seem to understand what I have been telling you. In the first place, I have no direct control over what the legislature will or will not fund. Second, the costs associated with your program appear to far exceed the benefits to the agency. Finally, you haven't provided me with strong enough evidence that your department could carry out this program, even if we had the money.

This exchange between Jane and Bill is an all-too-common occurrence in the relationship between many subordinates and their superiors. Bill had come to his boss with a program proposal that was not well conceived or well presented. Jane reported to the author that she later discovered that Bill's proposal had merit. However, at the time it was presented, "Bill's attitude and lack of skill in making his points killed the project." Many good programs go the way of this one, simply because the presenter is unfamiliar with the basic skills of subordinate-superior negotiations. As will be discussed later in this chapter, Bill could have had a much more positive response from Jane. If he had done his homework thoroughly, he would have been better prepared for her objections. Preparation is essential to effective negotiations.

A second category of negotiating relationships involves subordinates. Some managers frequently overlook the necessity for gaining the agreement and support of their staff for projects they wish to implement. Since they are in a strong position to demand conformity from the staff, they do not feel the need for negotiating with subordinate staff over departmental operations, policy changes, procedural modifications, or structural organization. That can be a critical error, particularly when the staff includes professionals. For example, a chief floor nurse at a large general hospital exercised great care in negotiating a change in nursing procedures on her floor with the head nurse, the medical director, and the hospital administrator. She was amazed when the floor nurses filed a formal complaint after reading the new policy, stating "the new procedure reduced their ability to provide adequate patient care." The chief floor nurse quickly learned that when considering basic nursing changes she would have to include her nurses in the negotiations.

Successful managers effectively utilize their subordinates. Keep in mind that the pivotal resource in any organization is the people who "do the work." No one person can do everything that is required to be effective as a manager—that person needs the commitment from subordinates to carry out the purpose, goals, and objectives of the unit, department, or bureau. If subordinates are not committed to the direction and mission of the organization, then they will be complacent. That does not foster good and productive organizational performance. Subordinates cannot be by-passed in the decision-making process. Had the head nurse included the floor nurses in the decision-making process, the decision would have been "our" decision, not "hers." The total staff should have an ego investment in the decision, and that will breed commitment.

The third set of negotiating relationships involves other managers in different departments, divisions, or agencies with whom you must work. Since an organizational unit is seldom given sufficient resources to perform all the tasks assigned, the manager must depend upon other work groups for assistance. Such aid must be negotiated with the heads of those work groups. In these negotiations, success will depend upon the mutual benefits to be derived from the agreement: "What's in it for us?" As the manager negotiates, he or she cannot lose sight of that question. For example, the Commissioner of Mental Health in a southern state was successful in negotiating the location of a maximum security mental health facility with local leaders, over the objections of community leaders, by emphasizing the facility's economic benefits to the community.

Even though these three sets of relationships have been discussed as separate categories, the reader should be aware that frequently a single proposal will involve all three categories. A single project may require the negotiation of additional resources with superiors, the renegotiation of roles within the department, and the negotiation of cooperation with one or more lateral managers—as could be the case with the preceding example. The construction of a maximum security mental health facility would require additional appropriations to be allocated by the legislative body. Therefore, the Commissioner of Mental Health would have to negotiate with the governor and convince him or her to include the necessary resources in the budget request made to the legislature. The new facility would have to be staffed and, often, that requires redeployment of existing staff as well as the hiring of new personnel. Important issues concerning staffing might have to be negotiated with appropriate personnel in the mental health system. And, finally, the construction of such a facility would need the support of the community and its leaders—a very sensitive area of negotiation. All three sets of relationships would go on simultaneously.

In summary, successful management of these negotiating relationships depends on knowledge of the basic elements of negotiation, knowledge of fundamental issues, ability to prepare for negotiations, and an understanding of the strategies and tactics involved in this process.

WHAT IS NEGOTIATION?

Morley and Stephenson (1977) formally define negotiation as "any form of verbal communication, direct or indirect, whereby parties to a conflict of interests discuss, without resort to arbitration or other judicial processes, the form of any joint action which they might take to manage a 'dispute' (difference) between them" (p. 26).

The desire to undertake a new program or the need to expand an existing activity may or may not contain the essentials for negotiation. Whether or not a manager is in a position to negotiate a proposal depends upon three factors. First, the manager must determine if the issue at hand is negotiable. A negotiable issue is one that is within the scope of authority of the parties to decide. For example, in the case of Jane and Bill, the size of the legislative appropriation was not controlled by either of them; therefore, it was not an issue about which they could negotiate. However, the level of funding allocated from the legislative appropriation to Bill's unit did constitute a negotiable issue between Jane and him.

A second essential element of negotiation is the readiness to trade something of value to obtain something else of value. In the successful negotiation, all parties gain something of value that fulfills a need. Thus, the skilled negotiator frames proposals to meet existing needs of the other party or parties involved. That may often require a willingness to compromise on an original position, but the necessity for such compromise is greatly reduced through the skillful development of proposals. For example, the incorporation of a cost-saving element into a new program proposal may meet a superior's need to show greater efficiency and enhance the prospects for obtaining approval with little compromise.

The third element of negotiation is a degree of trust among the negotiating parties. Each participant must believe that agreements made during the negotiation will, in fact, be carried out. The director of a state advocacy program for the developmentally disabled met with the administrators of the welfare department to negotiate a referral procedure between the two state agencies. An agreement was reached as to how such referrals would be handled, and each local county was advised of the new procedure. However, in a subsequent action the welfare department nullified the agreement, which created a great deal of strain between the two agencies. Fortunately, through further negotiations the matter was resolved, but the director of the advocacy program continued to be apprehensive in light of the entire experience. The integrity of the negotiator is a critical factor, without which there is no basis for negotiation.

THE INGREDIENTS OF NEGOTIATION

As we noted earlier, a successful negotiation allows all parties to gain something they value from the resulting agreement. We may conclude, therefore, that the unmet needs of the negotiating parties represent the common denominator of negotiation. That being the case, the parties devote considerable attention to the discovery of those unmet needs and to the formation of responses that will address those needs. People engaged in negotiations display their needs as well as their personality defenses, so the skilled negotiator must possess a thorough understanding of human behavior.

To recognize and respond to another's needs requires skill in interpersonal communications. Negotiations proceed through the exchange of ideas between the parties. That exchange occurs both verbally and through nonverbal cues exhibited by the negotiators. For example, an increase in the rate of involuntary eye blinking may indicate anxiety or fear; a lack of eye contact when speaking to another person may be an indication of the speaker's attempt to misdirect or mislead; and a change in posture (leaning toward or away from the speaker) may indicate the degree of interest an individual has in the point being discussed.

Finally, an individual's preconceptions developed from his or her background and experiences in life result in behaviors that may either help or hinder the progress of negotiations. For example, when a proposal is presented to a superior, it is with the preconception that the superior has the authority to accept or reject the proposal. That may not always be the case; thus, the preconception hinders negotiation in this instance.

The understanding of preconceived ideas that lead each of us to reach conclusions and take action is a valuable negotiating skill, since one of the primary objectives of a negotiator is to gain and maintain control over the course of discussions.

ISSUES IN NEGOTIATION

An important facet of negotiation involves the issues to be discussed. While specific bargaining issues abound, Walton and McKersie (1965) provide a convenient typology for grouping issues into four relatively discrete and independent categories. These groupings, in addition to allowing for simple classification, provide insight into the nature of the negotiating process.

Distributive Issues

If, during negotiations, you find that your objectives are in conflict with the objectives of the other party, you are probably dealing with a distributive issue. The parties are faced with the problem of obtaining benefits from a fixed sum. For example, budget allocations are a prime category of the distributive issue. If one party is successful in negotiating a higher budget level, others within the organization will have to accept less. Allocation of a limited number of staff is another example of a distributive issue. A large state human service agency in the South had to reduce its staff to compensate for a deficit in the budget. Where the cuts are made and how severe they are lead to frequent and heated debate. This is analogous to dividing a pie among several persons; the larger the piece obtained by one, the less there is to share among the others. As you might imagine, discussions of this issue tend to be more emotion-laden and difficult to resolve.

Integrative Issues

Many issues discussed during negotiations concern areas of administrative practice in which all parties have an interest. For example, the reduction of staff turnover is an issue concerning which all parties generally have the same objectives. Similarly, a program to improve the services offered by the agency will be supported by the majority. While there will be differing views regarding the approaches taken, discussions of this issue are more likely to be of a problem-solving nature. To continue the pie analogy, if the pie has not been baked and the discussions center on how the available ingredients can be combined to bake the largest pie possible, you are dealing with an integrative issue. Since the participants have common objectives, discussions about integrative issues are more likely to be characterized by rational discussion of a common problem, by a cooperative approach, and by a genuine desire to resolve the issue to the mutual benefit of all parties.

Attitudinal Issues

In addressing attitudinal issues, negotiators direct their activities toward changing the relationship between themselves and other participants in the negotiation. For example, a proposal to create a center to provide abortions may meet with initial hostility; therefore, attitudes must be changed before a successful outcome can be obtained through negotiations. Here, the negotiator is dealing with perceptions, attitudes, and motivations that must be modified before the primary issue can be addressed. The skillful negotiator deals with attitudinal issues by utilizing his or her knowledge of human behavior and how it can be modified.

An administrator of a medium-size community hospital wanted to implement a plan to modify the staffing configuration among the nursing staff. During the discussion phase, he elicited the opinions of staff nurses about the following proposals: a flextime schedule, a 4-10 proposal (four ten-hour days per week), and a plan that would allow nurses to work seven days a week and then be off seven days. Initially, the attitude of the nurses was that they wanted to leave the work schedule alone and continue as they had been working. However, after several meetings with a representative group of nurses, they came to a resolution. The nurses agreed to go on a flextime schedule. They were allowed to select their own hours of work, and the only condition was that the hospital had to be adequately staffed twenty-four hours a day, seven days a week. After several months, the attitude of the nursing staff was very supportive of the new schedule.

Intraorganizational Issues

The result of any negotiation carries with it the potential for creating problems among staff. A new program may mean a change in duties; a change in budget allocation may lead to resource allocation problems; or a change in staffing patterns may result in professional jealousies. In short, every negotiator faces the risk of failing to gain acceptance of an agreement by those who must ultimately implement the actions called for by the agreement. The responsible manager, therefore, must give attention to resolving any differences within his or her organizational unit and to being certain that agreements reached are acceptable to both the manager and the staff.

In recent years many human service agencies have begun to look to the use of computer technology as a way to improve the agency's activity. There has been substantial resistance to that among the staff. Attitudes have to be changed, and the effective manager is able to show the staff how their work can be facilitated by the computer. It is only as he or she is capable of defining the relationship between the mission of the agency and the new technology that attitudes will be modified. Once that has occurred, the issues of implementation can be focused upon and negotiated. Failure to handle such attitudes can lead to chaos. Several years ago a midwestern state developed and implemented a statewide criminal justice management system. A component of the new system dealt with juvenile probation—specifically, the number of juveniles who were on probation throughout the state. For this to work, the local probation officers had to fill out monthly reports, which would then be fed to the computer. The probation officers rebelled by giving no attention to the accuracy of their reports. Consequently, in one county of the state there were more juveniles on probation than there were juveniles in the state. What happened? The probation officers' attitude about the system was extremely negative, and they set out to sabotage the system. At no time during the development of the system were local probation officers involved in the decision-making process. The decision was made to have the system, and the probation officers were expected to implement it. The attitudes of people toward change must be recognized and handled, or the preceding illustration becomes the normal pattern of behavior.

PREPARATIONS FOR NEGOTIATIONS

The successful negotiator carefully examines any proposal to be sure that proper attention has been given to the basic negotiating ingredients. Once you are assured that you have incorporated those factors into proposals, you are ready to take the first step toward face-to-face negotiations.

Successful negotiators quickly agree that proper preparation is the key to their success. Once a proposal incorporates the objectives to be met, time must be devoted to marshaling support.

First, who are the persons to be involved in the negotiation and what is known about them? The most important person involved is you. How much do you know about yourself? What are your motivations? What is your emotional involvement with the project? What personal strengths and weaknesses may affect you as a negotiator? What is your ability as a communicator? You should answer those questions before undertaking negotiations. As for the other parties, you should learn as much as possible about their background and education, their behavioral patterns, the pressures of their jobs, and so on. After all, a major objective of negotiating is to be able to predict the behavior of others. The more knowledge you have about those individuals, the greater the likelihood that your behavioral predictions will be accurate.

A second facet of preparation is the collection of facts to support proposals. Much information can be easily obtained from existing budgets, operating plans, evaluations of existing programs, and agency reports. Care must be exercised in the development of those facts. Facts are like a double-edged sword in negotiations: When generally agreed upon, they are a source for leading the parties to agreement; when disputed, they introduce a new element that must be resolved before substantive discussions can continue. For example, a proposal to provide day-care services hinges, in part, upon the size of the client population. After investigation, a client population of 10,000 is decided upon. If all parties agree, that fact will aid in bringing about agreement. On the other hand, if the number is disputed, the issue of client population must be disposed of before the central issue, day-care services, can be dealt with. In short, when facts are to be used, they must be supportable.

The preparation phase should also include a careful review of agency guidelines, policies, policy interpretation, and any precedent for the action sought. Nothing can be more embarrassing during negotiations than to be caught offering a position that is contrary to established policy.

Next, a strategy should be decided upon and an agenda developed. The strategy incorporates the overall plan of attack or the approach to be employed during negotiations. For example, the negotiator may wish to begin with an attempt to resolve the more integrative issues, thereby establishing early an atmosphere of agreement and a cooperative attitude. As more difficult issues surface, the earlier agreements may be used as a mechanism to press on to a successful conclusion of all items on the agenda.

Finally, the complete proposal should be tried out in a practice session. Frequently, such a mock negotiation can reveal weaknesses in either the proposal or the approach. The time to repair such defects is before negotiations have begun.

Tactics

The strategy developed by the negotiator provides the overall direction, while the tactics employed relate to specific actions. For example, a trip to New York may be taken by plane, train, or automobile; however, once a mode of transportation is selected, specific actions (tactics) must follow if the destination is to be reached. Tactics are situational and are selected to fit the ebb and flow of the negotiations. Choosing the proper tactic is critical to the success of a negotiation. The wrong action at a crucial point in discussion can destroy the best proposals. Coffin (1973) provides a framework of useful negotiating tactics, which are summarized in Table 12-1. The basics should be observed during face-to-face discussions.

Summary

The preceding discussion and guidelines will not transform you into a professional negotiator, but they are essential as a beginning. Keeping in mind the changing nature of your negotiating relationships, the charac-

---

TABLE 12-1. Negotiating Tactics

Avoid marathon session. A tired negotiator makes a poor showing, and nothing is gained by trying to impress people with staying power.

Be the aggressor. You must take the initiative if you are going to accomplish your objectives.

Interruptions turn people off. When meeting in your facilities, see that your staff respects your privacy.

"Silence is Golden." It is your best reply to a totally unacceptable offer.

Be the first to bring up major items at the appropriate time. This is one of the most difficult maneuvers for a negotiator to master. Don't be afraid to "leave something on the table." You shouldn't be in negotiations if you don't know the values involved.

Break the tension. If you get the feeling that people are tightening up, inject humor or suggest a break.

Defer discussion of sensitive points. If you sense concern in certain areas, try to agree on as many other terms as possible rather than risk an early confrontation.

Don't end a meeting on a negative note. If you do, it could be the one thing to stick in someone's mind. After sleeping on it, that person might just change his or her mind about the deal.

Get agreement on next steps. If additional meetings are necessary, don't leave until you get a specific time and place for the next session.

Make it easier. The easier it is for others to do something or to agree with you, the quicker and more positive their response will be.

Disagree on a positive note. Instead of pointing out where others are wrong, stress the advantages to be gained.

Be courteous. Observing the common rules of courtesy adds greatly to your effectiveness.

Keep the meeting on track. Be alert for the guy who changes the subject. Keep your objective in mind and the meeting on the subject.

Don't react too unfavorably to your own mistakes. Life is one big negotiation, and if you are human you will make mistakes. Try to keep them to a minimum.

Don't rush the other side. This may be one of the most important decisions of a person's career, and he or she needs time.

When the mission is accomplished, leave. This maneuver reduces the chance that someone will change his or her mind and that you will continue to talk needlessly until you finally say the wrong thing.

---

teristics of the issues involved, the need to prepare your case, and the appropriate use of tactics will provide you with a starting point for success. To be successful as a managerial negotiator, you must actively participate in negotiations and sharpen your skills at every opportunity.

UNIONS—A SPECIAL CASE

The unionization of employees in human service organizations presents the manager with a different, although related, type of negotiating opportunity. While there are many unique aspects to management-union relations, four distinctives are of primary importance for the operating manager. First, when negotiating in this area, the manager is faced with the problem of reaching an agreement that will apply to all employees, through discussions with a third party (the union). Second, the negotiations themselves are usually governed by a law that may require discussion of certain subjects. Third, these negotiations generally involve the process by which the manager will manage rather than the content of a particular program. Finally, the impact of these negotiations on the organization may have a broader effect and greater ramifications than other types of negotiating activities.

The Union and Its Role

The union movement in the United States consists of three major elements: the federation, national or international unions, and local unions. Each of those elements performs functions directed toward serving the needs of individual members.

The federation is a "union of unions" in that its membership is drawn from the autonomous national and international unions who choose to affiliate with the federation. The primary functions performed by the federation include the chartering of new national unions, political action (lobbying and political organizations), organizing, and providing research and technical assistance to its members.

The national unions (or, more precisely, international unions, since they generally have local units in Canada) are the cornerstone of the American labor movement. They are the dominant force because they control the activities of the local unions and either conduct or have approval over the most important function of a union—collective bargaining.

The local union is the basic component of the labor movement. It is the unit in which the individual worker holds membership. The local is chartered by the national union and has primary responsibility for representing the membership at the workplace. This involves local union officials in the negotiation of grievances (worker complaints arising out of the interpretation or application of the collective bargaining agreement) with management. It is this level of union structure with which most managers will have contact.

Whether negotiating with the union about the terms of a new agreement or attempting to resolve the grievance of an individual employee, the responsible manager must keep in mind the objective of the union. The union's role is to obtain the most favorable terms possible for its members. Further, when an agreement is reached with the union on an issue, that agreement becomes agency policy and affects all employees in the bargaining unit (the group of employees or jobs that are combined for purposes of collective bargaining). Thus, the manager engaged in negotiations with a union must carefully consider the objectives sought and consider the impact of any agreement on the work force and on the operation of the organization. Agreements reached are difficult to modify and may become precedents during subsequent negotiations.

The Legal Setting

Most of the negotiating relationships discussed in the first sections of this chapter were voluntary in that the parties agreed to discuss an issue. Further, most of the negotiations were initiated by management. Management-union negotiations, however, most often have a legal foundation that requires recognition and negotiation.

Organizations in the private sector are regulated by the National Labor Relations Act of 1935 (the Wagner Act), which has had two major amendments: the 1947 Taft-Hartley Act and the 1959 Landrum-Griffin Act. This statute covers employees in the private sector, except agricultural laborers, domestic servants, those employed by a parent or spouse, independent contractors, and supervisors. Coverage does include employees of such human service organizations as private day-care centers, private voluntary agencies, private colleges and universities, privately operated health care institutions, and associations.

The provisions of this act guarantee employees the right to participate in unions and to engage in collective bargaining over wages, hours, terms, and conditions of employment. Further, the act prohibits both the employer and the union from interfering with, restraining, or coercing employees in the exercise of their rights. In addition, it requires the union and the employer to bargain in good faith over the terms of the employment contract.

There is no single statute that regulates the union-management relationship in the case of governments and their employees. Most agencies and employees of the federal government are covered by the Civil Service Reform Act of 1978. Title VII of this act controls the procedures for union recognition, outlines negotiable issues (subjects about which the parties are allowed to bargain), establishes unfair labor practices (actions by employer or union that interfere with the rights granted the parties), and requires that agreements include a grievance procedure with binding arbitration.

Most states and a substantial number of local governments and school districts have established frameworks for the conduct of union-management relations. These take the form of policies, statutes, executive orders, or local ordinances. Many of these are comprehensive, such as those in New York, Michigan, California, and Hawaii, in that they provide an administrative agency to oversee the act, specify bargaining rights, delineate the scope of bargaining, identify unfair labor practices and provide procedures for impasse resolution. Indeed, a few states even grant a limited right to strike, an activity that is customarily denied public employees. Other states, such as Alabama, provide only limited coverage (statutes limited to firefighters and so on) and limit the area of bargaining to narrow subjects (for example, grievance adjustment).

For the operating manager faced with the task of negotiating with a union, the multiplicity of policies and regulations may be confusing. The key element for the manager is preparation. It is particularly important that the manager know and understand the legal and policy position of the organization before undertaking negotiations.

The Content of Bargaining

The union agreement deals with the policies and practices the organization will follow in matters related to personnel. The collective bargaining agreement specifies the terms and conditions of the employment contract between the employer and each employee. The union, representing the employees, and management jointly determine the policies and practices the organization will follow in its dealings with employees. The functions and broad coverage usually found in collective bargaining agreements are presented in Figure 12-1.

The first function of the agreement is to specify the relationship between the parties. This section usually defines the employees who will be subject to the terms of the agreement (bargaining units); provides for the protection of the union by specifying a degree of union membership (union security); and delineates the scope of bargaining. This last function usually involves the rights of management, such as the freedom to determine the services to be offered by the organization or the right to discipline or discharge for "just cause."

The second function of the agreement is to set down the policies and practices to be followed with respect to personnel. Rates of pay and the relationship of jobs within the organization are included, as well as items such as holidays, vacations, and benefits (for example, life and health insurance). In addition, this section of the agreement deals with the performance expectations established for each job category and the process for determining the amount of work the employer may expect in return for the compensation paid to employees.

The protection of individual employees and the enforcement of the agreement are provisions normally found within the terms of the labor agreement. Generally, the concept of length of service (seniority) is used to protect the individual's job rights. Seniority is the customary means by which layoff and recall are determined, with the employee having the longest service being the last to be laid off and the first to be recalled. In addition, seniority may be an element in determining promotions and eligibility for additional benefits (for example, longer vacations).

The individual employee's right to due process is guaranteed through the operation of a grievance procedure, which terminates with final and

FUNCTION	CATEGORY	
I		
Union Security and Management Rights	a. The bargaining unit b. Form of recognition c. Duration and renewal d. Management rights	Who speaks for whom With what authority For how long Except in what conditions
II		
The Wage and Effort Bargain	a. Pay for time worked b. The effort bargain c. Premium pay d. Pay for time not worked e. Contingent benefits	Pay rates; job evaluation Standards Hours; duration Fixed labor costs Variable labor costs
III		

Individual Security	a. Job rights
	
	b. Due process
		Relative claim to available work—
		   seniority
		Absolute claim to fair treatment—
		   grievance procedures

IV		
Administration	a. Internal b. External	On the job representation; stewards Arbitration

FIGURE 12-1 Functions of the Labor Agreement. Reprinted, by permission of the publisher, from "How to Make Sure Everyone Understands the Contract," by Edwin F. Beal, PERSONNEL, Sept./Oct. 1962 © 1962 American Management Association, New York. All rights reserved.

binding arbitration. When a party to the agreement believes that the terms have been improperly applied or interpreted, the party files a grievance. This procedure for resolving conflicts arising out of the agreement provides a step-by-step process for working out a solution and for representation. A typical grievance procedure would contain the following: Step 1— the employee and the union representative (steward) present the complaint to the immediate supervisor. If they cannot work out the problem satisfactorily, the grievance moves to Step 2—negotiations between the chief union steward and the personnel officer. If no resolution is reached, the grievance moves to Step 3—negotiation between the local union president and the chief operating officer. If the problem is not resolved here, it moves to the final step—arbitration.

Arbitration grows out of the agreement of the parties to submit unresolved grievances to an outside neutral third party whose decision is final and binding. The agreement itself contains a method for choosing the arbitrator and specifies the power he or she is granted. That authority is usually limited to the interpretation and application of the agreement between the parties. That is, the arbitrator may not add to or subtract from the existing language of the agreement. The arbitration hearing is similar, although not identical, to a court proceeding, with the arbitrator acting as judge and jury. Each party presents its position on the problem, and the arbitrator renders a decision.

The operating manager should be familiar with the contents of the union-management agreement and particularly with the grievance-arbitration process. This latter element is the most likely point of contact between operating managers and the union. Further, agreements reached in grievance negotiations often have far-reaching effects and may establish precedents for the future.

The Impact of Unions on the Organization

The foregoing discussion illustrates many of the ways the existence of a union-management contract can affect the operation of a human service organization. Dollars bargained away for wages or other benefits may not be used to support programs or client service. Work rules that limit employee output diminish the productivity of the organization. The time of managers and employees devoted to resolving grievances is not available to clients or program management. Not all aspects of the relationship, however, are negative. A well-negotiated agreement with a union has advantages to the employer. The fact that the employees have a voice, through their union, in establishing the terms of their employment contract may lead to greater acceptance on their part. The fact that the union is ready to file a grievance may lead managers to consider the consequences of their actions more carefully and produce better decisions throughout the organization.

One area of the union-management relationship that has the potential for the greatest impact on the organization is the strike—the most powerful strategy the union has to support its claims during negotiations. The purpose is to demonstrate the strength of commitment to a position and to pressure management into agreeing to union terms. Strikes, while infrequent, do occur in both the private and the public sectors. Although strikes are generally banned in the public sector, there were 481 strikes, with a loss of working time of 1.7 million days, during 1978. Thus, the impact of unsuccessful negotiations in this arena can be devastating to the organization and emphasizes the need for adequate preparation and skilled conduct of negotiations by the parties.

SUMMARY

This chapter has focused on the manager as a negotiator. It has provided the reader with a basic understanding of the various relationships and issues that prompt a negotiating session. With this understanding, the manager can gain insight into a negotiating process. As these insights are mastered, a plan emerges for the conduct of the actual negotiation and specifies the preparation necessary for success. Whether the manager is involved in negotiating with a union, another agency, superiors, or subordinates, he or she must understand and apply the principles discussed throughout the chapter. The preceding discussion and guidelines will not transform the reader into a professional negotiator, but they are essential as a beginning.

REFERENCES

BEAL, E. T., WICKERSHAM, E. D., & KIENAST, P. (1967). *The practice of collective bargaining* (3rd ed.). Homewood, Ill.: Richard D. Irwin.

COFFIN, R. A. (1973). *The negotiator: A manual for winners.* New York: AMACOM.

MINTZBERG, H. (1973). *The nature of managerial work.* New York: Harper & Row.

MORLEY, L. E., & STEPHENSON, G. M. (1977). *The social psychology of bargaining.* London: George Allen & Unwin Ltd..

SAYLES, L. (1964). *Managerial behavior: Administration in complex organizations.* New York: McGraw-Hill.

WALTON, R., & McKERSIE, W. (1965). *A behavioral theory of labor negotiations.* New York: McGraw-Hill.

QUESTIONS FOR DISCUSSION

1. Assume that you have received a grade for this class lower than you feel appropriate. Develop a plan for negotiating a higher grade with the instructor.

2. Obtain a copy of a labor agreement from a nearby agency. Analyze the agreement from the viewpoint of a manager. What areas do you feel would present the most difficulties?

3. Interview a local agency manager who conducts negotiations on behalf of his or her organization. In the interview ask the manager to discuss the approach he or she uses when negotiating with a superior, a subordinate, and another manager.

4. Employees of human service organizations should have the right to strike to obtain higher wages, shorter working hours, and better working conditions. Discuss that proposition.

SUGGESTED PROJECTS

1. Divide the class into two teams (one union, one management). Using a current labor agreement, each team should (1) prepare a list of demands; (2) collect information to support those demands; and (3) develop a negotiating plan.

2. Using the information developed, the two teams are to conduct formal negotiations on each of the demands.

Selected Cases

appendix

Throughout this book we have attempted to stress the importance of integrated management action to ensure that the human service organization is successful in carrying out its mission. The student, by this time, should understand that the work of a manager involves a complex set of interrelated behaviors and the performance of integrated functions. Describing those behaviors and functions, however, does not provide a full understanding of how they operate together in the organizational setting. The case problems presented in this section will provide the student with an opportunity to apply the concepts discussed in the preceding sections in actual organizational situations. Each case presents an organizational situation, typical of those found in most human service agencies, in which the student will learn by doing. The cases are designed to aid the serious student in the development of his or her analytical skills and the application of those skills to "real world" situations; thus, it is important that each case be approached in a systematic fashion, using an analytical framework.

Good case analysis requires a thorough knowledge of the situation and pertinent facts. Much like a jigsaw puzzle, the various pieces of the organizational puzzle must be properly arranged before a solution is attempted. The student, therefore, should first become familiar with the situation by reading the case completely. After this initial familiarization, the vital facts related to the case should be abstracted for further analysis. An accurate and complete job of gathering the facts at this beginning stage will greatly facilitate the proper analysis of the case.

After the facts are gathered, the student should clearly state the problems and opportunities facing the manager in the organization under analysis. At this step the student should attempt to project himself or herself into the situation as fully as possible because the more actively one becomes involved, the greater the learning experience. It is likely that many of the problem statements will be related to or will be symptoms of a more basic issue. If you were the manager in this situation, how would you react? What is really going on? Such questions should be carefully analyzed to identify and state the major problems or opportunities present in the case.

After the major problems have been concisely restated, a situation analysis should be undertaken. A situation analysis involves the personalities, the environment, and the work setting. Solutions to organizational problems or the ability to exploit opportunities frequently depend on the personalities within the organization. Who are the people involved and what are their personal objectives? What competencies exist within the organization? Which persons or groups are most affected by the situation? What will be the likely reaction of those most affected? In each instance at least three groups—workers, administrators, and clients—should be included in the analysis. The environmental analysis should include information related to the overall organization. Is the agency public or private? Are there unique political (internal or external) aspects to the problem? Are there legal aspects to the problem? What organizational relationships (internal or external) are affected by the situation? Are there existing policies or procedures that will limit or guide actions? Those and other related questions should be analyzed to place the problem or opportunity under investigation into a proper environmental perspective. Finally, the situation analysis should include aspects of the work setting. Does the problem have an impact on direct service, or does it involve administrative work flows? What level of technology exists at the workplace? Is the work flow centralized or decentralized? Is the problem isolated within one unit or does it have organizationwide impact? An accurate assessment of the work setting will facilitate the analysis of alternative solutions. In summary, a good situation analysis outlines the boundaries within which a course of action is possible and is a necessary precedent to the development of sound alternatives.

With the situation analysis complete, the next step suggested for case analysis involves the development of alternatives, the selection of a course of action, and the development of a plan for implementing the chosen alternative. Rather than restating the steps involved in alternative development and decision making, the student should review the discussion of problem analysis, decision making, and action planning in the appropriate sections of the text, since those discussions are relevant to the case analysis process.

Students who thoroughly prepare and project themselves as active participants in the case situations will find ample opportunity to test their management skills. Further, prepared students will benefit from the discussions of the case problems with other group members. Testing your "solution" against those of other group members will increase greatly your insights into the management process.

A SUGGESTED CASE ANALYSIS FRAMEWORK

One method of analysis that has been found to be of value has six major steps:

1. Clearly define the central problem or problems in the case.
2. Divide the central problem into its significant aspects.
3. Analyze those aspects or factors through the creation of a logical series of questions, evaluating the evidence in the case.
4. Develop assumptions about the problem and the relevant data you have analyzed.
5. Develop alternative solutions for the central problem. Each alternative must be a complete proposal for appropriate action.
6. Select the alternative that you feel is the best and should be implemented. Document your choice by developing an impact statement.

1. The central problem.   A central problem of a case is defined as a basic issue that can be solved adequately without going deeper into the situation to solve another problem. It typically encompasses the subproblems that have been identified. If a deeper problem is found, it, by definition, is the central problem. It is impossible to carry analysis forward until the task to be performed has been clearly defined. Often, the business situations with which you will deal are so complex as to make this a difficult and significant part of your analysis.

A careful reading of the case will help to define its central problem. Such a reading, with a notation of the questions asked, is a preliminary setting for your analysis. It will help to determine the objectives of your analysis and to show which elements of the case are significant and which have little or no bearing on the solution of the central problem.

2. Significant aspects of the central issue.   It is a rare business problem that is so simple it can be solved by means of a single line of analysis. It is more typical to find the central problem of a business situation to be a complex bundle of major aspects and subsidiary factors. Each aspect will in turn depend upon various, more detailed considerations.

The reason for breaking down a problem into its elements is fundamental to the human mind. Our intellects are so constituted that we grasp only a single item at a time. We dissipate our mental powers by trying to focus our attention on more than one item at the same time. When a business problem is divided into its logical parts, the solution of the whole problem becomes a process of the solution of its parts.

3. Analysis of the aspects or factors.
a. *Questions.* After deciding upon the factors into which the central problem can be divided, create a series of questions whose purpose is the thorough exploration of each factor.

The exploration should not be a haphazard process but should be done systematically. In determining these questions, you will find your definition of the central problem helpful. It should show you what important questions need to be answered for each factor and which factors are the most significant and therefore require the most exhaustive list of questions for their solutions.

At this stage in your analysis, you will have before you a clear statement of the central problem of the case and an understanding of the proper line of attack on that problem. You will have divided the central problem into its subsidiary factors, which you intend to attack separately. Finally, you will have explored the case to arrive at a complete list of questions that must be answered before a satisfactory conclusion can be made about the factors. Now you must turn your attention to the evidence presented in the case.

b. *Marshaling the Evidence.* Generally, you will find that all the evidence necessary for adequate analysis of the cases will be included in the material that you will be asked to analyze. This circumstance does not mean that the evidence will always be in the form most useful to you or that the implications of all the data will be made clear in the case. It is your task to use the evidence satisfactorily in your own plan of analysis.

Sometimes, the evidence will be useful in its original form. At other times, it will be necessary for you to rearrange the data, to correlate the evidence, or to make further calculations from it in order to make it useful to your analysis.

Objectivity is necessary in the successful use of the pro-and-con method of evidence arrangement. In business problems it is the exception rather than the rule when a certain factor does not have both pro and con arguments attached to it. If you allow yourself to take notice only of those pieces of evidence that support a preconceived conclusion, you will seriously weaken your analysis. A good pro-and-con analysis remains completely objective until all the evidence has been applied to a factor. Only then is a sound decision on that factor possible.

In arranging and evaluating case evidence you will often find it helpful to study the source of the data. Are they fact or opinion? Have they been honestly stated, or do they come from a biased source? Can the evidence be reworked to have a bearing on more than one factor? These questions will often help you separate significant evidence from useless data in your analysis.

c. *Evaluation.* Once you have applied all the significant evidence in the case to the factors of the central problem, you are in a position to make decisions on the factors. Study the data, pro and con, that you have arranged for each factor. Which group of arguments seems the stronger in total? Are there greater dangers on the pro side than on the con side? Of all the arguments you have arrayed under a particular factor, which one seems most important? By evaluating the relative merits of each set of arguments, you will be able to arrive at a logical conclusion about the factor that is substantiated by the evidence in the case.

4. Assumptions. Assumptions are suppositions that you make about the data. They are those things that you take for granted but that may not be known to others and must, therefore, be articulated to create for the reader a context similar to the one in which you developed your alternatives. The assumptions establish the ground rules for your decision processes.

5. Developing alternatives. Inherent in the business problem is a choice of decisions even if it involves only a simple question of "make or buy." Not infrequently, the material in the case clearly defines the feasible courses of action from which the analyst makes his or her final decision. In such cases the possible courses of action will have been discussed, compared, and tested as part of the analytical process described above.

In instances where incomplete compilation of the information does not allow for a thorough study of possibilities, the alert student will recognize what other areas the company or individual would be advised to explore now or in the future. When pertinent and reasonably substantiated, such suggestions can give a more rounded picture of the analysis.

6. Selection of an alternative. With a logical decision on each of the factors before you, the last phase of the analysis is the gathering of those decisions together into a reasoned conclusion about the central problem in the case. The procedure is much the same as that used in the questioning. Which factors are of major importance in the problem? Which factors involve the greatest gain; which the largest risk? Which single factor, if any, seems most important to the decision? Is there a significant relationship among several factors that gives them more importance in the decision than other, unrelated factors? By asking such questions, you will arrive at a conclusion about the central problem that is based squarely on the evidence in the case.

A Word about the Cases

The first case, "Management Comes to the Mosaic County Welfare Department," illustrates the difficulties of management by edict within a human service organization. The case also demonstrates the impact of both formal and informal reporting relationships within the organization and addresses the problems associated with instituting organizational change within a complex organization. "Poindexter County Insight Center" involves the student in the planning process for a program to provide services to families receiving economic assistance. In addition to establishing clear results-oriented objectives, the student is called upon to identify activities and events necessary to accomplish the stated objectives and to identify resources necessary to support the overall program. In the third case, "Dover Municipal Hospital," students address problems associated with planning, decision making, and control in a health care setting. The case also illustrates many of the problems associated with managing professional staff in human service organizations.

The case "Selecting the New Commissioner" forces the student to select from among five candidates a new commissioner for the Yorkshire County Department of Social Services. The selection committee seeks someone to deal with problems of staff morale, client complaints, quality of work, staff turnover, and general community pressure for change. Further, the student is given the opportunity to analyze and assess a selection process involving the use of the assessment center technique. "The Teaching Hospital" demonstrates the impact of managerial leadership on the operation of a service delivery unit. The case also deals with the complex nature of organization structure and some of the conflicts that result. "Managing Reductions in the Work Force" presents problems faced by middle-level managers who must plan for a 30-percent reduction in staff budgets. The case deals with problems in cut-back management, with the reorganization of staff, with staff involvement in decision making, and with communication problems.

"A Case of Reasonable Time" focuses on a number of problems common to the management of human service organizations whose employees are represented by a union. The case deals with factors that influence public union membership, the influence of the political environment on labor-management relations, and the impact of unions on management practice. The final case, "Financial Planning for In-Service Training in the Midsize Department of Social Welfare," focuses on the financial planning responsibilities for a single unit. The student is called upon to analyze a financial report, to establish budget controls, and to develop a financial plan for a two-year period.

Management Comes to the Mosaic County Welfare Department

The federal government is responsible for public welfare programs on a nationwide basis. The states oversee these activities within their jurisdictions to see that they are carried out satisfactorily. In many states, units of local government are ultimately responsible for the administration of the programs.

Federal programs in the area of social welfare increased during the sixties and seventies, with a corresponding growth in the number of caseworkers and recipients. More recently, however, the downturn in the economy, coupled with the disenchantment of voters, has forced drastic reductions in the amount of money appropriated for social services. County offices have been forced to resort to a variety of strategies to cope with the future uncertainty of funding levels, ranging from cutting the size of their staffs to actively lobbying on their own behalf at the State Capitol and in Washington.

The State of New Amsterdam Department of Social Services has recently finished analyzing the net effects of federal cutbacks of funds, and the Governor's office was considering simply passing these cuts, estimated to be around 30 percent, directly along to the county offices.

Reprinted with permission. Continuing Education Program, Nelson A. Rockefeller College of Public Affairs and Policy, State University of New York at Albany, 1981.

MOSAIC COUNTY

Five years ago, Sam Pacific was appointed Commissioner of Mosaic County's Welfare Department after spending twenty years as a state legislative assistant and being very active in local politics.

Sam comes from a politically well-connected family. He was appointed several years ago with the change of administration. He accepted his current position as a "last hurrah" that would cap his lifelong career in public service. Since he became Commissioner, the department's caseload has doubled, while the number of assigned caseworkers has slightly decreased.

Even though he is currently facing the problem of losing additional funds and staff at a time when caseloads are up, Sam considers this a good opportunity to "clean house" and "trim the fat."

Sam has done everything he could to allay his staff's anxieties, including soliciting their opinions and encouraging full participation in all actions affecting them, but many remain concerned about their futures. (See Exhibits 1 through 4 for a more detailed description of the Mosaic County Welfare Department.)

EXHIBIT 1. Biographical Sketches

Bertha Clancey. Age: 52; B.S. (Education); employed ten years ago by County Welfare Department in first job, five years in present position.

Karen Dolenz. Age: 26; M.A. (Sociology); two years in present position.

Alex Henchley. Age: 55; B.A. (Accounting); in and out of politics and various agency assignments.

Ruth Lester. Age: 49; B.A. (English); twenty years in County Welfare Department with last six in current position.

Dave Lippman. Age: 38; J.D.; became active in local politics after brief stint in legislative assignments ten years ago.

Chris Luby. Age: 32; B.A. (Anthropology); formerly active in lobbying for social programs and plans on a lengthy career in social work.

Ken Monarchi. Age: 46; B.S. (Economics); built up a solid administrative unit with an emphasis on efficiency.

Sam Pacific. Age: 60; B.A. (Public Affairs); extensive experience in public policy and administration.

Phil Rappaport. Age: 42; B.A. (Communications); formerly worked for small town newspaper.

Arnold Steward. Age: 28; M.S. (Social Welfare); bright and ambitious, aspiring to management position.

EXHIBIT 2.   Organization of Mosaic County Welfare Department

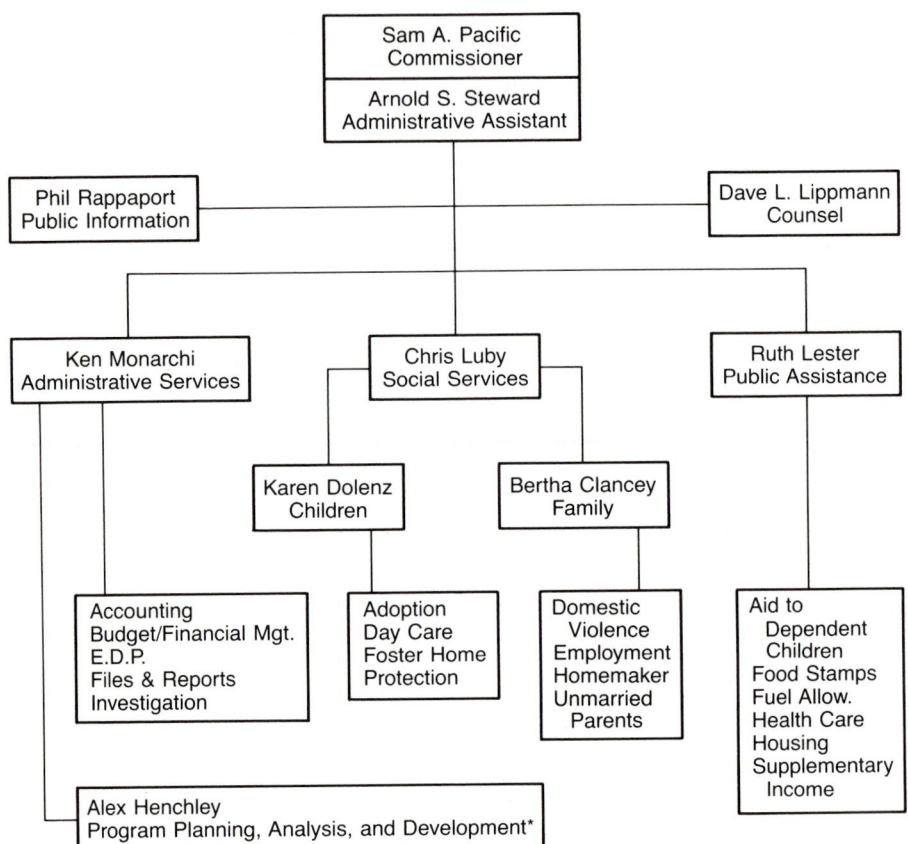

*Newly created

THE FIRST MEMO

Upon arriving at work one Monday morning, staff members at the Mosaic County Welfare Department were astonished to find the following note from the Commissioner on the bulletin board:

Memorandum

TO: All Staff, Mosaic County Welfare Department
FROM: Commissioner Pacific
RE: Reorganization

As you all know, our workloads have been increasing over the years. In an effort to serve our clients more efficiently, I am creating a new office for

EXHIBIT 3. Current Budget Estimates

	LOCAL CONTRIBUTIONS	STATE CONTRIBUTIONS	FEDERAL CONTRIBUTIONS	TOTAL
Director's Office	$ 60,000	$ 60,000	$ ——	$ 120,000
Administrative Assistant:				
Operations	10,000	——	——	10,000
Audit and Control	50,000	110,000	150,000	310,000
MIS	50,000	80,000	100,000	230,000
Public Information	15,000	——	——	15,000
Counsel	——	20,000	——	20,000
Administrative Services	370,000	240,000	——	610,000
(Program Planning, Analysis, and Development)	(165,000)	(175,000)	(——)	(340,000)
Social Services	1,200,000	1,250,000	1,500,000	3,950,000
(Children)	(75,000)	(50,000)	(25,000)	(150,000)
(Family)	(590,000)	(1,080,000)	(1,590,000)	(3,260,000)
Public Assistance	25,000,000	25,000,000	25,000,000	75,000,000
(Medical)	(10,000,000)	(15,000,000)	(20,000,000)	(45,000,000)
TOTALS:	$ 26,755,000	$ 26,760,000	$ 26,750,000	$ 80,265,000

EXHIBIT 4. Approximate Casework Loads

	NUMBER OF CASEWORKERS		NUMBER OF RECIPIENTS	
SERVICE	THIS YEAR	5 YRS. AGO	THIS YEAR	5 YRS. AGO
Adoption	3	4	100	100
Aid to Dependent Children	3	4	600	500
Day Care	3	3	2,000	900
Domestic Violence	1	1	70	25
Employment	2	2	100	100
Food Stamps	3	4	600	500
Foster Home	2	3	1,100	1,100
Fuel Allowances	2	1	300	100
Health	2	2	100	75
Homemaker	1	1	1,200	1,000
Housing	3	2	1,300	1,000
Information	1	1	6,500	300
Protection	2	2	1,800	1,000
Supplementary Income	2	2	100	75
	30	32	15,870	6,775

Program Planning, Analysis, and Development. It will be run by Al Henchley, and he will report to Ken Monarchi of Administrative Services.

Al worked with me on several projects when we were state legislative assistants, and I can assure you that he is a most competent and conscientious individual. He will be responsible for coordinating the programs of the Social Services and Public Assistance offices and will be assisting me with overall department planning and management. I am sure that you will find most useful his ability to provide you with extensive, current, and accurate information. This should help you to reduce duplicate payments, ineligibility, fraud, and waste, and generally help to improve your planning of caseloads and public assistance payments.

Please welcome him aboard as enthusiastically as I do, and give him your full cooperation.

This memo is only one of a number of steps that Pacific has taken to make the best of this opportunity. One of the people that he has utilized in this process is Arnold Steward. Steward joined the staff as Sam's administrative assistant four years ago, having then just received his master's degree in social welfare. Young and enthusiastic, he got along well with many of the caseworkers at the office. Sam immediately made him his right-hand man, giving him general office responsibilities that included planning and monitoring operations, audit and control of activities, and implementing a management information system.

Two weeks before the memo was posted, Arnold had been given a new assignment. Sam asked Arnold to help him establish an aggressive and creative organization that could cope with the inevitable stress that would result from trying to improve services in the face of budget cutbacks. Arnold attacked this challenge by getting ideas from fellow staffers. He initially met with Chris Luby, Director of Social Services, and her two assistants, Karen Dolenz and Bertha Clancey. Their conversation follows.

KAREN: I've lost two people since Sam arrived. During that time, our average caseload has doubled—and I'm still told to operate on a shoestring budget.

BERTHA: Fortunately, we've been able to help each other out. Like that time some lady told us her husband beat her up. She was worried about her kids, and so one of my caseworkers also filled in to help Karen's caseworker. We don't stand on formality when things get hectic around here.

CHRIS: My people have been able to get their jobs done, in spite of all the obstacles thrown in their way. They pitch in whenever they can. Karen hasn't been around that long, but I can remember when Bertha and I spent all of our time helping our clients.

BERTHA: Right. But now, we have to spend too much time helping our own staff fill out our forms!

KAREN: I wouldn't mind the red tape, if I only knew that it was doing some good.

ARNOLD: I hope you appreciate the position I'm in. If it was up to me, I'd approve your funding requests, but since I only work for Sam, we'll have to make do as best we can with what we've got.

CHRIS: It never seems to be enough, does it?

ARNOLD: No, it doesn't.

Arnold's session the next day was with the people responsible for administrative services. This meeting consisted of Phil Rappaport, Director of Public Information; Dave Lippman, Counsel; and Ken Monarchi, Director of Administrative Services.

PHIL: It seems that the more our budget is reduced, the more applicants we get. I spend all day either directing the traffic through here, or I'm on the phone.

DAVE: We're getting a lot of inquiries about eligibility, you know. It seems as though everyone is trying to benefit from some program or other.

KEN: We'll cooperate with you in every way we can, Arnold, but it's becoming very difficult to keep track of all the activity around here. I think I could do a better job of answering your requests for information if we could update our computer system and get some more bodies around here.

ARNOLD: I know, Ken.

(At that moment, Ruth Lester, Director of Public Assistance, abruptly entered the meeting.)

RUTH: Arnold, I just borrowed two of Karen's staffers so we can process the food stamp recipients today. What a line of people out there!

ARNOLD: O.K., Ruth, but in the future, please ask Chris first, and let me know beforehand.

RUTH: Sure. By the way, Phil, I think that many of these people in line don't really belong there.

DAVE: Now, now, Ruth. I don't think they would be here if they were ineligible.

KEN: We would be able to check their requests more thoroughly if we had modern facilities, updated records, and more people.

ARNOLD: I know, Ken. I'm working on it.

(Just then, Sam Pacific calls Arnold to come into his office alone. Arnold entered Sam's office, ready to present some of his ideas.)

SAM: Arnold, what would you think about centralizing all data flow and analyses in one office?

ARNOLD: I think that would relieve a lot of the pressures around here. I could . . .

SAM: Thanks. I'll get back to you later.

ENTER THE PROFESSIONAL MANAGER

It was a few days after Arnold's meeting with Sam that Sam's memo appeared on the bulletin board. The following Monday morning, Alex ("Al") Henchley arrived to begin his new job. His first act was to send the following memorandum to all of the Welfare Department employees, including Sam:

Memorandum

TO: All Employees, Mosaic County Welfare Department
FROM: Al Henchley
RE: Data Analysis

As you are undoubtedly aware, it is my responsibility to gather and analyze data. As such, it will be vital that you submit to me your plans, schedules, and workloads so that we can better allocate our resources, be they time, money, or people.

Over the next few weeks, Henchley received information from everyone and had to work late into the evenings to sort it all out. It seemed that as hard as he tried, he never had time to get through it all. He finally requested a meeting with Sam.

AL: The amount of information I'm getting is overwhelming.

SAM: Well, Al, we do need to get a handle on what's going on. Just try the best you can.

AL: But, Sam, much of what I get is useless. I'm not really interested in knowing the details of specific client problems.

SAM: Do you think our people know that?

AL: No. Perhaps I shouldn't depend on their input and go ahead and just design a new reporting and management system that will provide us with the information that we really need.

SAM: I don't know if that will go over too well.

AL: Maybe it won't, but if we wait for consensus, we will still be talking a year from now and nothing will have changed.

SAM: You're probably right. Why don't you draft something and run it by me before we issue it.

AL: O.K., I'll put something together for you within two weeks.

About three weeks later on a Friday, Chris, Ruth, Karen, and Bertha were discussing how difficult their jobs had become recently.

CHRIS: I just don't understand Sam. You would think he would go easy on us just before his retirement.

RUTH: He isn't so bad. But his friend Al just doesn't understand how we do things around here.

KAREN: That's not unusual—neither do I! You never know from day to day who'll be doing what.

BERTHA: Things sure have changed. I can't wait to retire myself.

Later that afternoon the following memo was circulated to all staff in the Department.

Memorandum

TO: All Employees, Mosaic County Welfare Department
FROM: Al Henchley
RE: Reporting and Management System

A little over two weeks ago, I requested comprehensive data from all divisions focusing upon: (1) division planning; (2) scheduling of activities; and (3) actual workloads. It is essential for me to obtain such detailed information so that it can form a basis for improved program planning and development. Furthermore, it will allow for more efficient allocation of resources. I have thoroughly reviewed the data that has been submitted, and as result of this review, certain issues have become quite clear:

1. Management reporting is inadequate. Data is not standardized from division to division and, therefore, is fragmented, incomplete, and often conflicting.

2. In all program areas there is far too much emphasis upon reporting the details of individual client problems. Such information is valuable for social workers who work with the clients, but it is totally useless for my purposes.

3. There is a pressing and immediate need for an agencywide reporting and management system designed to address the information needs of the Office of Program Planning, Analysis, and Development.

Given the above, I have developed a system that will utilize standardized forms specifically geared to meet my data needs. All staff will be expected to use this system in reporting of activities, etc. Next week I will be meeting with all division heads in order to explain thoroughly how the system will work, staff responsibilities, and my expectations concerning these responsibilities. In turn, they will relay this information to their staffs. I expect that this system will be fully operating throughout the agency within thirty days.

ASSIGNMENT

Within fifteen minutes of the appearance of this memo, Arnold Steward's office was crowded with the division heads. Because both Pacific and Henchley were out of the office until Monday, they took turns threatening Steward with their resignations if the Commissioner didn't put Henchley on a leash. They demanded that Steward deliver this message to the Commissioner on Monday.

You are Arnold Steward. You have the weekend to analyze this situation, develop a strategy for approaching the Commissioner and develop a solution to this crisis. You may wish to consider the following issues in completing the assignment.

1. How adequately is the County Welfare Department currently organized and run? What changes would you recommend?
2. Evaluate Sam Pacific's management style.
3. Could Sam have introduced Al Henchley more effectively?
4. How would you have overcome the problem of data overload, which Al Henchley experienced as a result of his first memo?
5. Was Al Henchley's second memo an appropriate action? If not, what alternatives were available?

Poindexter County
Insight Center

DEMOGRAPHIC CHARACTERISTICS
OF POINDEXTER COUNTY

Poindexter County is located in the west-central part of the state in the "heart of the sun belt." The county and its principal city, Southtown, constitute the major economic center for that region of the state. There are approximately 175,000 residents in Poindexter County, and they are supported by major industrial and agricultural businesses.

Industry in the county includes an automotive tire plant, a chemical plant, coal mining operations, an international corporate headquarters for

Reprinted with permission. Continuing Education Program, Nelson A. Rockefeller College of Public Affairs and Policy, State University of New York at Albany, 1981.

a paper manufacturer, an automotive carburetor assembly plant, an oil refinery, and numerous small manufacturers.

The State University with a student population of 20,000 is located in Southtown along with a small church-supported college, a community college, and a technical school. Southtown is the major retail center for that region of the state, with people driving 60 to 100 miles to shop in Southtown's malls and shopping centers.

Southtown is a transportation hub for the region with two interstate highways, railroads (including AMTRAK), and air service by a major airline.

Agriculture is also a major industry in the county with 619 farms producing 24.991 million dollars of agricultural income in the county.

All of this makes Poindexter's economy broad based and relatively stable.

THE ORIGIN OF A NEW PROGRAM

In 1974 the Poindexter County Department of Social and Rehabilitation Services (DSRS) saw the need to provide additional services to families (generally single-parent families) receiving economic assistance through the various programs of the county. Cathy Johnson, assistant director in charge of Economic Assistance Programs, had convinced Bert Owens, County DSRS director, that the heads of these households needed assistance in such areas as social adjustment, home management, homemaking, family planning, and health related activities. Cathy and Mr. Owens talked at length about the possibilities of a program to provide these services and finally decided that the department should make an effort to provide for client needs in these areas. A survey of AFDC clients was made, and it was determined that the primary needs of this client population were in the areas of social adjustment, nutrition, and primary health care.

Bert asked Cathy to give some additional thought to the matter and to draft a proposal that would include the purpose or mission of the program(s) and what objectives she would hope to accomplish in the first year. She was to include some cost figures as well. Cathy spent several days trying to develop a complete set of plans for the program. She finally worked up the following plan.

Purpose: To provide assistance to Economic Assistance recipient families so that they might develop skills and knowledge in the areas of social adjustment, nutrition planning, family planning and homemaking, and primary health care.

Objectives: To train 180 clients per year in each of the following: (1) to prepare nutritionally balanced meals for their families; (2) to maintain clean homes and to be economic in their household purchasing activities; (3) to use appropriate techniques of family planning, birth control, and child rearing; (4) to recognize the dangers of alcohol abuse; and (5) to be familiar with basic health concepts and to identify and use available medical assistance resources.

Accomplishment of these objectives would involve the commitment of resources of between $15,000 and $20,000 annually. This was based on the following estimates made by Cathy:

Personnel Services	$ 12,500
Program director (¼ time)	
Assistant (½ time)	
Secretary (½ time)	
Operating Expenses	2,200
Supplies, telephone, mileage reimbursement, special activities, insurance, rent	
Capital Outlay	-0-
None planned	
Administrative Overhead	2,612
20.8926% of Personnel services	
TOTAL	$ 17,312

Cathy presented the plan to Bert and he asked for two days to study the plan. At the end of the second day Bert was convinced that the program had merit and called Cathy in to tell her that he would approve the program. It was agreed that the program would be funded through Title XX and that the services should be contracted. Bert called Will Price, the Title XX contract officer, into the meeting to advise him of the desire to secure a contract for the program. Will pointed out that there were several organizations in Poindexter County that would be suitable agencies for implementing the desired programs within the stated purpose of the project. Bert left the project in Cathy's and Will's hands at this point with instructions to keep him informed of the progress being made.

Cathy and Will drew up a request for a proposal (RFP) and sent it to those agencies that were on the Department's list to receive RFPs. A local welfare organization, Tri County Community Services (TCCS), was awarded the contract on the strength of both the technical and the financial aspects of their proposal.

THE IMPLEMENTATION AND EXPANSION
OF THE INSIGHT CENTER

TCCS's proposal included some unique features. These were (1) an advisory committee composed of persons drawn from the Economic Assistance client population, local ministers, and professionals from the fields of medicine, social work, home economics, sociology, or psychology; (2) a registered nurse as the principal or director of the project; (3) a project office in the west end of Southtown, the center of the low income community within Poindexter County; and (4) transportation for clients to the programs.

Beatrice Washington, a registered nurse and social worker with considerable experience, was assigned by TCCS to the project. Her assistant was Jo Lynn, and Meg Duram was assigned to be the secretary. Dan Tice, a young college student who worked part-time for TCCS, was designated to work in the program. Dan's tasks would primarily involve driving the van to pick up and deliver clients. The salaries of three part-time employees brought the total budget for the project to $18,750.

A house was located on the edge of the west end area (for $100 per month) in August of 1974. A meeting of the advisory group was called, and Rev. Dorsey Blake was elected chairman. Beatrice and her staff shared with the advisory group the purpose that the RFP set out for them to accomplish and the specific objectives established by the Poindexter County DSRS. The Advisory Committee quickly accepted the challenge as set forth in the purpose and objectives and committed themselves to help clients to participate in planned programs and to secure resources for the program. A number of resources were secured to make the house adequate for program needs: a stove, a sink, wiring, paint, flooring, and several days of free labor.

On October 3, 1974, the Insight Center, the name the Advisory Committee has chosen for the house, opened with the following scheduled hours:

Monday	7 P.M.–9 P.M.
Tuesday	closed
Wednesday–Thursday	1 P.M.–5 P.M.
Friday	closed
Saturday	9 A.M.–1 P.M.

The initial focus of the programs was nutrition and home economics education. Classes of sixty people (mostly women) were conducted each Monday evening from 7 P.M. to 9 P.M. and Saturdays from 10 A.M. to 12 noon at the Insight Center. Jo Lynn was especially good in this area, since she had spent several years in the field and had attended numerous short courses on nutrition given by the Home Economics Department of State University in Southtown.

Beatrice began a program of home visitation in her efforts to assess the health care needs of the client population. In the months of October and November, she averaged twenty home visits per week. These efforts produced two groups: one of expectant mothers and one with special health problems.

The expectant mothers were organized into a class where prenatal care was taught on Wednesdays and Thursdays, from 1 P.M. to 3 P.M. at the Insight Center. At the end of these classes, a new class on caring for the newborn baby was conducted in the same time slot for this group of women.

The special health problem in the district that Beatrice identified was alcoholism. Beatrice had grown up in the west end of Southtown, and she knew that alcohol consumption was a problem among many of the residents. She attempted to gain the confidence of the clients and soon had several people (again mostly women from the community) enrolled in a class on alcoholism, its symptoms, and what to do when faced with the problem.

After one year of operation, the Poindexter County DSRS evaluation of the Insight Center and its programs indicated that the objectives set forth by Cathy in the original RFP had been substantially met and that the contract with TCCS should be continued.

A new proposal was requested from TCCS. TCCS's proposal recommended an expansion and proposed that the center be maintained on a full-time basis and that the programs be expanded accordingly. The proposal was accepted and funded at the level of $30,800, making Beatrice, Jo, and Meg full-time on the project. The new hours at the center were:

Monday	10 A.M.–9 P.M.
Tuesday	closed
Wednesday	10 A.M.–3 P.M.
Thursday	8 A.M.–5 P.M.
Friday	8 A.M.–5 P.M.
Saturday	10 A.M.–1 P.M.

Programs in social adjustment for teenagers and family planning were added to the expanded programs of nutrition, health care, alcoholism, and home economics. The center also served as a drop-in center and a disseminator of information to families receiving economic assistance on all services for which they were eligible.

The Insight Center continued to operate at its initial location until

---

EXHIBIT 1.   Program Purpose and Objectives

PROGRAM NAME: INSIGHT

PROGRAM PURPOSE AND DESCRIPTION:

The overall goal of this program is to maximize each person's development through education. This program serves young children and clients receiving economic assistance from Poindexter County Department of Social and Rehabilitative Services.

The program provides classes in homemaking, nutrition, family planning, health-related areas of pre- and post-natal care, caring for the infant child, alcoholism, and social adjustment.

The social problem this program attempts to solve is the upgrading of family life for DSRS clients. This is attempted through increasing the functioning level of the clients by providing basic knowledge in those areas listed above.

No fees are charged.

PROGRAM OBJECTIVES:

---

1. To train 180 clients per year to prepare nutritionally balanced meals for their families.
2. To train 180 clients per year to maintain clean homes and to be economic in household purchasing activities.
3. To train 180 clients per year in appropriate techniques in family planning, birth control, and child rearing.
4. To train 180 clients per year in the dangers of alcohol abuse.
5. To train 180 clients per year in basic health concepts, and to identify and use available medical assistance resources.

EXHIBIT 2. Form B: Performance Objectives

Organizational Unit_____
Program Name_____
Sheet Number _____
of Total Sheets_____

Effective Objectives: Assist 75% of the family heads of households to prepare a nutritionally sound meal on a daily basis within the workload established in #1 above by the end of February 1980.

Workload Objectives: Provide a training program to 31 clients for an average of 25 contacts; a minimum of 30 hours per client. This gives an average annual cost per client of $1,259.

MEASUREMENT	CORRES. OBJEC.	PRIOR YR. ACTUAL	CURRENT YR. ESTIMATED	NEXT YR. PROJECTED
Heads of households w/ little or no nutritional standards knowledge	All	318	165	165
Clients served	2	34	37	31
Days of service	2	850	925	775
Hours of service	2	1020	1110	930
Cost per client served	2	1957.50	1846	1259
Cost per day	2	78.30	73.84	50.36
Cost per hour	2	65.25	61.53	41.96
Provide 1 nutritious	1	70%	72%	75%
meal per day		60%	62%	65%

Budget Justification:

September 1978. A different facility was secured at 9003 West 19th Avenue, that was more centrally located, larger, and more structurally sound. The rent was the same as that of the old site. Programs continued to meet the needs of the community and the objectives of the County DSRS.

By 1980, The budget had grown from the original $18,750 to the following (see Exhibits 1, 2, 3, and 4 for details of the budget categories):

Personnel Services	$103,850
Operating Expenses	16,930
Capital Outlay	-0-
Administrative Overhead	15,860
TOTAL	$136,640

EXHIBIT 3. Resource Allocation

PROGRAM: INSIGHT	PRIOR YEAR ACTUAL 1979	CURRENT YEAR ESTIMATED 1980	REQUESTED 6/12/79	APPROVED 6/27/79

POSITIONS	NO. OF POSITIONS				EXPENDITURES			
	PRIOR	CURR.	REQ.	APPD.	PRIOR	CURR.	REQ.	APPD.
Principal	1.00	1.00	1.00					
Secretary	1.00	1.00	1.00					
Social Workers	2.00	2.00	2.00					
Janitor	——	——	.5					
Teacher	2.0	2.0	2.0					
Teaching Assistant	1.0	1.0	.5					
Pediatric Nurse	.5	1.0	1.0					
Total Salaries					87,734	93,044	53,598	
FRINGE BENEFITS 11, 11.6 & 12%					9,651	10,793	6,432	
TOTAL	7.50	8.00	8.00		97,385	103,837	60,030	

DESCRIPTION OF EXPENDITURE	PRIOR	CURR.	REQ.	APPD.
Supplied, telephone, postage, staff improvement, mileage, reimbursement, special activities, food, rent, utilities, depreciation, insurance, etc.	21,105	16,927	5,519	
TOTAL	21,105	16,927	5,519	

DESCRIPTION OF EXPENDITURE	PRIOR	CURR.	REQ.	APPD.
None planned				
TOTAL	-0-	-0-	-0-	-0-

EXHIBIT 4.

DESCRIPTION OF ALLOCATION METHOD	PRIOR	CURR.	REQ.	APPD.

Indirect Cost Rate * × Personal Services
    = 20.892% × $60,030
    = FY 1979–80 Allocation
	14,367	14,857	12,541	

TOTAL	14,367	14,857	12,541	

THE IMPACT OF FUNDING REDUCTIONS

On June 1, 1981, time to begin renewal activities on the contract, Bert Owens advised Cathy Johnson that the Title XX funds available for the Insight Center would be reduced by 25 percent or a total of $25,960. TCCS was called and notified of the cut in Title XX funds and asked to meet with Cathy and Will Price to discuss the upcoming contract negotiations. Jim Ward, Director of TCCS, Beatrice Washington, Jo Lynn, Meg Duram, and Frances McKinley, a social worker who had joined the staff of TCCS in the past year, met with Cathy and Will to discuss the project and its purpose, goals and objectives, and plans for FY 1982. All agreed that the purpose of the program had not changed, only the level of funding. The purpose as restated by the group was to provide training to Poindexter County families receiving economic assistance from DSRS in nutrition, home management, homemaking, social adjustment, family planning, and health related areas.

The group proceeded to discuss the activities of the Insight Center and to exchange ideas on what could be done to maintain the programs at their previous high level of effectiveness. Cathy pointed out that in the initial stages of the program back in 1974, she had set out some clear objectives that were specific, measurable, time bound, and accomplishable with the resources available. She expressed the opinion that she thought that maybe it was time for DSRS, meaning herself, to develop a new set of objectives that the Department would like to accomplish with the approximately $75,000 that would be available for the project. After another hour of discussion, questioning, and "brain storming," Cathy thanked Jim, Beatrice, Jo, Meg, and Frances for their time and help. She assured them that she would have the objectives for the program completed, written, and approved by Mr. Owens no later than Friday, June 19. At that time she and Will would draft an RFP, and TCCS would be asked to submit a proposal to act as a contract provider, just as they had done for the past seven years.

Cathy felt certain that the only way the clients could be assured of getting services that would be comparable to those received in the past was for her to draw up a clear set of objectives. Also, specific measurement criteria, detailed plans and a budget that TCCS could implement would have to be a part of Cathy's job in this critical period of fund reduction. She began this task with the intention of finishing it by Friday of the following week, June 19, 1981.

ASSIGNMENT

Place yourself in Cathy Johnson's position and develop a plan complete with objectives, budgets, and control mechanisms that will ensure that the clients of Poindexter County receive the services outlined in the statement of purpose drawn up in the joint meeting between DSRS and TCCS.

‖ Dover Municipal Hospital*

> *I knew the hospital either made money or lost it based on its professional services. And I knew that you came in contact with the whole hospital through those services; so I said that's what I want to run. I also knew that professional services was filled with the biggest prima donnas on the staff—radiologists, biochemists, cardiologists—each more difficult than the others, and that my predecessor at age 28, had developed a bleeding ulcer and left.*
>
> Chuck Graham, Assistant Administrator
> Dover Municipal Hospital

So thought Chuck Graham when he had accepted responsibility for professional services at Dover Municipal Hospital in Delaware. The past few months had given him a much better insight into just how difficult it was to manage those prima donnas, and now, he had to decide whether or not, how, and how tightly, to put the lid on this business of sending tests to outside laboratories.

THE DOVER MUNICIPAL HOSPITAL

The Dover Municipal Hospital (DMH) was a complex of five buildings located in one of the poorest sections of Delaware's capital city. Constructed mostly in the 1930s, the physical plant was drab, and security was tight. After 5 o'clock in the evening, heavy chains and padlocks secured the doors to passageways leading from one building to another. Nearly all of DMH's patients arrived via the hospital's emergency room, and most of the remainder came through its ambulatory care unit. The Dover police department brought DMH most of the hospital cases it picked up; and other hospitals sent their "dump jobs"—indigent, uninsured patients that these hospitals were "too full" to accommodate.

Case prepared by Professor John R. Russell, Associate Dean, Boston University, under a grant from the National Training and Development Service.
*Names and locations have been disguised.

Throughout its history, DMH had been a teaching hospital, and was currently affiliated with Delaware University's medical school. The hospital was staffed entirely by residents and interns who worked under a salaried senior medical staff that provided both teaching and supervision. No physicians in private practice had staff privileges. All the senior medical staff committed only one quarter to one half their time to the hospital. They were paid an administrative salary by the city, which was all that third-party reimbursers would pay for, and which was only a fraction of what a doctor could earn in private practice or from a full-time job at a private hospital. Most of the physicians augmented their DMH salaries with teaching stipends from the university, salaries received as principal investigators on research grants, jobs managing outside laboratories, and other means. In addition, a special physicians' billing corporation culled the hospital's records to identify patients with third-party reimbursement resources, such as commercial medical insurance, that could be billed for the doctors' services. According to one observer, these arrangements created friction:

> The city wants to pay for clinical care for indigent patients. It doesn't want to pay for research or teaching, or try to make DMH a great research center. The medical staff, on the other hand, are the kind who are willing to give up the money available in private practice because they *are* researchers. And this is where they expect to do their research and their teaching.

The breakdown of billing for inpatient care was Medicare, 20 percent; Blue Cross, 3 percent; Medicaid, 40 percent; commercial insurance, 5 percent; and "self-pay," 35 percent. In practice, the hospital sent all its patients a bill, but did not expect to recover from any of the self-payers. Each year, DMH estimated the cost of the services it would deliver next year, subtracted the amount of third-party and self-paid reimbursements it expected, and submitted the remainder as its annual budget proposal to the city. The city usually cut several million dollars from this proposal, and it was up to the hospital to determine how to absorb the cuts. The current city share of hospital expenses was about $10 million.

At one time, the hospital's capacity had been about 750 beds, but demand for its services had slackened when the advent of Medicaid and Medicare gave many indigents the option of going to other Dover hospitals. Eventually, over half of DMH's beds had been delicensed. The staff currently numbered about 2,000, of whom approximately 150 were interns, residents, or senior medical staff; and the remainder were nurses, technicians, clerical help, maintenance people, messengers, orderlies, and so forth.

The *medical* staff was organized into two major departments—medicine (which included pediatrics, cardiology, gastrointestinal, hematology, pulmonary, and other internal medicine subservices) and surgery (which included obstetrics/gynecology). There was also an outpatient department. The hospital's *administrative* staff reported to an associate director and three assistant directors, one for medicine, one for surgery, and one for professional services. The assistant director for professional services had administrative responsibility for the laboratories and other diagnostic services as well as various support services such as medical records, admitting, social services, messenger, pharmacy, and transportation. (In a few instances, such as the biochemistry laboratory, these professional services subdepartments reported on medical matters to the department of medicine and on administrative matters to the assistant director of professional services.) Both the associate director and the heads of the two medical departments reported to the hospital director, who was hired by the city. The relative influence of the director, the associate director, and the medical staff depended on the individuals who occupied the various positions at a particular time.

CHUCK GRAHAM

In the spring of 1975, the old director of DMH retired and was replaced by Donna Breen. The two were a study in contrasts. Whereas her predecessor has been described as a wily and cautious civil servant who had managed, nevertheless, to alienate city hall, Breen was young, active, and had excellent relations with the city manager and his staff. She had just completed three years as Delaware's assistant commissioner for social services. Breen was without experience in medicine or the health system, but believed firmly that a hospital could be managed well by people who were good managers, but who were not necessarily doctors. She also believed in change and innovation. Good ideas should be tried and mistakes tolerated. Within a few days of Breen's arrival, the associate administrator resigned, and Breen herself decided to occupy the position until a suitable replacement could be found. In the weeks that followed, a great many junior administrators left DMH and others were shifted to new responsibilities. One of the latter was Chuck Graham.

Like Breen, Graham had no medical background. As an undergraduate, he had been a summer intern at DMH and decided he liked working in health. After three years as a Peace Corps volunteer in South America, he returned to DMH, this time as unit coordinator for three wards and the intensive care unit. In this capacity, he was responsible for administrative operations—that is, making sure the units were properly stocked with supplies, dealing with the demands and complaints of the physicians and nurses, supervising the secretaries, and handling other administrative chores. Graham characterized the work as middle management, which to him meant solving whatever problems came up in the wards, and "doing what head nurses used to do but don't want to do anymore." After six months, he had been promoted to assistant manager for the unit coordination department and, after a year, to head of the department. In a few months, he had been promoted again, to junior administrator in charge of 12 support service departments including messenger, transportation, housekeeping, mail, central supply, laundry, kitchen, and several others.

During the fall of 1975, Breen offered Graham any of the three assistant administrator slots, and Graham elected professional services:

I went from managing 12 departments to managing over 20. They said I could give up transportation and messenger, but I decided to keep them. I knew if I wanted to make the labs work, I'd have to control the process from the time a specimen was drawn to the time the results were delivered back to the doctor.

The main additions to Graham's responsibilities were five large decentralized clinical laboratories and several small research labs that performed one or two tests of clinical importance to the hospital. The five were hematology, biochemistry, bacteriology, pathology, and the blood bank. They employed about 200 people. A physician had medical responsibility for each of the labs, and as administrator, Graham would "more or less," as he put it, be in charge of personnel and budget.

If a lab wanted to buy a new piece of equipment, I'd have to sign off on it. On the other hand, if I wanted a lab to do a particular test, the doctor could say, "No, I won't do it." Or, he could say, "I'll do it, but it will cost you two technicians and $100,000 in equipment." In other words, the doctors controlled what went on in the labs. And I had to avoid practicing medicine.

Since the lab chiefs were there only part-time, the day-to-day operations were run by chief technicians who ordered supplies, signed documents, scheduled work, and trained other technicians. Bringing outside work into the labs (except under a contract to which the city was a party) was against the law. While the lab chiefs had the final say on hiring technicians, Graham, theoretically, could fire anyone, including the lab chief himself. In practice this was difficult, because replacing a lab chief for $15,000 to $20,000 meant finding someone in the area who had enough other activities to augment his DMH salary, but who still had enough time left to work one-quarter time for the hospital.

THE TEST LIST

During his early days on the job, Graham was plagued by his own ignorance of the labs and by a barrage of complaints from the doctors:

The physicians, when they're unhappy with the administration, think their best leverage is to complain. Donna [Breen] was moving strongly to shift the balance of who ran the hospital—from the physicians to the administration—and the physicians were fighting it. One thing they did was to complain about the service they were getting from the labs and other support departments. What really was bothering them was Donna's demands that they devote more time to clinical work and less to their research and teaching. She didn't want to support those activities with public funds.

One discovery Graham made was that no one in the hospital knew every test that was offered by the laboratories. His predecessor had tried to compile a list, but failed. Graham decided to try for himself and visited each lab chief:

They all said, "All we've got is a partial list." I said "May I see it?" and they said, "Sure, but it's out-dated. We've added a few tests and dropped a few others. Also, I'm short a few people because of layoffs, and I really don't have time to put a list together for you now."

I began to think that most of the lab chiefs didn't want the administration to know what tests they could perform. It gave them more flexibility.

After two months of trying, Graham had virtually nothing of any value from biochemistry, pathology, or hematology. Bacteriology and the blood bank, on the other hand, had provided him with lists that he thought were complete.

What I did was design a form [see Exhibit 1]. Then I said, "I want a completed form for every test you do. It's getting close to budget time; and if you give me ten tests, that's what I'll base your budget on. If you do 50 more on the sly, you'll have to find the funds on your own." Suddenly, I began to get a little cooperation, and the number of tests that everyone was doing began to go up.

I also began to call the chief lab technicians into my office and deal with them because the physicians were only there part of the time.

It took almost six months, but at the end of that time Graham believed he had a collection of forms that represented, quite accurately, the tests currently being performed. He had also developed the following impressions of the five labs:

Hematology.   The lab consisted of two units: the main hematology lab, where a staff of 30 technicians, blood drawers, and clerks provided round-the-clock service and performed the bulk of hematology testing, and an outpatient laboratory that ran simple tests on ambulatory patients. Little or no research was done in the lab.

The lab chief, who also ran the hematology lab at another Dover hospital, was extremely independent. Said Graham:

If he feels like doing a test, he does it. If he doesn't feel like it, you're out of luck. He's very difficult to get along with, but he's a very skillful hematologist and he runs a quality lab. No matter what you want, though, it's push, shove, and toe-to-toe, and there's always a price attached to it.

He runs the lab like a dictator, and the techs do what he tells them to. But he sends them home two hours early if he thinks that's good for them. And he won't let his techs help with some of the chores that all the other lab techs share.

I've been told that he asks only for new equipment in his budget request, even when he knows some of the most vital older equipment will probably break down soon. Then when it does, you have to add money to his original budget so he can go on performing the tests.

Biochemistry.   Staffed 24 hours a day, 7 days a week, biochemistry was the largest producer of tests in the hospital. It was also the biggest money maker and the best equipped. Daily operations were supervised by a Ph.D.

EXHIBIT 1. Sample of Completed Test Inventory Form

LAB: Central Hematology

1. *Lab test name:*
   White Blood Count (WBC)
2. *What it does (What is its purpose? What does it test for? What sample (Blood, urine, etc.)? Is it a common test?):*
   Very common test
   Blood sample
   Test for:
     infection—leukemia—surgical conditions
3. *How many tests are done per year?:*
   85,000
4. *Is it part of a larger test (i.e., CMC, SMA 12)?:*
   Yes (CBC)—Usually done on Coulter Counter
5. *Charge of this test as of 8/25/76:*
   Manually—$ 4.00
   Coulter —$10.00
6. *Cost of the test as of 10/1/76:*
   $0.50
7. *Automated or manual test (batches or individual)?:*
   Either—Automated = 95%
          Manual   = 5%
8. *How long does it take to perform?*
   Coulter —45 seconds
   Manually—10 minutes
9. *Emergency nature or routine (How quickly is it needed)?:*
   Either
10. *What reagents and equipment are used to perform this test?:*
    Reagents: 2% Acetic Acid—Manually (unopette)
                  Isoton—Lyse S—Coulter
    Equipment: Microscope—coverglass—counting chamber—Tally counter
                  (manually)
                  Coulter models
11. *The hours the test is offered (What is the turn-around time)?:*
    24 hours
    STAT Turn-Around Time—30 minutes or less
12. *Procedure used to perform the test (i.e., radioimmunoassay, etc.):*
    Manual Unit Count by Hand
    Particle Count on Coulter
13. *Who takes the specimen? What container is used? How is it transported?:*
    Phlebotomist—Lavender Top Tube (EDTA)
    By hand to tech—messenger service—pneumatic tube
14. *Amount of sample required:*
    At least half-filled Lavender Top Tube

in chemistry who presided over a staff of about 45 technicians and support personnel. There was also a consulting biochemistry lab which consisted of two people, on a normal 40 hour week, working on research grants and doing a few sophisticated clinical tests.

The chief of biochemistry was new at DMH. He had come to Graham with several requests from his technicians concerning longer lunch hours or shorter work days—all of which Graham had refused. He spent almost all his time either teaching or working on his research in the consulting biochemistry lab. The Ph.D. in chemistry appeared to run the laboratory.

Bacteriology.   From a technical viewpoint, this was the showpiece laboratory. More than in the other labs, the work in microbiology—which involved planting specimens in culture media—was an art form. While the output of the hematology and biochemistry labs was sometimes criticized, the quality of microbiology's output was never questioned. The 40 technicians and bacteriologists worked a five-day week, and because bacteriologists would not read anything that someone else had planted, delays sometimes developed over weekends.

The lab had a degree of fiscal independence that the other labs did not. Almost two thirds of its budget came from a local foundation and another 15 percent from contracts to perform work for Memorial Hospital. DMH paid for only that part of the lab's budget that was not supported by these outside sources.

The lab chief was one of the DMH's medical statesmen. He stayed out of hospital politics and hospital administration, seemed always to have a good word for everyone, and made few demands of his own. When he did ask for something—such as a new piece of equipment—the request was invariably reasonable.

Pathology.   Pathology, with about 90 people, was concerned with the analysis of disease. Its lab chief, who was to retire at the end of 1976, had earned a national reputation in anatomical pathology research. His fundraising efforts had paid for most of the equipment in the building where the lab was housed, and his continuing success at acquiring research grants kept more than a dozen physicians working at the hospital, providing services for which the city did not have to pay. In return for these benefits and the high quality of his work, he expected to be given a budget and then left alone. No one on the Dover University medical staff, except the senior surgeons, ever set foot in the laboratory. Graham visited the area once, but discovered that most of the doors were locked and that keys were not available.

Blood bank.   The blood bank managed DMH's inventory of blood and performed the simple tests necessary to dispensing that inventory properly. Nominally, one of the staff surgeons was the lab chief, but the bank was actually managed by a very pleasant and capable nurse.

THE FREE T-4 INCIDENT

As he was developing the list of tests and becoming more familiar with the laboratories, Graham learned that almost $150,000 in testing (10 percent of the total DMH lab budget) was being sent to labs outside the hospital. After securing a breakdown of these outside tests from the DMH accounting department (see Exhibit 2), he noted that over $20,000 was being spent annually just to perform Free T-4 tests at Memorial Hospital, Dover, where the biochemistry lab was run by a doctor who had recently left DMH. He asked several doctors why this was being done:

> Their answer was something like, "Well, young man, this is a superior methodology being used by a superior laboratory. We've done it that way for three or four years, and it's really none of your business."

Rather than let the issue drop, Graham asked other doctors about the Free T-4 test. He discovered that there was a more advanced method of doing the test that could be set up in the DMH biochemistry lab for an initial cost of about $20,000.

> So I went to my laboratory advisory committee (the group of doctors who advise me on the technical and medical aspects of the labs) and asked them if they thought it would be all right to switch to the new method. They said no. Then I went to biochemistry—since Free T-4s are basically biochemistry tests—and asked if he'd be willing to do them in-house. I was told that it was none of my business, that I wasn't a physician, that Memorial's method was much better, and that biochemistry reported to the department of medicine anyway.
>
> I didn't buy it. I called an out-of-state friend who was a hospital administrator and talked to his clinical pathologist, and he convinced me that the new method was not only better, it was cheaper. He also said the Memorial Hospital method cost a lot less than they were charging us, which made me think our money was being used to support teaching and research over there.
>
> I went back to biochemistry and said, "Will you do it?" But he wouldn't. So I talked to hematology, and he said he'd do it provided I gave him another $15,000-a-year technician.

THE OUTSIDE TESTING ISSUE

In the midst of his efforts to resolve the Free T-4 issue and to compile a complete list of tests, Graham received a phone call from the city's auditor. The auditor, too, was concerned about the amount of outside testing. What was even more disturbing to him, many of the outside labs that DMH used were receiving more than $2,000 in business. The law required that dealings of this amount be covered by a contract, and that these contracts be awarded on the basis of competitive bidding. None of DMH's outside sources were under contract.

EXHIBIT 2. Summary of Outside Laboratory Tests for January 1976

TEST	NUMBER OF TESTS	PRICE	TOTAL
Ag titer to crystococcus	3	$ 20.00	$ 60.00
Alcohol level*	42	16.00†	672.00
Alkaline phosphatase-fractionated*	2	10.00	20.00
Alpha fetoglobin	2	11.00	22.00
Amino and organic acids	1	10.00	10.00
Aminophylline level	1	23.00	23.00
Analysis of kidney stone	2	9.50	19.00
Analysis of urinary calculus	2	9.50	19.00
Anti-mitochondrial antibodies	1	16.50	16.50
Anti-smooth muscle antibodies	1	16.50	16.50
Anti-toxoplasma antibodies	1	18.00	18.00
Australian antigen (HAA)	77	4.75	365.75
Barbiturate level	3	16.50	49.50
Calcium*	64	6.50	416.00
Carcinoembryonic antigen	11	30.00	330.00
Catecholomines	1	16.00	16.00
Chromosomes	1	100.00	100.00
Cortisol*	12	20.00	240.00
CPK—fractionated*	1	8.00	8.00
CPK—isoenzymes	22	19.50	429.00
Digitoxin level*	1	25.00	25.00
Digoxin level*	19	21.00†	399.00
Dilantin level*	20	25.00†	500.00
Dilantin and phenobarb level	1	25.00	25.00
Drugs of abuse	1	35.00	35.00
Elavil and thorazine level	1	20.00	20.00
Estradiol level*	13	38.00†	494.00
Fats*	1	6.00	6.00
Febrile agglutinins	1	10.00	10.00
Fluorescent treponema antibodies	1	9.00	9.00
Free T-4	90	18.00	1,620.00
FSH*	15	22.00†	330.00
Gamma glutamyl transpeptidose	1	10.00	10.00
Gastrin level	5	22.00	110.00
Histoplasma compliment fixation	1	29.25	29.25
Immunoglobulin E	1	15.00	15.00
17-Ketogenic steroids*	1	18.00	18.00
17-Ketosteroids*	1	12.00	12.00
Lap stain*	1	5.00	5.00
Latex fixation*	1	11.00	11.00
Leucine amino peptidose	1	5.00	5.00
LH	15	22.00†	330.00
Lithium level	1	9.00	9.00
Luteinizing hormone	1	19.50	19.50
Mercury level*	2	6.00	12.00
Metanephrine	1	20.00	20.00
Myoglobin	1	10.00	10.00

EXHIBIT 2 (*cont.*)

TEST	NUMBER OF TESTS	PRICE	TOTAL
Mysoline level*	2	$ 18.00†	$ 36.00
Parathyroid hormone	13	49.50	643.50
Phenobarb level*	2	16.50	33.00
Phenothiazine screen	1	3.50	3.50
Phosphorus*	2	4.40	8.80
Pregnanetriol	13	23.00†	299.00
Progesterone*	15	24.00†	360.00
17-OH Progesterone	3	25.00	75.00
Prolactin assay*	13	30.00	390.00
Protein analysis*	1	38.50	38.50
Protein electrophoresis	1	24.00	24.00
Rast profile	1	70.00	70.00
Renin level*	16	25.00	400.00
Rubella	18	8.00	144.00
Salicylate level*	1	5.00	5.00
Semen analysis	1	10.00	10.00
Sensitivity to 5 FC	1	15.00	15.00
Sub B unit level	1	21.00	21.00
Sweat test*	1	35.00	35.00
Tegretol	1	18.00	18.00
Testosterone*	16	32.00†	516.00
Testosterone doxycortisol	1	20.00	20.00
Theophylline level	10	12.00	120.00
Toxic screen (blood)	70	13.00†	910.00
Toxic screen (urine, gastric)	35	13.00†	455.00
Valium level*	2	15.00	30.00
Zarontin level	1	15.00	15.00
	690		$11,634.30

*Can be performed at DMH.
†Average cost.

In response to the auditor's prompting, Graham set out to learn, in detail, how the process worked. He found that physicians who wanted a test performed by an outside laboratory filled out a four-part form and delivered it (together with the specimen) to the secretary of one of the medical staff (see Exhibit 3). (There were about 10 or 12 secretaries throughout the hospital who processed these requisitions.) The secretary sent a messenger, with one copy of the requisition, to the invoice office where the requisition was assigned an invoice number, authorizing payment for the test. The invoice number was filled in on the remaining three copies, the secretary obtained a cab voucher, and the messenger delivered the specimen and two copies of the requisition, via cab, to the outside lab. The remaining copy stayed with the secretary and was eventually filed in the patient's record. When it had performed the tests, the lab returned the results and one copy

EXHIBIT 3. **Requisitions for Outside Laboratory Tests**

/ /

Date   Name of Patient

Hospital Number   Medical Service   Ward or Clinic

USE ADDRESSOGRAPH PLATE OR PRINT LEGIBLY

Requisition for Special Laboratory Tests

Indicate Source of Request:

CPD ☐   Emergency Floor ☐   Ped Walk-In ☐   House Patient ☐

INDICATE IN WRITING LAB DESIRED	SERVICE ORDER NUMBER	TEST NUMBER	ESTIMATED COST

ATTENDING PHYSICIAN-EXTENSION NO.	AUTHORIZED BY:
SPECIMEN SUBMITTED	TEST DESIRED (Do not abbreviate)

D I R E C T I O N S

Specimen containers must be properly labeled with patient and hospital identification prior to being granted a requisition number.

House officers are not to deliver specimens to labs in person, however it is incumbent upon them to specify the lab to which the specimen is to be sent.

Special Instructions:

1. REQUISITION OFFICE

City of Dover — Dover Municipal Hospital — 900 Washington Street of the requisition to the DMH secretary (who transmitted the results to the doctor) and retained the second copy for its records. Periodically, the lab submitted a bill to the DMH invoice office, listing all the tests it had performed by invoice number. The invoice office matched the numbers with its copies of the requisitions, paid the outside lab, and sent the requisition copies to the hospital's billing office, so the costs could be billed to patients and third-party reimbursers.

The system seemed to work reasonably well except for several problems. First, messengers from the outside labs who delivered test results (and sometimes picked up requisitions and specimens) often got lost in DMH and delivered material to the wrong location. Second, the invoice office's copy of the requisition frequently did not arrive in the billing office until long after the patient had been dismissed. Finally, there was no way for the invoice office to know if a test for which it was billed had actually been performed. It was standard practice for the invoice office to pay outside laboratory bills even if the invoice number could not be matched.

When a physician wanted a test done by one of the DMH labs, he obtained the specimen and filled out one of several different in-house, four-part requisition slips, depending on which lab did the test and what test it was. . . . He then stamped the requisition with the patient's name and hospital number. One copy of the requisition stayed in the doctor's department for inclusion in the patient's record, and three copies, together with the specimen, were sent to the laboratory where the test was performed. The lab kept one copy of the requisition, sent one back with the test results, and sent the third to the DMH billing office so the patients and third-party reimbursers could be billed. (Instead of doing the work themselves, physicians could simply ask that a test be performed. In that case, a technician drew the specimen and a secretary filled out the requisitions.) The only substantial problem in this procedure occurred when a physician failed to provide the patient's name and number, or did so illegibly, so that subsequent billing was impossible.

Graham discovered several reasons why physicians sent tests to outside labs:

> Sometimes the senior staff just decided that it made sense to use tests we couldn't or hadn't been performing. We also had some senior staff who ran laboratories outside DMH, and they might say to the house officers, "When you need an Australian antigen, send it to my lab, because I know they do it the way I like it done." They might even ask—as they made their rounds with the house staff—why Australian antigen tests hadn't been ordered for some patients and direct that they be ordered.
>
> A lot of other tests went out because the physicians thought our labs did poor work or because they'd had a fight with the lab chief. The head of hematology had chewed out a lot of interns and residents for criticizing, so they tried to avoid his lab. Sometimes a fleeb (the person who draws the blood sample) would mix up specimens, so a physician would get wildly fluctuating results and conclude it was because the lab wasn't testing properly. Some of the newer interns and residents just didn't know what tests our lab could do.

Graham also discussed, with several house physicians and lab chiefs, the issue of contracting for outside laboratory services. They were all adamantly opposed to the concept.

> City Hall had suggested that we give all the outside work to one laboratory, but there were some reasons why this didn't make sense. If you go to the lowest bidder, you may get someone with poor quality control. Then, once they've got your contract, they may begin to cut corners or reserve their fastest service for other customers. We also were using some small specialty labs that were doing work for us almost as a favor, and the price at a big lab under contract would almost certainly be much more.
>
> I told all this to the auditor, but he wouldn't budge. He wanted everything over $2,000 under contract. He didn't care about the difficulties, and he didn't care if it cost more money. Those were my problems. He just wanted to satisfy the legal requirements for a contract.

Selecting
the New Commissioner

A commissioner for the Yorkshire County Department of Social Services was to be appointed by the County Legislature. The major consideration was to find a person who would be the best equipped to handle a troubled situation. The members of the Legislature agreed that they would not rush into the appointment, but would take their time to find someone who had the potential for turning the department around. The Legislature appointed a three-person selection committee whose responsibility would be to screen the applicants and to submit a recommendation to the full legislative body.

THE SCREENING COMMITTEE

The committee members met to develop criteria that they would be looking for in those individuals who applied for the position. The composition of the committee included John O'Brien, an attorney with 25 years of practice in Yorkshire County. In his practice he specialized in civil cases, but would occasionally take a criminal case if it was of interest to him. He was viewed as a very successful and respected lawyer throughout the community. He lived in a fashionable suburb, was a member of the Northern Estates Country Club, and had previously been the chairman of the United Fund campaign. His commitment to civic concerns was well known throughout the community, and he was frequently referred to as "a person you can depend upon to get the job done." John had been a member of the Legislature for 12 years.

Reprinted with permission. Continuing Education Program, Nelson A. Rockefeller College of Public Affairs and Policy, State University of New York at Albany, 1981.

Mary Santini was a relatively new member of the Legislature. She was in the second year of her term and had gained the respect of her legislative peers. Ms. Santini was viewed as a thoughtful and realistic legislator who frequently was able to bring her colleagues to successful compromise on important issues. Initially, the more seasoned members of the Legislature were reluctant to accept her as a peer, because of her age and the fact that she was the only female member of the Legislature. Additionally, she had been an outspoken supporter of the Equal Rights Amendment as well as a leader in the community on the pro-abortion issue. Mary's husband was the owner of the Ford dealership and had always successfully bid for the county's fleet contract. Mary was a graduate of Marymont College with a bachelor's degree in Fine Arts.

The third member of the screening committee was O. D. Roosevelt. As one of two black members of the Legislature, he had been reasonably successful in gaining the respect of the other members. Mr. Roosevelt was in his sixth year as a legislator and had spent much of his time campaigning to upgrade the predominantly black sections of the community. He worked for the regional labor council as a union organizer and had performed very well in this capacity. On several occasions he found himself "on the other side of the table" from the industrial leaders in the community, many of whom moved in the same circles as the legislators. O. D. was viewed as a "trouble-maker" who stirred up the workers, yet he was respected for his skill in bringing labor and management together to improve working conditions. His mother was retired and was currently receiving Social Security benefits. She often complained to him about the attitudes of the workers at the local Social Security office as well as her frequent problems with the social workers with whom she talked about her Medicare benefits. In two separate situations O. D. accompanied his mother to the local office of the Department of Social Services to assist her in "dealing with the bureaucracy."

THE CRITERIA FOR SELECTION

The committee agreed to recommend that the announcement for the position should be open and not limited to individuals already working for the Department of Social Services. This recommendation was approved by the Legislature and an announcement was prepared. (See Exhibit 1.) The overriding concern was that whoever was appointed should be a "good manager." It was the judgment of the committee that the problems which had developed over the past three years in the department were the result of poor and inadequate management. Someone was needed who could make sound decisions. There was a great deal of discussion as to whether or not the new commissioner should have had previous experience in the social services field. After much debate, it was concluded that such experience would be preferable but not mandatory. Mr. O'Brien stated, "What we need is someone who can get the job done."

The committee was aware that the state office in Albany had devel-

EXHIBIT 1.   Commissioner of Social Services

Yorkshire County, New York, is seeking candidates for the position of Commissioner of Social Services. Yorkshire County is located in central New York and has a population of 400,000 and a large private university.

Qualifications for the position include a bachelor's degree from a recognized college or university and, preferably, a post-graduate degree in social work, public administration, hospital administration, education administration, or business administration. Previous experience should include at least six years of responsible full-time paid experience in an administrative or management position, where there was responsibility for planning, directing, and coordinating the work of a substantial staff working in several units or performing several separate functions.

Interested applicants should submit a detailed résumé, including present and previous management experience, to the Screening Committee, Yorkshire County, New York 16123.

Salary and fringe benefits are competitive.

An Equal Opportunity Employer

---

oped guidelines for the commissioner's position and that there were state statutes that affected the selection. They also knew that the Legislature made the appointment. The state's guidelines and the Statutes were rather general and left a lot of room for interpretation. (See Exhibit 2.). The committee members intended to exercise their responsibility to influence the appointment. The committee reviewed various state and federal regulations relative to Affirmative Action guidelines and other material dealing with discriminatory practices and agreed that these would have to be taken into consideration.

The announcement for the position was sent out and placed in several publications, including the *New York Times.* It was agreed that the search would be kept open for 90 days. The committee would not review any of the applicants until the search was closed on October 15.

THE METHOD OF SELECTION

A procedure for processing the applicants was developed by the committee. Each member of the committee would go over all of the applicants and sort them into two groups: those who qualified and those who did not. Then they would go over those that qualified and individually rank the applicants. Once this was done by each of the committee members, they would then get together and share their individual rankings. The final list of applicants would be determined by a consensus of the committee. It was agreed that the final list should not exceed five candidates.

Once identified, the five candidates would be contacted and if they continued to be interested, they would remain on the list. If any of the top five individuals was no longer interested, then he or she should be removed

EXHIBIT 2.

Title 18, New York State Social Services Law, Part 679

Specifications for Local Social Services Commissioner and Deputy Social Services Commissioner

679.5 Commissioners of districts in Group II: minimum qualifications for appointment. Candidates shall have the following minimum training and experience:

(a) *Training.* Graduation from a recognized college or university with a bachelor's degree for a four-year course of study, and

(b) *Experience.* (1) Six years of satisfactory full-time paid experience in a health, education, or social services agency, four years' services of which must have been in a satisfactory administrative or supervisory capacity, or (2) Six years of responsible full-time paid experience in an administrative or management position where there is responsibility for planning, directing, and coordinating the work of a substantial staff working in several units or performing several separate functions.

(c) *Experience as local social services commissioner.* Each year of experience as a chief executive officer of a social services district, within six years immediately preceding the date on which he or she is appointed, shall be the equivalent of two years of the above prescribed experience.

(d) *Post-graduate training.* Post-graduate training at a recognized college or university in social work, public administration, hospital administration, educational administration or business administration shall be the equivalent, on a year for year basis up to two years, of the above prescribed experience. However, no such post-graduate training shall be the equivalent of the administrative or supervisory experience prescribed in paragraph (1) or subdivision (b) of this section.

---

from the list and replaced by the next person with the highest ranking. From the final five, one name would be submitted to the full legislative body as the person recommended for appointment.

The committee concluded that the most appropriate method of identifying the "best manager" was to use the assessment center technique. The state had been using this technique for selection for the past three years and the consensus was that it was the most unbiased and defensible approach. Prior to establishing the specific assessment center, they agreed that they should consult with the State Department of Personnel as well as with the personnel office in the State Department of Social Services. This would be done during the ninety-day period that the search was open.

THE ASSESSMENT CENTER

Following several meetings and discussions with personnel in the respective state offices, it was concluded that there were eight key factors that should be assessed in the assessment center. This was determined through extensive consultation with the individuals in the Department of Personnel who were responsible for assisting agencies in the development of assessment

EXHIBIT 3. Assessment Centers

An assessment center is a system of management and supervisory simulations used to evaluate dimensions that have been identified as important for a particular position in an organization. There are three ways in which it differs from other evaluation techniques:

1. It uses multiple job-related simulations to elicit behavior.
2. It evaluates groups of individuals at the same time.
3. Trained observers assess and evaluate the performance of the candidates.

The assessment center is tailored to evaluate those dimensions that have been identified for a specific employee population. As a technique for selection and development of managerial and supervisory personnel, it has been widely used in the private sector. In recent years it has been utilized in various facets of the public sector. It is a fair, job-related, and defensible method for identifying potential for success at supervisory and managerial levels. Individuals who have been chosen by this method have been found to be two to three times more likely to be successful at higher management levels than those who have been promoted on the basis of supervisory judgment. Further, the method has been found to be equally accurate for all protected groups.

A typical assessment center will involve four to six participants and will last for two days. Participants take part in exercises, such as an interview simulation, a group discussion, a fact-finding exercise, and an in-basket exercise, that have been designed to expose dimensions deemed important for a particular targeted position. Trained assessors observe each participant as he or she goes through the exercises. Each participant will be observed by a different assessor for each of the exercises. For example, if four exercises are used in the assessment center, then four different assessors would observe a participant. Following the two days the participants spend in the center, the assessors share their observations and reach agreement on the performance of each participant.

DIMENSIONS

LEADERSHIP—Utilization of appropriate interpersonal styles and methods in guiding individuals (subordinates, peers, superiors) or groups toward task accomplishment.
> This refers to the ability of an individual to get others to follow his or her direction toward task accomplishment, for example, contributing ideas and suggestions in a group discussion that are accepted by the group. Additional examples would be allocating time, monitoring the group discussion, attempting to achieve consensus.

PLANNING AND ORGANIZING—Ability to establish a course of action for self and/or others to accomplish a specific goal; planning proper assignments of personnel and appropriate allocation of resources.
> This dimension refers to the process of planning one's own time and the time of subordinates. Examples include the use of a calendar, tickler file, "to do" lists establishing times and dates for follow-up meetings, memos, reports. It also requires the demonstration of awareness of available resources and the establishment of priorities of tasks and activities.

DELEGATION—Utilizing subordinates effectively. Allocating decision-making and other responsibilities to the appropriate subordinates.
> This refers to the utilization of appropriate subordinates by understanding where a decision can best be made appropriately. This includes giving clear instructions to subordinates about assigned work, and the proper delegation of information-gathering tasks and decision making.

EXHIBIT 3 *(cont.)*

PROBLEM ANALYSIS—Identifying problems, securing relevant information, relating data from different sources, and identifying possible causes of problems.

An individual must display the understanding of background information, be able to identify major problems, relate available data to the major problems, and assimilate and use new information appropriately.

JUDGMENT—Ability to make decisions based on logical assumptions that reflect factual information and the ability to develop alternative courses of action.

This refers to the candidate's ability to make decisions based on logical assumptions from factual information available. This dimension requires evidence that alternative courses of action have been considered and that the candidate is aware of the ramifications of his/her decisions.

SENSITIVITY—Actions that indicate a consideration for the feelings and needs of others.

The candidate can demonstrate this by showing an awareness of and respect for the needs of others, both in face-to-face discussions and in writing, by acknowledging the needs of others' projects, showing concern for subordinates in handling sensitive situations, acknowledging extra effort by subordinates.

COMMUNICATION SKILLS—Effective expression in individual or group situations including gestures and other forms of nonverbal communication.

The candidate should demonstrate the ability to state ideas in a clear, audible, concise manner. Examples would include both one-to-one and group situations: presenting a budget proposal to the Legislature, interviewing perspective employees, acting as a member of a task force.

DECISIVENESS—Readiness to make decisions, render judgments, take action, or commit oneself.

Individuals must make decisions when information is available or when a due date requires it and remain committed to a decision unless presented with new information that would require a modification of the original decision. A poor performer would shun decisions by not making a decision—this is indecisiveness, i.e., "pass-the-buck."

centers. The new commissioner would have to be particularly well suited to demonstrate the ability or skills defined by the eight factors or dimensions. Three simulation exercises were selected that would provide the opportunity to assess each candidate's performance. (See Exhibits 3 and 4 for a list of the dimensions and the exercises.)

Through consultation with the State Personnel Office and the State Department of Social Services, the following priority ranking for the dimensions was agreed upon:

DIMENSION	RANK
Leadership	1
Planning and Organizing	2
Delegation	3
Problem Analysis	4

DIMENSION	RANK
Judgment	5
Decisiveness	6
Oral Communication Skill	7
Sensitivity	8

In light of the problems in the Yorkshire office, it would be crucial that the new commissioner be a strong leader; hence, it was the number one priority.

Prior to conducting the assessment center procedure, 10 individuals were trained as assessors. Each of the ten assessors was in a top management position at either the county or state level. In selecting the assessors, the basic criterion was that they would have an understanding of the commissioner's position.

THE YORKSHIRE OFFICE

The Yorkshire office has experienced considerable difficulty during the past three years. Staff morale has reached an all-time low, client complaints have become more frequent, the error rates in the AFDC and Food Stamps programs have been alarmingly high, and turnover among the staff exceeded 40 percent in the last year. To complicate the situation, the Welfare

EXHIBIT 4. Dimensions Observable by Exercise

IN-BASKET

Sensitivity
Planning and organizing
Delegation
Problem analysis
Judgment
Decisiveness

GROUP DISCUSSION

Communication skill
Leadership
Sensitivity

INTERVIEW SIMULATION

Communication skill
Sensitivity
Leadership
Problem analysis
Judgment
Decisiveness

Rights Organization demonstrated at the office on six occasions during the past year, and one of their demands was that a black commissioner be appointed. In general, the office was in chaos.

The previous commissioner, Matt Smart, was in the position for seven years. He came to the position highly recommended and with a good background in social services. Prior to becoming the commissioner, he had been a deputy commissioner for Social Services in one of the counties of New York City. In this capacity he had performed in outstanding fashion. In his interview with the County Legislature he impressed everyone as the person for the job. For the first three years, his performance as commissioner was quite good. The staff, at all levels, appreciated his openness and availability. He effectively utilized his staff, and the office was frequently used as an example of how a public social service agency should function. However, in his fourth year, following a traumatic divorce, the situation began to change. His interest in the job deteriorated. He often was not in the office, and when he was there, he frequently refused to see anyone. If a member of the staff tried to talk to him about a problem, his typical response was, "That's your problem." As a result of the manner in which he was handling his job, others in the office began to take an "I don't care attitude." When it became public knowledge that he was living with one of the supervisors in the Protective Services Unit, it was decided that the only answer was to remove him from the job and to look for a new commissioner.

The Yorkshire office was relatively large. The number of cases served in the past year was 23,531. Of these, one-third were receiving Aid to Families with Dependent Children payments, and another third were receiving Medical Assistance. A substantial number of the recipients were members of minority groups. At the end of the last fiscal year there were 375 employees in the office, one-third of whom would be considered professionals. Last year's expenditures exceeded $57,000,000, a significant portion of which was federal money.

YORKSHIRE COUNTY

Yorkshire County is located in the center of the state. Its population is approximately 400,000. Of this number, 20 percent are black and 5 percent are of Latin-American origin, with many of the latter having moved to the area from New York City in search of employment opportunities. There is one major metropolitan center with a population of 200,000, and most of the remaining population is located in four smaller cities in the county. Approximately 15,000 people live in the rural areas. The county is heavily Republican and supported Ronald Reagan by a five-to-one ratio in the last presidential election.

In the county there is a large private university with 22,000 students. The university has an international reputation and is particularly noted for its outstanding engineering programs. The relationship between the university and the community is very compatible, and the resources at the university have often been drawn upon to deal with issues and concerns within the county. Over one-third of the population is either directly or indirectly reliant upon the university for employment; therefore, it is the highest source of employment in the county.

There are also two sizable manufacturing companies in the county, each employing over 2,500 employees. The remainder of the labor force is employed in smaller manufacturing and retailing firms or in industries related to agriculture. The unemployment rate in the county fluctuates between 7 and 8 percent. Meanwhile, 8.3 percent of the population is considered below the poverty level.

THE CANDIDATES

Martha Simpson is 42, white, recently divorced, and has had extensive supervisory and managerial experience with a sizable insurance company in Hartford, Connecticut. She has been with the insurance company for 12 years and was selected for their management development program after being there for two years. Her present position is manager of the small claims division. As a native of New York, she is interested in coming back to an area closer to her family. Her only child, a daughter, will be a senior in high school and has been interested in attending the university in Yorkshire County. Ms. Simpson graduated from the University of Pennsylvania with a bachelor's degree in business and completed her M.B.A. degree by attending night classes at the University of Connecticut. She is very ambitious, has moved rapidly "up the corporate ladder." A colleague at the insurance company described her as "a lady who looks out for number one." In response to the question of why she was interested in the commissioner's position, she stated, "I see it as a challenge and I am getting a bit stale in the insurance business."

Thomas McKinney is 45, white, and has worked for the Department of Social Services in one capacity or another for twenty-two years. He is currently the deputy commissioner of Administrative Services in Yorkshire County, a position he has held for nine years. During the interim period since the previous commissioner was removed, he has been the acting commissioner. Most of the people in the office like Tom, but feel that he is too concerned about money issues rather than quality services for the clients. However, since he has been acting commissioner, he has worked closely with the County Legislature as well as the state office to maintain sufficient funding to keep services at an acceptable level. He has been able to establish a good rapport with the county legislators and has been described by some as a welcome relief from the past commissioner. Tom is married and has five children; two still live at home. He has a bachelor's degree in accounting from the State University.

Susan Trost is 37, single, black, and has been the deputy commissioner of Social Services in Yorkshire County for the past three years. She is very active in civic and community affairs and is a recognized leader in the black community. Ms. Trost has an M.S.W. degree from Columbia University, and prior to becoming the deputy commissioner, she was a supervisor and caseworker in the department. She was born and raised in Yorkshire County and has not expressed interest in leaving. She describes herself as one who has come up through the ranks and knows what it is like to carry a caseload. While she has been an effective administrator, she has alienated some of her staff who complain that she identifies with the clients too frequently. When it was decided that the previous commissioner would be removed, Ms. Trost felt that she was the best qualified person to be the acting commissioner and continues to harbor resentment toward the Legislature for not appointing her. She has been successful in getting a cadre of the professional staff to support her and this group has been "a thorn in the side" for McKinney. To put it mildly, there is some bad blood between Trost and McKinney. Another issue that has caused some concern is that Ms. Trost is presently living with a man, and this has caused some repercussions in the conservative environs of Yorkshire County.

Samuel Johnson is 35, white, and has substantial support among the legislators. He is currently the director of the United Fund, and the general opinion within the community is that he got the position because of his family's standing in the community. The Civic Center bears the name of his grandfather, Myron Johnson, signifying the role the family has played over the years. Mr. Johnson has been described as an eager, bright, well-intentioned individual, yet often his motives have been suspect. He has been very active in the Young Republicans and four years ago was the state chairman of that organization. Prior to coming to the United Fund, he was a legislative aide to the Speaker of the State Assembly and also served on the staff of Senator Ritwing in Washington. His credentials for the position are impressive. In addition to his bachelor's degree in history from Harvard, he also has an M.P.A. degree from a reputable university on the East coast. During his three-year tenure with the United Fund, the annual goal has doubled. He is married to the daughter of the county executive and has two young children.

Marvin Leibowitz is 54, white, and currently director of the Family Service Association in a large suburban area outside of New York City. Prior to moving into his present position, Mr. Leibowitz had worked with the Department of Social Services in supervisory and managerial positions in the Lake Erie region of the state. For 10 years he was commissioner of a medium-size county department located twenty-five miles east of Buffalo. During his time with the department, he was viewed as a successful commissioner and one the system did not want to lose. A massive heart attack, which immobilized him for several months, required that he find a less stressful work environment, and at that time he took the position he currently holds. Mr. Leibowitz is considered one of the leading authorities on public welfare policy and has written numerous articles and three books on this area. An intellectual, he has often demonstrated impatience with the "nitty-gritty" matters of welfare, and the one complaint from those that worked for him was that he is only comfortable with those of similar intellectual ability. This led to some problems with his staff, but from all indications, nothing that was insurmountable. He was born and raised in New

York City and earned his bachelor's degree in economics from City College and his M.S.W. degree from Yeshiva University. He has completed all but his dissertation for his doctorate in social work from Columbia University.

THE SELECTION PROCESS

On November 5, the five candidates came to the assessment center. Each of them completed the three exercises: an in-basket exercise, an interview simulation, and a group discussion exercise. During their session at the center, each was observed by a trained assessor. Each assessor had been trained to observe only the candidate's behavior—what actually was said or done.

After each of the candidates completed the exercises, the assessors got together with the center administrator, and a consensus was reached on ratings for each of the candidates. The following rating scale was used for each of the eight dimensions:

5 = Much more than satisfactory
4 = More than satisfactory
3 = Satisfactory
2 = Less than satisfactory
1 = Much less than satisfactory

With this scale, a rating of 3 indicates that a satisfactory amount of the dimension was evident during the assessment center exercises. Any rating above 3 indicates that the performance exceeded what would be considered satisfactory to do the job.

The profiles for the five candidates were as follows:

DIMENSION	SIMPSON	MCKINNEY	TROST	JOHNSON	LEIBOWITZ
Leadership	5	3	4	5	4
Planning and Organizing	4	4	2	3	5
Delegation	4	2	3	4	4
Problem Analysis	4	4	2	5	5
Judgment	5	4	3	5	5
Decisiveness	5	2	4	5	5
Oral Communication Skill	5	3	5	4	3
Sensitivity	2	4	3	4	2

It was now the committee's decision to select the individual who would be recommended for the commissioner's position.

ASSIGNMENTS

1. Of the five applicants, who would be the "best manager" for the commissioner's position? Evaluate the strengths and weaknesses of each applicant in developing a rationale for your selection. What might be the ramifications of your selection?

2. Evaluate the process that was used for selecting the new commissioner. Was it fair? Were there any flaws in the process? If so, what were they? Provide an alternative process that would be better, keeping in mind the situation presented in the case.

3. Evaluate the use of the assessment center technique for selection. Identify the strengths of this approach as well as its weaknesses. Was the assessment center that was used adequate? Should it be used as the only basis for selection? If so, why? If not, why not?

4. What is your assessment of the choice of the screening committee? Was it equipped to make the critical decisions that were required? Again, provide your rationale for the position you take.

5. What are the pros and cons of open competition vs. promoting someone from within. What are some potential problems that might arise by not promoting from within the ranks of those initially qualified? What are some of the advantages of bringing in someone from the outside?

The Teaching Hospital

Dr. Robert Uric was the head of the Renal Medicine Unit at a large university medical school and teaching hospital. A regional medical center, the teaching hospital had over 1,000 beds and was considered a reasonably prestigious assignment, although no one fooled himself that it was the Mayo Clinic.

There was a steady undercurrent of hostility and competition between the hospital and the medical school. A state school, and state-supported hospital, the two institutions had only one official in common—the provost. From the provost down, the organization split in half, with the medical school, its M.D. faculty, and nursing faculty on one side, and the hospital administrator, nonmedical hospital employees, and technicians on the other.

The physical plant paralleled and accentuated the organizational structure. Designed in the shape of an "H", the medical school ran east-west, ten floors high on the north side, and the hospital ran east-west, eight stories high on the south. They were connected only by the bar of the "H", an officeless corridor connecting the medical school and the hospital on each of the first six floors.

A large part of the problem was the unusual nature of the financial arrangements. The physicians, as faculty members, received salaries, but no money for patient services. Patients were billed for professional services, but the revenues went into department funds which were disbursed at the discretion of the department chairmen. The hospital, on the other hand, turned in every patient-revenue dollar to the state and then had to turn around and beg for, and account for, every penny of operating revenue they got.

Grant monies further complicated the situation, especially in the area of salaries. Hospital employees were civil service, strictly regulated by job classifications and wage scales; no exceptions were made. The medical school faculty, however, could frequently use grant money to supplement state salary scale, hire people outright at higher salaries, or use the grant money to provide nonsalary perquisites. Because of this, working conditions were also frequently better on the medical school side, and they had money for more equipment, more travel, and even more parties.

The inconsistencies between the operations of the hospital and the medical school were highlighted by the integration of medical school faculty into hospital functions; the situation was aggravated by the reports of technicians, patient-floor employees, and clinical clerks. These hospital personnel worked directly under the physicians and nurses from the medical school faculty, who were also administrative heads of clinical hospital departments, and were in rather good positions to observe and hear of differences between the hospital and teaching sides. (Qualified physicians were felt to be necessary in heading clinical hospital departments because of the technical natures of the departments' functions and from medical necessity.)

Assistant hospital directors were in charge of most administrative matters, including administration of wage and benefit programs; department heads (physicians), however, were responsible for supervising departmental activities, evaluating employees, and recommending raises and promotions. It left the employees in a situation of very divided responsibilities. Further, the general disdain which the physicians felt for hospital administrators left the assistant directors in the position of mere figureheads in the area of clinical services. The hospital personnel, seemingly from the administrators down to the clinic clerks, complained that the physicians were prima donnas who considered themselves the next best thing to being divine. The medical personnel, on the other hand, complained that hospital personnel were civil service, time-serving incompetents.

One exception was Dr. Robert Uric, head of the Renal Unit. Despite the difficulty of his job, and his apparent membership in the faculty group, Dr. Uric was roundly liked by the hospital employees with whom he worked. One reason was that he shared whenever possible the largess of his grant monies with the hospital employees in his Renal Unit. Financially and emotionally, the hospital Renal Unit, not the medical school Department of Medicine, was Dr. Uric's home and favorite child.

The Renal Medicine Unit at the teaching hospital, like many other renal units, received what might be termed stepchild treatment, banished to a subbasement where most of the other faculty and staff could avoid the painful realities of chronic kidney patients. Nevertheless, the Renal Unit was a cheerful place. The staff, under Uric's leadership, maintained high morale, remarkably high in view of the hopelessness of many cases and the frequent deaths of patients who spent years visiting the unit and who became, in time, almost members of a large family. The job done by the renal staffers—residents, interns, and technicians alike—was sincerely appreciated by the patients and their families and was a source of wonder to those outside faculty and staff who were familiar with the conditions in the dungeonlike Renal Unit. As a matter of fact, Dr. Uric himself was something of a wonder.

On nice afternoons he could be seen strolling the grounds, pop bottle and hero sandwich in hand, trailed by a half-dozen students, teaching Socratic-style among the birch trees and the squirrels. Brown-bagging his lunch was not the least of Uric's peculiarities; many stories circulated including the tale of his being given a ticket for speeding down one of the steep campus hills on his bicycle. Also, through those who knew someone in the Renal Unit, other stories began to leak out; tales of Friday afternoon parties fueled with grain alcohol and Hawaiian Punch, and worse yet, rumors of a monthly rabbit roast in which experimental animals whose transplants didn't take were put away painlessly and barbequed over a pair of Bunsen burners.

Other faculty members found Uric to be a constant source of embarrassment and discomfort. His actions were "undignified"; for a research physician he was entirely too involved with his patients. He actually cried, openly, when his patients died; most unprofessional! Still, he was a fine director of renal medicine, and a remarkable teacher, and he was, after all, an inside joke.

That all changed with Flower Life.

Dr. Uric had several federal grants from the National Institutes of Health (NIH) to pursue research on kidney transplantation. He had begun doing active research within the first year after taking over the Renal Unit. Not the type of man to become fascinated by academic questions, Uric had become almost obsessed with the need for answers when he saw his patients suffering and dying because treatments were not available. He began by solving small, individual problems for specific patients and then generalizing and publishing the solutions. Gaining confidence from his initial successes, Uric applied for, and got, grant money and began working on the larger problems facing patients with chronic kidney failure.

A major problem in transplantation is keeping the kidney properly diffused (alive and full of fluid) between donor and recipient, and Uric was involved in this aspect of the problem. In the course of his work he discovered a fluid that was absorbed much faster than water at the cellular level. Testing showed it to be ineffective as a solution for diffusion, but it occurred to Uric that if plants absorbed it as well as cells it might make a good fluid for cut flowers, extending their life. After finding the right combination of fluid and an acid substance to keep the cut stem end from closing, Dr. Uric decided he did have a substance superior to anything on the market.

As required by the grant agreement, Uric reported his discovery to NIH. They said they didn't want it. Ownership next belonged to the university, and Uric offered it to them. They smiled indulgently and said he could keep it. Not a man to be easily discouraged, Uric next offered his discovery to a large nursery supply manufacturer. They bought it, named it Flower Life, and began making millions. All of a sudden, NIH had a change of heart and filed suit. The story broke in the newspapers, first locally, then regionally, then nationally; needless to say, Dr. Uric made "fun" copy.

Uric and his peculiarities were no longer a private joke, and the faculty became concerned for the "reputation of the school." At the next Executive Committee meeting, the heads of the clinical departments discussed the situation with the dean and suggested that perhaps Uric should be put in a "less visible" position until things quieted down. The dean agreed. The Executive Committee felt they should move carefully; Uric was, after all, tenured and very popular with the students and house staff. It wouldn't do to let this look like persecution. They finally settled on approaching the provost with a plan to establish a new research chair in medicine. Backed by the dean, and financed by donated money from the chairman's department funds, the plan was approved and Uric was hastily offered the position. At first he refused, but it was made subtly clear that if the university were to be expected to back him in the impending litigation, he would have to help out by surrounding himself with an air of respectability. Uric accepted and was given a big raise and transferred to a beautifully equipped new lab on the tenth floor of the main building; the chief resident on renal medicine, Dr. George Conrad, was placed in charge of the dialysis unit.

The chief resident had a reputation for being a "hard nose." He had gone to medical school at a smaller university and had been very happy to get an internship and residency at a large teaching hospital. An excellent student, Conrad had also applied to Bellevue, the hospital arm of N.Y.U., and to several other major teaching hospitals. This had been his only acceptance, and the evaluation committee had looked long and hard at his application before accepting him. While his grades and aptitude tests showed him to be an extremely bright and an extraordinarily dedicated young man, his reference letters revealed an inflexible and rather ruthless individual. Born and raised in very poor surroundings, George Conrad was determined to become a doctor and surround himself with that safe and apparently impenetrable aura of the physician—financially, socially, and professionally secure. He had an image of the "physician"—wise, aloof, self-controlled, and as close to infallible as a man can get. Somewhat insecure about his origins, Conrad had long ago assumed the facade of what he thought a physician should look like, and by this time it was hard, even for him, to tell whether it was still facade or had become reality.

With Uric's removal, the members of the Executive Committee felt that this man was ideal to assume the reponsibility for the unit. They felt Conrad would apply "a strong hand." The assignment was turned over to him by the chairman of the anesthesiology department, a powerful and respected member of the committee. The chairman told Conrad that the committee was certain he could handle it, and that they didn't expect to hear of any problems from the unit under his capable guidance. The chairman also suggested that Conrad be firm in asking Uric to stay away from the unit and thereby allow the transition of authority to proceed most quickly.

The Executive Committee expected a period of adjustment, but disruptions of routine exceeded anything they imagined. Employees in the dialysis unit became serious personnel problems with increased absences and constant grievances about impossible working conditions. While these complaints were pouring into the Hospital Personnel Office through grievance procedures, few or no messages were coming through to the Executive Committee or the dean. The hospital administration, unable to alter matters without the concurrence of the department head, in this case Dr. Conrad, waited for appropriate authorization to investigate the matter and attempt to improve conditions.

By the end of the first month the turnovers had started; after three months ninety of the old employees were gone. Dr. Conrad did not believe in becoming involved with patients on a personal basis, and he appeared to feel the same way about subordinates. Interns on rotation through renal medicine complained bitterly about Conrad's attitude toward, and treatment of, them; the roster of residents applying to the service dropped dramatically.

Meanwhile upstairs, Uric's research work was stale, and his disposition matched. He failed to turn in a grant progress report on time, and the granting agency flexed its muscle and canceled the remainder of his funding.

The dean was not happy and the Executive Committee was far from delighted, but everyone still believed it would all straighten itself out. Nobody, however, believed the problem to be serious enough to investigate the effects on the kidney patients and how the patients were doing down in the subbasement. They might have even forgotten that the dialysis unit was down there. When news did come out, its effects were far more damaging than any tales of Dr. Uric's weird habits could possibly have been.

A patient who had been on dialysis (three times a week) for several years had given up her place and gone home to die. A rare blood and tissue type, the woman had been waiting a long time for a transplant. She had seen many other patients die waiting, and had seen still more get transplants while her odds appeared ever slimmer. Sometime after Uric left the unit she had made her decision; the story leaked out after she died.

Shocked by realization of how bad the situation had actually become, the dean and the Executive Committee immediately placed Uric back as head of the Renal Unit: they then began to analyze what had happened, and what could be done to put the Renal Unit—and the hospital's reputation—back together again.

Managing Reductions in the Work Force

In contrast to the experience of the last two decades in which the size of most social services staffs increased, during the 1980s officials must learn to manage reductions rather than growth in the work force. Taxpayer resistance at the state and local levels and budget reductions in human service areas at the federal level have produced this situation. As a result, cutbacks have been ordered in income maintenance, medical assistance, food stamps, and other services at state and local levels.

In many ways it is more difficult for the administrator to manage reduction than it is to manage growth. Legal, administrative, and human relations considerations compound the tasks. Removing people from their chosen jobs is a burdensome activity.

This case study has been developed to stimulate thinking about the problems that might be encountered by those with management responsibility who must deal with cutbacks in staff.

THE SETTING

The setting is a medium-size district office of a state-supervised, locally administered Department of Social Services. The unit facing a reduction in employees is the one administering the income maintenance program. This unit is composed of sixty persons having income maintenance or eligibility position titles.[1]

The staff is grouped into eight work units, each having a Supervisor I in charge. There are two Supervisor II's, each responsible for three work units, and one Supervisor II responsible for the remaining two units and acting as second in command to the Income Maintenance Director. The Income Maintenance Director reports to the Commissioner of Social Services as do the Director of Social Services, Director of Finance and Administration, and the Director of Personnel.

In this particular state, all public employees engaged in this type of work for a local district are considered employed by a civil division of the state and are subject to the state civil service code and rules.[2] Although hiring, firing, creating new positions, and reducing old positions are the responsibilities of the local division and the district Commissioner of Social Services, these acts must be carried out within the requirements of state law.

The income maintenance caseload of the district office is a heterogeneous client population. As might be expected in an area of mixed ur-

Reprinted with permission. Continuing Education Program, Nelson A. Rockefeller College of Public Affairs and Policy, State University of New York at Albany, 1981.

[1]See Exhibit 2, p. 234.
[2]See Exhibits 5 and 6, pp. 237 and 239.

ban, suburban, and rural settings, there is a heavier concentration of minority clients in the urban settings and a somewhat more homogeneous, white client population in the more sparsely populated rural areas. Because the major urban center is in the center of the service area, the total staff is housed together in a central office. Each IM work unit is assigned cases on a geographical basis; five of the work units serve the urban and suburban areas, and three of the units serve the rural areas.[3]

THE ACTORS

Commissioner Faye Downs.   Fay is politically oriented, having spent a number of years working in the Social Services office and coming from a politically well-connected family. She was appointed several years ago with the change of administration. She has caught the current spirit of social services frugality and is viewed as one who supports the cutbacks at the federal level. As long as expenses and error rates are kept in line, she lets her directors run their sections. Now and then she "suggests" that a politically useful person be helped to qualify for an open position.

Director of Finance and Administration John Crain.   John is Faye's first administrative appointment and shares her philosophy of fiscal conservatism. He has a background in accounting and finance in the private sector and has taken the position with a certain "missionary" zeal to clear up the waste, fraud, and incompetence he believes exist in this office. After trying to create major changes, he has become increasingly upset. He feels there are unnecessary constraints on his ability to make personnel and budget shifts because of state and federal statutes and the rules and regulations governing the office.

Director of Personnel Ed Palaski.   Ed has served for many years in the area central personnel office. Ed is politically connected and is proud of having completed his M.P.A. in an evening program at the local state university. He is friendly, likes people, and has become enamored of the concepts of modern personnel management. He sought the position so he could directly implement those concepts. He has already tried to get other directors to practice a greater amount of participatory management. This has run into resistance, because of the long tradition of fairly rigid management in the district office.

Income Maintenance Director Matt Lukeridge.   Matt, a protégé of Ed's, has recently been appointed to the position from another local governmental office. He has the reputation of being a competent manager and was brought in to try to improve the operations of the IM program, which has been having considerable trouble with high error rates, high staff turnover, and poor staff morale.

[3]See Exhibit 1, page 233.

Supervisor II Sam Stone.   Sam, who has been with the office for fifteen years, has responsibility for the three units serving the predominantly rural areas. He is a "survivor" with a philosophy of keeping as low a profile as possible in order to last out one more administration. Although under the current administration his performance rating is quite low, he believes his seniority and the network of "friends" he has developed over the years will keep his position secure. He is not one to stand up for the staff working for him and generally provides little overall direction to the three units under him.

Supervisor II Maria Rodriguez.   Maria, who acts as Matt's assistant, has responsibility for two of the units which serve the major urban center. She has worked her way up in the program during the last fourteen years by dint of solid work. She is most knowledgeable regarding IM policy and procedures and often is involved in drafting policy interpretations and training staff on policy implementation. She is quite aware that the IM program management has tended to be run by white males and she considers her fairly recent designation as number two in the IM section as a significant step.

Supervisor II Peter Bell.   Pete came to the district office six years ago with his M.P.A., as part of an experimental management development program being tried out by local government. He has proved to be a quick learner and has developed into a competent manager. He is responsible for two units serving the urban center and the one unit serving the other urban area to the southeast. Pete is viewed with some skepticism by some of the "old timers" in the office. Sam believes Pete hasn't "paid his dues" and is too interested in "rocking the boat."

THE NARRATIVE

The Commissioner, Faye Downs, is in her office thinking over the potential effects of the increasing tension developing between John Crain, her finance director, and Ed Palaski, her personnel director. She receives a phone call from an old friend in the state Capitol. The friend tells Faye that the State Department of Social Services has finished analyzing the effects of federal cutbacks in Title IV-A funds and the governor's office is considering simply passing the cuts directly along to each local district. The friend indicates she has heard that it would mean a probable 30 percent reduction in available IM funds for personnel salaries.

Realizing that this is probably a deeper cut than can be handled through staff attrition, Faye decides to hold a meeting the next day with John, Ed, and the IM Director, Matt Lukeridge, to explore the implications of this type of cut. She calls John and asks him to bring a salary breakdown by individual staff members. She then calls Ed and asks him to check whether any state regulations deal with staff reductions. Ed indicates that there are civil service rules affecting this, and that he will get hold of the current set. She then calls Matt and asks him to bring an organization chart showing individual staff positions. She does not tell them the nature of the meeting, but each realizes that something fairly serious is occurring.

She opens the meeting by telling the three men that they need to keep this discussion confidential, and then she shares with them the information she has received from her friend. Matt is shocked at the implications of losing additional staff at a time when caseloads are increased. John's immediate reaction is that it would provide a good opportunity to "clean house" and trim some of the fat out of the program. Ed suggests that his review of the Civil Service code and rules indicate they do not have a completely free hand in trimming staff, and there is a major emphasis on protecting seniority among the staff. He also raises the issue of whether it isn't premature to plan cutbacks before they have official word from the state department, and that this could pose major morale problems for the staff.

The Commissioner indicates, with strong support from John, that she wants to get a jump on this and to have a clear plan of action to handle a cut of this size. John indicates that with 60 staff in IM, a 30 percent cut in funds would mean that approximately 18 employees, depending on their level, would be eliminated. He indicates that the current salary budget is $805,738 and 30 percent of this, or $241,721, is to be cut. He suggests looking at performance ratings and trimming those staff members who don't rate highly. Matt cautions that he would want to look carefully at how the staff is currently deployed and wants to involve the Supervisor II's in this type of review. John argues against involving anyone else in this planning, while Ed says it is only good personnel management to involve all the staff in a major restructuring.

Faye tells the group she believes that Matt would need to involve the Supervisor II's in developing a cutback plan, but that it would not be useful at this time to get the whole staff upset by news of possible cutbacks. She asks Ed to elaborate on the legal requirements of developing a cutback plan, and he indicates that there are rules governing both initial reductions and what is referred to as "bumping rights." The latter are rights of a staff person who loses his or her job to replace another staff member at a lower classification who has less seniority.[4] He points out that extra seniority is given veterans and as long as the employee "bumping" another did not have an unsatisfactory performance rating, he or she should retain bumping rights.

John suggests that they immediately review those workers with marginal work histories and give them unsatisfactory performance ratings prior to having to institute reductions so they could be terminated instead of bumping better staff members with less seniority. Ed replies that that certainly isn't a fair way to treat workers. He adds that civil service rules govern how to give performance ratings, how to remove an incompetent, and what kind of appeal rights an employee has. Faye suggests they review the rules and determine if they can use the performance ratings and removal systems as a way to keep the better employees.

[4]See Exhibits 5 and 6, pp. 237 and 239.

Faye asks Ed to get information on appointment dates, performance ratings, and other pertinent data on all staffers and to check out the performance rating rules.[5] She asks Matt to meet with his three Supervisor II's and review how best to restructure the organization to serve the area with fewer staffers, and to work with Ed in making up a list of those he recommends should be cut.

She asks all three to think about how to communicate this to the staff if the time comes, how much lead time in notification should be given staff, whether to share a reduction in force list with all staff or to just notify those affected, whether to break the news at a large staff meeting or in work units, to speak with individuals personally, or to notify them via memo. She indicates that they will meet again in a week and review Matt's and Ed's recommendations. Upon leaving the meeting, Ed mentions to Matt that he strongly feels that all staff members should know what is going on, and Matt cautions that the Commissioner feels that a lid should be kept on this.

Matt immediately calls in Sam Stone, Maria Rodriguez, and Peter Bell to consider how they could best cope with the cuts. Both Maria and Pete are aghast at the implications of a 30 percent reduction in staff in both personnel and service. Sam shrugs his shoulders as if to say, "So what's new about another round of cuts?" Matt reviews with them the importance of keeping this information within this group and shares with the group the civil service information he has received from Ed. He suggests that they have three major tasks to complete before he meets with the Commissioner next week. These are: (1) to analyze their current staffing plan and recommend how to reorganize with approximately 18 less staff; (2) to come up with a recommended list of staff to be cut; and (3) to develop a plan of communicating this to staff.

After hearing Matt review the civil service issues, Maria indicates her concern that this might have a negative effect on retaining minority staff as a number of them are relatively recent hirees. Pete asks how they will know which staff members are to be eliminated until they exercise their "bumping" rights. Sam just smiles, thinking to himself that some of the young "upstarts" in the office will finally get theirs. Matt asks whether they should consider eliminating several whole units or trim some staff from all the existing units. Pete argues that it would be better for those remaining to function in fully staffed units while Sam argues that there would be better geographical coverage by keeping all eight units. Sam suggests the possibility of eliminating the technician category altogether, since they got along without them in former years. Maria stresses that that class was created to provide career opportunities for a greater number of minorities and it would be a travesty to eliminate the whole class.

Pete suggests that they take a hard look at performance ratings and at least try to reduce staff members with low ratings wherever possible. Maria believes they should consider such things as minority status, sex, and whether the person is the sole income producer for the family, and how many dependents a person has. Sam indicates he is satisfied with the principle of seniority spelled out in the civil service rules and that loyalty to the office as shown in longevity on the job is what really counts.

Matt asks Sam to work with Maria in drafting alternative staffing plans, one with a reduced number of units and the other with fewer staff members in each unit. He also asks Pete to work with Maria in roughing out a preliminary reduction list which meets the requirements of the Civil Service Law but takes into consideration some of the other important variables mentioned. He indicates that they will meet in three days to review progress and to discuss specifically how the plans should be shared with staff.

After the meeting Maria remains behind to share with Matt how concerned she is about how this cut would affect those staff who will lose their jobs. She indicates that no one knows better than they how many people are currently out of work and how difficult it is to find jobs. She wonders if there might be a way to institute the kind of job sharing arrangements found in some industries where some jobs can be restructured and staff members kept on part time, rather than losing their jobs altogether. Matt says that that's an intriguing idea and asks her to develop it in more detail.

Three days later, shortly before Matt would meet again with Sam, Maria, and Pete, the Commissioner is interrupted by a phone call from her secretary who excitedly tells her there is a whole delegation of IM staff demanding that they meet with her to get the straight story on the rumored major cutback of IM staff.

After reviewing the exhibits, turn to the assignments on page 243.

EXHIBIT 1. Income Maintenance Service Area

Work Units 1–8

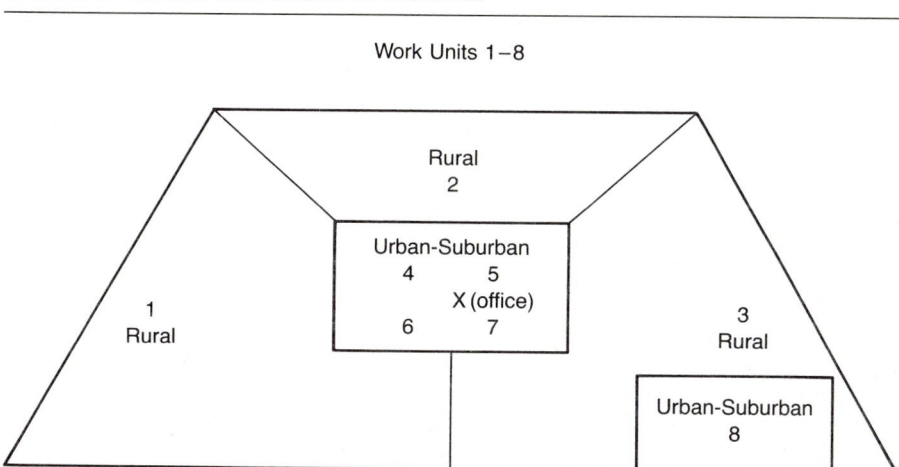

EXHIBIT 2. Organizational Chart Income Maintenance Staff

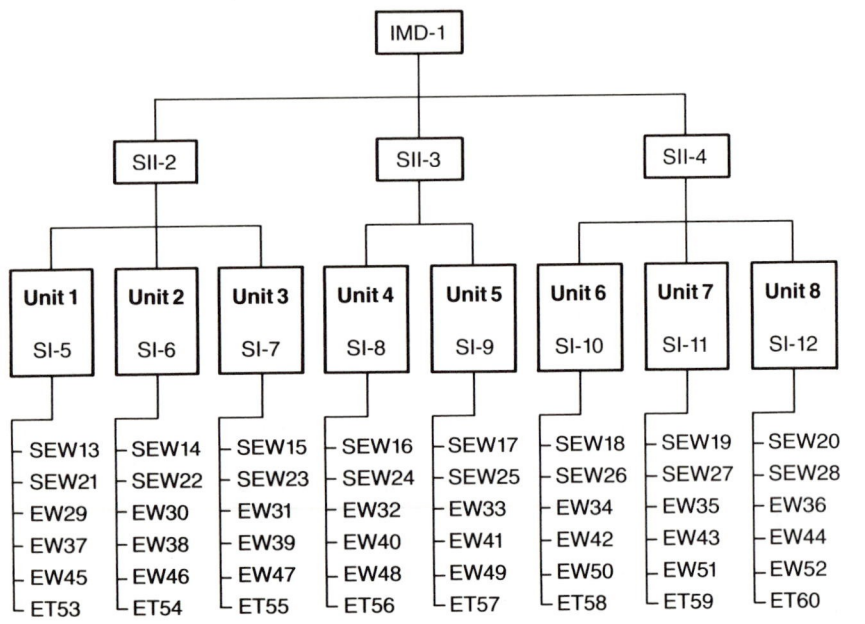

Class Title Legend: IMD - Income Maintenance Program Director
SII - Income Maintenance Supervisor II
SI   - Income Maintenance Supervisor I
SEW- Senior Eligibility Worker
EW - Eligibility Worker
ET   - Eligibility Technician

EXHIBIT 3. Income Maintenance Staff Roster

STAFF	CLASS TITLE	GRADE	APPT. DATE	LAST PERF. RATING[1]	SALARY	STATUS[2] VET.	MIN.
Matthew Lukeridge	IMD	13	181	8	$27,040	X	
Sam Stone	SII	11	166	4	20,628	X	
Maria Rodriguez	SII	11	667	6	25,271		X
Peter Bell	SII	11	475	9	22,072		
John Wallace	SI	9	276	8	15,737		X
Fred Dillard	SI	9	373	7	20,628	X	
Edna Crawford	SI	9	1174	3	15,737		X
Kyoto Yamamitzi	SI	9	776	9	16,839		X
Margot Kane	SI	9	970	8	18,018		
Ralph Willard	SI	9	366	5	19,279	X	
Betty Walker	SI	9	772	6	16,839		
Lewis Brown	SI	9	1075	7	18,018		
Marge Princeton	SEW	8	670	8	18,018		

EXHIBIT 3 (*cont.*)

STAFF	CLASS TITLE	GRADE	APPT. DATE	LAST PERF. RATING[1]	SALARY	STATUS[2] VET.	MIN.
Bob Bundange	SEW	8	1175	4	$ 13,746		
Joe Cook	SEW	8	177	2	14,708	X	
Wilma Black	SEW	8	1278	8	12,846		X
Jane Dottson	SEW	8	569	6	16,839		
Sue Gable	SEW	8	375	7	15,737		
Milford Clark	SEW	8	976	8	14,708		
Jose Ramirez	SEW	8	673	5	16,839		X
Ellen Marol	SEW	8	274	6	14,708		
Frieda Tillman	SEW	8	875	6	15,737		
Percy Adams	SEW	8	1172	4	18,018	X	
Casey Jones	SEW	8	777	9	14,708		
June Lockwood	SEW	8	574	5	14,708		
Judy Suller	SEW	8	1076	6	15,737		
Will Randal	SEW	8	369	5	16,839		
Kathy Dance	SEW	8	1273	8	15,737		
Joe Fong	EW	6	881	—	9,800		X
Lucy Medford	EW	6	1179	9	10,486		
Charles Keg	EW	6	378	6	11,220		X
Casandra Smith	EW	6	780	8	10,486		X
Clark Kent	EW	6	481	—	9,800		
Jessie James	EW	6	977	4	12,006		X
Lois Lane	EW	6	579	7	10,486		
Jim Renfrow	EW	6	1277	6	12,006	X	
Maria Garcia	EW	6	280	7	10,486		X
Mary Motts	EW	6	379	6	10,486		
Allan Alder	EW	6	1075	6	12,846		
Henry Help	EW	6	178	3	11,220	X	
Ruby Lindner	EW	6	1180	9	10,486		X
Travis Gossit	EW	6	980	7	10,486		
Josh Block	EW	6	579	6	10,486		
Lena Lorn	EW	6	375	4	13,746	X	X
Susy Wong	EW	6	980	5	10,486		X
Mary Ann Nobly	EW	6	679	7	11,220		
Walter Patter	EW	6	677	5	12,846		
Lloyd Richards	EW	6	978	9	12,006		
JoJo Musari	EW	6	480	6	10,486		X
Cindy Blue	EW	6	281	8	10,486		
Mickie Rodney	EW	6	1080	7	10,486		
Henry Runningwater	EW	6	481	—	9,800		X
Hugh Hungry	ET	4	681	—	7,477		
Raul Hernandez	ET	4	1080	5	8,000		X
Saul Linski	ET	4	281	4	8,000	X	
Kenny Shingles	ET	4	381	7	8,000		X
Tina Labor	ET	4	1180	6	8,560		X
Michelle Marston	ET	4	979	9	8,560		
Elma Norton	ET	4	780	2	7,477		X
Suki Yaki	ET	4	481	—	7,477		X
TOTAL					$805,738		

[1]Scale 1–10 with 3 = unsatisfactory
[2]Vet. = veteran   Min. = minority

EXHIBIT 4. Income Maintenance Section Salary Plan

POSITION	GRADE	STEP 1	STEP 2	STEP 3	STEP 4	STEP 5	STEP 6
Eligibility Technician	4	7,477	8,000	8,560	9,159	9,800	10,486
Eligibility Worker	6	9,800	10,486	11,220	12,006	12,846	13,746
Senior Eligibility Worker	8	12,846	13,746	14,708	15,937	16,839	18,018
IM Supervisor I	9	14,708	15,737	16,839	18,018	19,279	20,628
IM Supervisor II	11	19,279	20,628	22,072	23,617	25,271	27,040
IM Program Director	13	25,271	27,040	28,932	30,932	33,125	35,443

EXHIBIT 5.   State Civil Service Code

K75. *Removal and other disciplinary action.*

1. *Removal and other disciplinary action.* A person described in paragraph (a), or paragraph (b), or paragraph (c), or paragraph (d) of this subdivision shall not be removed or otherwise subjected to any disciplinary penalty provided in this section except for incompetency or misconduct shown after a hearing upon stated charges pursuant to this section.

(a) A person holding a position by permanent appointment in the competitive class of the classified civil service, or

(b) a person holding a position by permanent appointment or employment in the classified service of the state or in the several cities, counties, towns, or villages thereof, or in any other political or civil division of the state or of a municipality.

2. *Procedure.* A person against whom removal or other disciplinary action is proposed shall have written notice thereof and of the reasons therefor, shall be furnished a copy of the charges preferred against him and shall be allowed at least eight days for answering the same in writing. The hearing upon such charges shall be held by the officer or body having the power to remove the person against whom such charges are preferred, or by the person or persons holding such hearing shall, upon the request of the person against whom charges are preferred, permit him to be represented by counsel, or by a representative of a recognized or certified employee organization, and shall allow him to summon witnesses in his behalf. The burden of proving incompetency or misconduct shall be upon the person alleging the same. Compliance with technical rules of evidence shall be not be required.

3. Notwithstanding any other provision of law, no removal or disciplinary proceeding shall be commenced more than three years after the occurrence of the alleged incompetency or misconduct complained of and described in the charges provided, however, that such limitation shall not apply where the incompetency or misconduct complained of and described in the charges would, if proved in a court of appropriate jurisdiction, constitute a crime.

K76. *Appeals from determinations in disciplinary proceedings.*

1. *Appeals.* Any officer or employee believing himself aggrieved by a penalty or punishment of demotion in or dismissal from the service, or suspension without pay, or a fine, imposed pursuant to the provisions of section seventy-five of this chapter, may appeal from such determination either by an application to the state or municipal commission having jurisdiction, or by an application to the court in accordance with the provisions of article seventy-eight of the civil practice law and rules.

K80.

Suspension or demotion upon the abolition or reduction of positions.

1. *Suspension or demotion.* Where, because of economy, consolidation or abolition of functions, curtailment of activities or otherwise, positions in the competitive class are abolished or reduced in rank or salary grade, suspension or demotion, as the case may be, among incumbents holding the same or similar positions shall be made in the inverse order of original appointment on a permanent basis in the classified service in the service of the governmental jurisdiction in which such abolition or reduction of positions occurs, subject to the provisions of subdivision seven of section eighty-five of this chapter; provided, however, that the date of original appointment of any such incumbent who has transferred to such governmental jurisdiction from another governmental jurisdiction upon the transfer of functions shall be the date of original appointment on a permanent basis in the classified service in the service of the governmental jurisdiction from which such transfer was made. Notwithstanding the provisions of this subdivision, however, upon the abolition or reduction of

EXHIBIT 5 (*cont.*)

positions in the competitive class, incumbents holding the same or similar positions who have not completed their probationary service shall be suspended or demoted, as the case may be, before any permanent incumbents, and among such probationary employees the order of suspension or demotion shall be determined as if such employees were permanent incumbents.

2. *Units for suspension or demotion in civil divisions.* Upon the abolition or reduction of positions in the service of a civil division, suspension or demotion shall be made from among employees holding the same or similar positions in the entire department or agency within which such abolition or reduction of positions occurs. In a city having a population of one million or more, the municipal civil service commission may, by rule, designate as separate units for suspension and demotion under the provisions of this section any hospital or institution or any division of any department or agency under its jurisdiction. Upon the abolition or reduction of positions in such service, suspension or demotion, as the case may be, shall be made from among employees holding the same or similar positions in the department wherein such abolition or reduction occurs, except that where such abolition or reduction occurs in such hospital or institution or division of a department designated as a separate unit for suspension or demotion, suspension or demotion shall be made from among incumbents holding the same or similar positions in such separate unit.

3. *Displacement in civil divisions.* A permanent incumbent of a position in a civil division in a specific title to which there is a direct line of promotion who is suspended or displaced pursuant to this section, together with all other such incumbents suspended or displaced at the same time, shall displace, in the inverse order of the order of suspension or demotion prescribed in subdivisions one and two of this section, incumbents serving in positions in the same layoff unit in the next lower occupied title in direct line of promotion who shall be displaced in the order of suspension or demotion prescribed in subdivisions one and two of this section; provided, however, that no incumbent shall displace any other incumbent having greater retention standing. If a permanent incumbent of a position in a civil division is suspended or displaced from a position in a title for which there are no lower-level occupied positions in direct line of promotion, he shall displace the incumbent with the least retention right pursuant to subdivisions one and two of this section who is serving in a position in the title in which the displacing incumbent last served on a permanent basis prior to service in one or more positions in the title from which he is suspended or displaced; if: (1) the service of the displacing incumbent while in such former title was satisfactory and (2) the position of the junior incumbent is in (a) the competitive class, (b) the layoff unit from which the displacing incumbent was suspended or displaced, and (c) a lower salary grade than the position from which the displacing incumbent is suspended or displaced; provided, however, that no incumbent shall displace any other incumbent having greater retention standing. Refusal of appointment to a position afforded by this subdivision constitutes waiver of rights under this subdivision with respect to the suspension or displacement on account of which the refused appointment is afforded. The municipal civil service commission shall promulgate rules to implement this subdivision including rules which may provide adjunctive opportunities for displacement either to positions in direct line of promotion or to formerly held positions; provided, however, that no such rule shall permit an incumbent to displace any other incumbent having greater retention standing. For the purpose of this subdivision suspension is the equivalent of demotion pursuant to subdivision one of this section.

EXHIBIT 6. State Department of Civil Service Rules and Regulations

K5.5 *Layoff of competitive class employees.*

(a) *Definitions.* In connection with the suspension, demotion and displacement of competitive class employees authorized by section 80 of the Civil Service Law the following terms shall mean:

(1) *vertical bumping* shall mean displacement by an incumbent of another incumbent serving in a position in the title not in direct line of promotion in which the displacing incumbent served at a prior time as provided in subdivision 6 of section 80 of the Civil Service Law.

(2) *retreat* shall mean displacement by a permanent incumbent of another incumbent serving in a position in the title not in direct line of promotion in which the displacing incumbent served at a prior time as provided in subdivision six of section 80 of the Civil Service Law.

(3) *next lower occupied title* shall mean the title in direct line of promotion immediately below the title from which the incumbent is suspended or demoted, unless no one serves in that title in direct line of promotion in that layoff unit in which one or more persons do serve.

(4) *satisfactory service* shall mean service by an employee during the final rating period of which he did not receive an "unsatisfactory" performance rating and was not found guilty of misconduct or incompetency pursuant to either section 75 of the Civil Service Law of a disciplinary procedure provided by labor contract which in either case resulted in the imposition of any of the following penalties upon such employee:

(i) dismissal from the service

(ii) suspension without pay for a period exceeding one month or

(iii) demotion in grade and title.

(b) *Advance decisions.* An appointing authority may take such steps as it may deem necessary in order to secure binding written commitments in advance of suspension, demotion or displacement from employees potentially affected by such suspension, demotion or displacement as to their willingness to accept reassignment or displacement.

(c) *Order of displacement.* When two or more permanent incumbents of positions in a specific title are suspended, demoted, or displaced at the same time, the order in which they displace shall be determined by their respective retention standing, with those having the greater retention standing entitled to displace first. This principle shall apply to both vertical bumping and retreat.

(d) *Displacement by probationers.*

(1) *Probationer having a right to a permanent position.* An employee who is serving a probationary term and who has a position formerly held by him on a permanent basis being held open for him has no displacement rights from the position in which he is serving the probationary term pursuant to section 80 of the Civil Service Law and is afforded none by these rules.

(2) *Probationer without a right to a permanent position.* An employee who is serving a probationary term and who has no position formerly held by him on a permanent basis being held open for him shall nevertheless have the possibility of displacing upon being suspended or displaced from the position wherein he is serving a probationary term; provided however,

(i) he has previously completed at least five years of continuous service which shall also have been satisfactory service and

EXHIBIT 6 *(cont.)*

  (ii) he shall not be allowed to displace ahead of any permanent incumbents. The order of displacement among such probationers shall be determined by their respective retention standing, with those having the greater retention standing entitled to displace first.

 (e) *Refusal or failure to accept appointment to a position afforded by displacement.* The refusal or failure of a person to accept appointment to a lower-grade position to which he is entitled through displacement shall not affect his right to be placed on a preferred list for the position from which he was suspended, demoted, or displaced.

 (f) *Retreat where title of position has been changed.* A permanent incumbent who has been suspended or displaced shall be allowed to retreat to a position in which he last served even though the title of such position has been changed; provided however, that there has been substantial change in duties.

 (g) Preferred list standing for competitive class employees on and after October 1, 1972, shall be as follows:

  (1) On and after October 1, 1972, those employees whose positions were abolished prior to that date and who therefore have their standing on the preferred list determined by the date of their original appointment on a permanent list on a permanent basis in the competitive class shall retain among themselves such preferred list standing including the preferences to which they were entitled as blind, disabled veterans, and nondisabled veterans.

  (2) Blind employees whose positions are abolished on or after October 1, 1972, shall have their preferred list standing determined by the date of their original appointment on a permanent basis in the classified service, whether or not they are also disabled veterans or nondisabled veterans; provided however, that the blind shall be granted absolute preference on the preferred list over all other employees except those disabled veterans and blind employees whose positions were abolished prior to October 1, 1972, with whose names theirs shall be interfiled.

  (3) Disabled veterans whose positions are abolished on or after October 1, 1972, shall have their preferred list standing determined by the date of their original appointment on a permanent basis in the classified service; provided however, that the date of such original appointment shall be deemed to be 60 months earlier than the actual date, determined in accordance with section 30 of the General Construction Law.

  (4) Nondisabled veterans whose positions are abolished on or after October 1, 1972, shall have their preferred list standing determined by the date of their original appointment on a permanent basis in the classified service; provided however, that the date of such original appointment shall be deemed to be 30 months earlier than the actual date, determined in accordance with section 30 of the General Construction Law.

  (5) Nonveterans whose positions are abolished on or after October 1, 1972, shall have their preferred list standing determined by the date of their original appointment on a permanent basis in the classified service.

  (6) The names of all persons encompassed by paragraphs (3), (4), and (5) above whose positions are abolished on or after October 1, 1972, shall be interfiled on the preferred list with the names of all nonveterans whose positions were abolished prior to October 1, 1972.

 (h) *Adjunctive opportunities.* (Pursuant to the authority to provide adjunctive opportunities for displacement granted by subdivision 6 of section 80 of the Civil Service

EXHIBIT 6 (*cont.*)

Law.) If a permanent incumbent of a position in the State Service is suspended or displaced from a position in a title for which there are no lower-level occupied positions in direct line of promotion, he shall displace the incumbent with the least retention right, pursuant to subdivisions 1 and 2 of section 80 of the Civil Service Law, who is serving in a position in the title with a lower salary grade in which the displacing incumbent last served on a permanent basis prior to service in one or more positions in the title from which he is suspended or displaced, if:

(1)   the service of the displacing incumbent while in such former title was satisfactory; and

(2)   the position of the junior incumbent is in:

(i)   the competitive, noncompetitive, or labor class;

(ii)   the layoff unit from which the displacing incumbent was suspended or displaced; and

(iii)   a lower salary grade than the position from which the displacing incumbent is suspended or displaced; provided, however, that no incumbent shall displace any other incumbent with greater retention standing.

K5.8 *Placement roster in the competitive class*

Where it is known or expected by a department or agency of the State that an abolition or reduction of positions in such department or agency will occur within six months and will require the suspension or demotion of permanent employees, such department or agency shall give notice thereof to the Department of Civil Service and shall submit to such department the names and titles of permanent employees expected to be suspended or demoted. The Department of Civil Service shall enter such names on a placement roster if in the judgment of such department so doing would facilitate fairness and efficiency. If a placement roster is created, the following principles shall apply:

(a)   Vacancies in positions in any State department or agency for which one or more employees on such placement roster are eligible and willing to accept transfer or reassignment shall be filled by such transfer or reassignment before appointment or promotion to such positions may be made from an open competitive or promotion eligible list; (b) Any other employee in the department or unit for suspension or demotion wherein the abolition or reduction of positions will occur who holds a position to which an employee on the placement roster could be reassigned may receive transfer or reassignment to other positions in the State service, provided the vacancy created thereby is filled forthwith by the reassignment thereto of an employee from the placement roster; and (c) Employees on such placement roster who are not so transferred or reassigned prior to the abolition or reduction of positions shall, upon suspension or demotion, have their names entered on an appropriate preferred list pursuant to the Civil Service Law.

Part 35. Administration of Performance Rating.

PREAMBLE

The purpose of this Part is to provide for periodic evaluations of the performance and promotability of employees of the State.

K35.1 *Definition of terms*

(a)   The term *performance rating* shall mean an annual summary judgment of the value of an employee's performance and conduct prepared by his supervisors for the

EXHIBIT 6 (*cont.*)

purpose of determining the employee's eligibility for salary increment and promotion. Such summary judgment shall be recorded only as "satisfactory" or "unsatisfactory."

(b)   The term *appraisal* shall mean a continuing evaluation of an employee's performance, conduct, skills and abilities for the purpose of facilitating the employee's development and the most effective utilization of his abilities.

K35.2 *Applicability*

(a)   The provisions of the Part shall apply to all employees in the executive branch of the State Service holding positions in the competitive class, or positions in the noncompetitive or labor classes which are allocated to salary grades.

(b)   The provision of the Part concerning appeal from performance ratings are not applicable to probationary employees.

K35.3 *Powers and duties of the Civil Service Commission*

The Civil Service Commission shall:

(a)   have discretion to exempt an agency from these rules, during a prescribed period, provided there exists in the agency a performance rating plan approved by the commissioner, and provided further that for purposes of determining eligibility for promotion and salary increments under any such performance rating plan only the ratings "satisfactory" and "unsatisfactory" shall be used;

(b)   consider and determine appeals from employees whose performance was rated as unsatisfactory and modify such ratings if appropriate;

(c)   conduct or designate representatives to conduct investigations of any matters pertaining to the performance rating program in any agency.

K35.5 *Powers and duties of the agency*

(a)   For purposes of increment and promotion eligibility:

(1)   Each agency shall rate, in the manner or form prescribed or approved, the performance of each employee who will have completed three months' continuous service as of the last day of the rating period.

(2)   Each employee shall, so far as reasonably possible, be rated by the person or persons who supervised his work or who were responsible for the supervision of his work during the rating period. However, no employee shall be rated by a provisionally promoted examination. The rating shall be reviewed by one or more successive levels of supervision. In the event of a difference of opinion as to the rating of an employee, a final determination shall be made by the agency head or by a person so designated by that agency head.

(3)   Except where an unsatisfactory rating is appealed to the Civil Service Commission, the agency head is empowered to make the final rating of any employee of his agency.

(4)   Each agency shall notify each of its employees of his satisfactory or unsatisfactory performance rating, provide the employee an opportunity to review his rating with his supervisor, and give to each employee whose performance is rated as unsatisfactory a copy of his rating.

(5)   Each agency shall withhold the salary increment of any employee whose performance is rated as unsatisfactory.

(6)   Each agency shall insure so far as practicable that rating standards are applied uniformly within the agency.

(b)   For purposes of employee development and effective utilization of employee abilities:

EXHIBIT 6 (*cont.*)

(1)   Each agency shall develop and administer, subject to the approval of the Department of Civil Service, procedures for the continuing appraisal of the performance, conduct, skills, and abilities of its employees.

(2)   An employee shall be given an opportunity to examine any written appraisal of his performance, conduct, skills, and abilities, to discuss the same with his supervisor, and to submit comments thereon to his supervisor and agency head.

K35.6 *Performance Rating Board*

(a)   The Performance Rating Board of an agency shall consist of not less than three nor more than five members who shall be employees of the agency with permanent status, at least two of whom shall be in the competitive class. If the agency head shall so authorize, they may be elected by the employees of the agency for a term specified by the agency head. In a large agency, separate boards may be designated for geographically separated units, districts, or institutions.

(b)   As directed by the agency head, the Performance Rating Board in each agency shall

(1)   develop and administer procedures for the appeal of performance ratings;

(2)   allow any employee to appeal from an unsatisfactory performance rating, review the appeal, and inform the employee of its decision. In the case of an unsatisfactory rating where the appeal is denied, the board shall notify the employee of his right to appeal his unsatisfactory rating to the Civil Service Commission.

ASSIGNMENTS

1.   Assume the staff did not find out about the cuts. How would you advise the Commissioner to communicate the news to staff? Include considerations of timing, form, and substance of such a communication.

2.   You are Sam and Maria. Develop the alternate staffing plans for Matt with arguments pro and con for each alternative.

3.   You are Pete and Maria. Develop the reduction list keeping in mind your staffing plans. Would each alternative make a difference? Keep in mind some of the criteria in addition to seniority. Indicate which you would recommend using. Why? Draft a memo explaining why those on the list were chosen.

A Case
of Reasonable Time

BACKGROUND

Col. John E. Bickle, U.S.A., Ret., was employed by the Any County Legislature as the Director of the Any County Department of Social Services. He started his new duties on October 1, 1980, after having served in the

Reprinted with permission. Continuing Education Program, Nelson A. Rockefeller College of Public Affairs and Policy, State University of New York at Albany, 1981.

military for thirty-three years. During his final three years in the military, he served as the Chief of Management Services at a large military installation where he was responsible for the direction of 800 military and 300 civilian employees.

The legislative committee that employed John indicated that they were very upset with the direction of the agency. They revealed that administrative costs were increasing at a rate of 18 percent per year. Further, the error rates in all programs for Any County were well above the state average and the number of complaints from clients about the poor quality of services delivered by DSS had more than doubled in the previous year. The situation had come to a head six months before when the state uncovered a case of fraud in the AFDC program amounting to approximately $75,000. The situation, involving one individual who had been receiving payments under eleven different names, had received national news coverage and led to the resignation of the director. The charge given John by the committee was to "clean up the mess in the welfare department" and to restore efficient and effective management.

Upon taking charge of the agency, Bickle was instantly overwhelmed by the "country club" attitude that prevailed. Staff members were reporting for work as much as one hour late, lunch hours were being unreasonably extended, coffee breaks were frequently turning into half-hour bull sessions, and there was a general feeling of indifference toward clients. Of particular concern to John was the seemingly limitless power of the Public Employees Union within the department. Bickle had never worked in a union setting and was amazed at the influence the union had upon the operation. At the end of his first month, the new director decided to hold a meeting with all supervisory personnel to discuss the situation.

The meeting began with the director outlining his observations to the supervisory staff. He asked for their input. Initially the supervisors were reluctant to discuss the situation but soon began to speak candidly. After three hours of listening, the new director had obtained a much clearer picture of his department. Later, in his office, John summarized the major points developed by the supervisors.

First, the previous director, Helen Dougle, had led the agency for seventeen years. During the first ten years she had been extremely successful in obtaining budget increases and new staff positions, while maintaining a good image within the community for the Department of Social Services. In short, she had been an effective manager. As resources became more difficult to obtain during the 1970s and the agency began to be more closely scrutinized by the legislative body, Helen became concerned about staff morale. To compensate for increased work loads and stagnating salaries, Helen began granting special privileges to the staff. At first, these extras were helpful in maintaining staff morale; however, soon both the number and the cost of privileges began to get out of control. When Helen tried to regain control of the department, a group of staff members contacted the Public Employees Union, and an organizing campaign was begun.

The union was certified following an election conducted by PERB in which it obtained 87 percent of the votes cast. During initial contract negotiations with the union, Helen attempted to obtain an agreement that would satisfy both the union and her own management needs. After long and often heated negotiating sessions lasting approximately six weeks, Helen finally signed the first agreement, which contained virtually every item the union had sought. As the years passed, Helen had increasing difficulty in managing the union relationship, and according to one of the supervisors, "she simply allowed the union to run the organization for the last three years that she was director."

Second, the supervisors appeared (to John) to be mature, hardworking, and willing individuals who viewed their role under Helen as "glorified clerks." They were unwilling to make decisions since they felt that Helen would not back them up. For example, one supervisor related the following incident. "One of my social workers was missing appointments with clients. Upon investigation, I learned that she was out looking for a new apartment. I informed her that this was not acceptable and placed a reprimand in her personnel file. She immediately went to the union steward, who talked with Helen. The reprimand was removed. Helen later told me that she didn't "want to be bothered with a grievance."

Third, the union president, Bill Turnbull, is an ardent and devoted trade unionist. He has been with the agency for twelve years and was one of the founding members of the local union. Since his election as president four years ago, Bill has maintained a militant posture toward the management of the agency. The supervisors agreed that Bill is a competent and effective social worker and that his position within the union has not interfered with his devotion to his clients.

Finally, Any County is considered to be a union stronghold. A community of approximately 200,000, the county is heavily industrialized and has a long history of trade union support. At present, 34 percent of the labor force are members of a union. The trade union movement is a strong political force, having been responsible for the election of two members of the county legislature who are themselves union members. Many feel that one of them, Mickey Turnbull (Bill's uncle), is the most powerful member of the body.

After reviewing the information, Director Bickle knew that he would have to take strong and quick action or the situation would get further out of hand. He immediately called his supervisors back together and informed them of his position. He made it clear that he wanted to be fair and that he was not out to break the union; however, he was going to insist upon adherence to all rules, regulations, and policies of the department. He instructed the supervisors to begin at once to enforce all policies with particular attention to adherence to work schedules and client contacts. He assured them that he wanted them to assume their full supervisory responsibilities and that he would back them "to the hilt."

THE INCIDENT

The supervisors initially were reluctant to act, fearing that John would not support their actions. After further discussion, the director's continued urging, and his full assurance that he would support their decisions, the supervisors began to take the initiative. They informed staff that attitudes toward clients would have to improve and that work schedules were to be rigidly adhered to in the future. The staff, suspicious of John's military background, considered these new instructions as a form of "military regimentation not appropriate for a professional work group." Thus, they generally continued to disregard the supervisors' insistence upon conformance to policy.

After two weeks of repeated warnings, supervisors began issuing reprimands to the worst offenders. During the third week of the new program, twenty written reprimands were issued to various staff members. Each of these actions was appealed by the Public Employees Union through the grievance procedure. The processing of this large number of grievances led to a major confrontation in one unit.

Jim Johnson is a social worker in the Adult Services unit and a union steward. As called for by Article VI of the agreement, he had been elected to represent twenty employees in four small units. With the increased number of grievances being filed, Jim was spending more and more time away from his work station. On each occasion he informed his supervisor, Evelyn Brown, of his destination and the reason for his absences. At about 9:00 A.M. on Thursday, Jim informed Evelyn that he was going to be out of the unit for approximately two hours to work on a grievance. Evelyn informed him that he had been spending an unreasonable amount of time on union business and that she could not spare him for more than thirty minutes. Jim responded that he would be gone only the time necessary to complete his union business.

When Jim returned to the unit at 10:45 A.M., Evelyn informed him that he had missed a 10:00 A.M. appointment with a client, and as a result, she had to fill in for him. She restated her earlier position that Jim was spending too much time on union business and that in the future he would have to limit his time away from the unit. She supported her contention by pointing out that Jim had been out of the unit a total of sixteen hours (approximately 40 percent of his time) during the week and that she felt this was excessive. Jim responded that he had only spent the time necessary to satisfy the requirements of his position as union steward.

On the following Monday at approximately 1:45 P.M., Jim informed Evelyn that he was going to be out of the unit assisting with the processing of a grievance of an employee who had been reprimanded for returning late from lunch. Evelyn informed Jim that thirty minutes should be sufficient for this activity and that she expected him to be back by 2:15 P.M. Jim responded that he would spend no more time than was necessary.

Upon his return to the unit at 3:15 P.M., Jim was notified by Evelyn that she was docking him one hour's pay and placing a letter of reprimand in his personnel file for excessive absence. After a heated discussion of the issue, Jim informed Evelyn that her action violated Article VI of the agreement and that he intended to file a grievance. (See Exhibit 1 for Articles VI and VII.)

Jim's request for the removal of the written reprimand from his personnel file and the restoration of the one hour's pay was denied at both the

EXHIBIT 1. Article VI Representation

6.1—The Union shall be entitled to one (1) representative (steward) for each twenty (20) employees. Where units do not contain twenty (20) employees, smaller units will be combined for the purposes of representation.

6.2—The Department shall grant a reasonable amount of time to each union representative for the implementation of this contract and the handling of grievances. Such time may not be used to solicit Union membership.

ARTICLE VII
GRIEVANCE PROCEDURE AND ARBITRATION

7.1—Grievances may be filed by an employee in the bargaining unit on his/her behalf, or by the Union on its behalf, or on behalf of any employee or group of employees in the bargaining unit. A grievance must be filed by an employee or the Union within a reasonable time from the date it was found to exist. Any grievance shall be deemed waived by the grievant.

Step 1. A grievance must be stated in writing setting forth the basis therefor, and the remedy requested. The grievance shall be filed with the employee's immediate supervisor. The Supervisor shall within three (3) calendar days of the receipt of the grievance meet with the grievant and a representative of the Union for the purpose of discussing the grievance. The Supervisor shall within three (3) calendar days after the grievance meetings issue a decision with reasons in writing to the grievant and to the Union.

Step 2. If the grievance has not been settled at Step 1, within five (5) calendar days after the receipt of the written decision of the Supervisor, or the expiration of the time limits for making such decision, the grievant or the Union may submit the grievance in writing to the Personnel Officer or his/her designee, together with a copy of the decision of the Supervisor. The Personnel Officer or his/her designee shall within five (5) calendar days of the receipt of the grievance meet with the grievant and a representative of the Union for the purpose of discussing the grievance. The Personnel Officer or his/her designee shall within five (5) calendar days after the grievance meeting issue a decision with reasons in writing to the grievant and to the Union.

Step 3. If the grievance has not been settled at Step 2, then within seven (7) calendar days after receipt of the written decision of the Personnel Officer or his/her designee, or expiration of the time limits for making such decision, the grievant or the Union may submit the grievance in writing to the Director or his/her designee, together with a copy of previous decisions. The Director or his/her designee within seven (7) calendar days of the receipt of the grievance shall meet with the grievant and a representative of the Union for the purpose of discussing the grievance. The Director or his/her designee shall within seven (7) calendar days after the grievance meetings issue a decision with reasons in writing to the grievant and to the Union.

7.2—Step 4. Arbitration. If the grievance has not been settled at Step 3, then within ten (10) calendar days after receipt of the written decision of the Director or his/her designee, the grievant or the Union may request arbitration by giving notice to that effect, by registered mail, directed to the Director or his/her designee and to the Arbitration Panel. The Arbitration Panel shall be jointly chosen by the Department and the Union, and shall consist of three (3) members who are familiar with the customs, practices, and nature of the Department. Each member is to serve in turn as sole arbitrator for a given case. Where a member of the Panel is unable to serve for any reason, the next member in sequence shall then serve. The arbitration procedure shall be in accordance with the rules of the American Arbitration Association. In no event shall the arbitrator have authority to add to, subtract from, modify or amend the provisions of this agreement. The final decision of the arbitrator shall be binding upon the Union, the Department, and the employees affected thereby. The cost of arbitration shall be borne equally by the parties.

EXHIBIT 2.   Statutory Provisions

Sec. 208. Rights Accompanying Certification or Recognition.

1.   A public employer shall extend to an employee organization certified or recognized pursuant to this article the following rights:

(a)   to represent the employees in negotiations notwithstanding the existence of an agreement with an employee organization that is no longer certified or recognized, and in the settlement of grievances; and

(b)   to membership dues deduction; upon presentation of dues deduction authorization cards signed by individual employees.

2.   An employee organization certified or recognized pursuant to this article shall be entitled to unchallenged representation status until seven months prior to the expiration of a written agreement between the public employer and said employee organization determining terms and conditions of employment. For the purposes of this subdivision, (a) any such agreement for a term covering other than the fiscal year of the public employer shall be deemed to expire with the fiscal year ending immediately prior to the termination date of such agreement, (b) any such agreement having a term in excess of three years shall be treated as an agreement for a term of three years and (c) extensions of any such agreement shall not extend the period of unchallenged representation status. [As amended by Ch. 503, L. 1971.]

3.   (a) Notwithstanding provisions of and restrictions of sections two hundred two and two hundred nine-a of this article, and section six-a of the state finance law, every employee organization that has been recognized or certified as the exclusive representative of employees of the state within a negotiating unit of classified civil service employees or employees in a collective negotiating unit established pursuant to this article for the professional services in the state university, for the members of the state police or for the members of the capitol buildings police force of the office of general services shall be entitled to have deducted from the wage or salary of the employees in such negotiating unit who are not members of said employee organization the amount equivalent to the dues levied by such employee organization, and the state comptroller shall make such deductions and transmit the sum so deducted to such employee organization. Provided, however, that the foregoing provisions of this subdivision shall only be applicable in the case of an employee organization which has established and maintained a procedure providing for the refund to any employee demanding the return of any part of an agency shop fee deduction which represents the employee's pro rata share of expenditures by the organization in aid of activities or causes of a political or ideological nature only incidentally related to terms and conditions of employment. Nothing herein shall be deemed to require an employee to become a member of such employee organization. [Paragraph (a) as last amended by Ch. 122, L. 1978.]

Sec. 209-a. Improper Employer Practices; Improper Employee Organization Practices; Application.

1.   Improper employer practices. It shall be an improper practice for a public employer or its agents deliberately (a) to interfere with, restrain, or coerce public employees in the exercise of their rights guaranteed in section two hundred two for the purpose of depriving them of such rights; (b) to dominate or interfere with the formation or administration of any employee organization for the purpose of depriving them of such rights; (c) to discriminate against any employee for the purpose of encouraging or discouraging membership in, or participation in the activities of, any employee organization; or (d) to refuse to negotiate in good faith with the duly recognized or certified representatives of its public employees.

2.   Improper employee organization practices. It shall be an improper practice for an employee organization or its agents deliberately (a) to interfere with, restrain or coerce public

EXHIBIT 2 (*cont.*)

employees in the exercise of the rights granted in section two hundred two, or to cause, or attempt to cause, a public employer to do so; or (b) to refuse to negotiate collectively in good faith with a public employer, provided it is the duly recognized or certified representative of the employees of such employer.

  3. Application. In applying this section, fundamental distinctions between private and public employment shall be recognized, and no body of federal or state law applicable wholly or in part to private employment, shall be regarded as binding or controlling precedent. [As added by Ch. 24, L. 1969.]

first and second steps of the grievance procedure. In its response, management pointed to the length of time Jim devoted to union business (40 percent of his scheduled time), the instructions of his supervisor to limit such time to thirty minutes, the missing of appointments with clients, and management's right to direct the work force. For its part, the union pointed out that the agreement provided an unqualified right to union stewards to represent employees in processing grievances, that Jim was in fact (verified by the supervisors involved) engaged in appropriate union business while away from his unit, that at least two other stewards had spent more time out of their units on union business without receiving reprimands, and that management was in fact responsible since they precipitated the large number of grievances through their own actions.

At the meeting between the union president and the director, both men took hard-line positions. John Bickle maintained that management had the obligation to provide for the efficient and effective operation of the agency and that this management prerogative was being infringed upon by the union's insistence upon unlimited time spent on processing grievances. Bill Turnbull, on the other hand, stated emphatically that the right to union representation for each employee was guaranteed both by the agreement in Articles VI and VII and by state law in Section 208.

As the meeting proceeded, more and more issues were addressed by the two men. Bill pointed out that this situation was precipitated by management's own actions. He stated, "If you had not tried to change the rules without fair warning and discussion with the union, there would not have been grievances for him to handle." John responded that he had not changed the rules, but rather that he was simply enforcing the existing policies, an action protected by management prerogatives. Bill responded, "In this situation past practice governs and management has an obligation to confer with the union before instituting any new rules or regulations affecting terms or conditions of employment."

John, seeing that the meeting was accomplishing nothing, suggested the grievance be submitted to arbitration for final resolution. Bill angrily responded, "This is not an arbitrable issue since union representation is a guaranteed right under Section 208 of the state law, and, further, you are not bargaining in good faith by refusing to confer with the union on this matter." Bill further stated, "Unless you drop all disciplinary actions against employees presently pending in the grievance procedure and unequivocally guarantee the right of unlimited time for representation, the union will file an unfair practice charge with the Public Employee Relations Board under Section 209." John, recognizing that he was in a difficult position, asked for time to consider a response to Bill's proposal. A meeting was scheduled for the next Tuesday at 9:00 A.M.

ASSIGNMENT

John Bickle has employed you as a consultant and asked you to develop a position statement. He asks that you develop the issues related to arbitration and handling the unfair practice charge. In your treatment of the issues, he requests that you give consideration to the impact of any proposals upon supervisors and the operation of the agency. Finally, after choosing an alternative, how can Bill Turnbull be convinced to cooperate?

Fiscal Planning and Control of In-Service Training in Midsize Department of Public Welfare

INTRODUCTION

This case centers on the financial planning responsibilities of the Staff Development Unit of the Midsize State Department of Public Welfare. The new staff development director is challenged to bring the in-service training budget under control and develop financial plans for the next two fiscal years. Priority is to be given to economic assistance training.

Although the case focuses on a limited aspect of the unit's responsibilities, the economic assistance in-service training program, the budgetary problems presented are found in simpler as well as more complex organizations. The budgetary planning and control strategies applied in resolving the issues are also used in diverse situations, as they are based on fundamental fiscal planning and management principles.

In January 1980, Mr. John Burke was appointed director of Staff Development and Training for the Midsize Department of Public Welfare (DPW). The previous director had resigned after a year and a half to relocate to another part of the country. The director of Administrative Services, Burke's immediate superior, pointed out that there had been some dissatisfaction with the previous director's management of training

Reprinted with permission. Continuing Education Program, Nelson A. Rockefeller College of Public Affairs and Policy, State University of New York at Albany, 1981.

funds, although the staff rated highly most of the training that was provided. Burke was instructed to bring the in-service training budget under control for the current fiscal year and to develop a comprehensive financial plan for the next two years. Priority was to be given to the economic assistance in-service training program, since training of economic assistance staff was to be a major component of future efforts to reduce DPW's eligibility error rates.

Burke's review of the financial situation revealed two major problems in managing the budget. First of all, program planning and budgeting were independent, rather than integrated, efforts. Training plans were not costed out, although data were available to compute the cost of different training activities. When costs for training programs and projects were determined, they bore little relationship to the nature or level of activities actually implemented. Second, the unit's financial reports did not provide the information needed to control spending. Sometimes last-minute training was done to use surplus funds, while at other times training was abruptly cancelled because the budget was exhausted.

Burke's successful implementation of a comprehensive in-service training program would necessitate a more systematic approach to budgeting than had previously been employed. Equally important would be the need for relevant and timely financial data to control the budget for the current and upcoming fiscal years.

BACKGROUND

DPW administers public welfare programs through ten district offices, each for an assigned geographic area. Four of the offices serve urban areas, with at least one city having a population of over 100,000 persons. The other areas are primarily rural.

Each of the district offices provides economic assistance and social services to area residents. Different staff are utilized for the two services except in very small offices in the rural areas where these services are combined. Several functions, including personnel administration, staff development and training, and fiscal administration, rest at the state level. An organization chart for DPW is presented in Exhibit 1.

DPW has over 5,000 employees. Economic assistance field staff number 1,500 eligibility specialists and 250 supervisors. The social services staff is larger and has 2,500 casework staff and 83 supervisors. The annual turnover rate of personnel at the lower level is 40 percent. At the supervisory level, it is 20 percent. For the past two years, new staff have been hired only to fill vacancies left by persons terminating or transferring to other positions. This policy is expected to continue indefinitely.

Economic eligibility specialists determine initial and ongoing eligibility of residents for food stamps, income maintenance, and medical assistance. Social services workers determine eligibility of residents and provide social services and child welfare services.

EXHIBIT 1.   DPW Organizational Chart

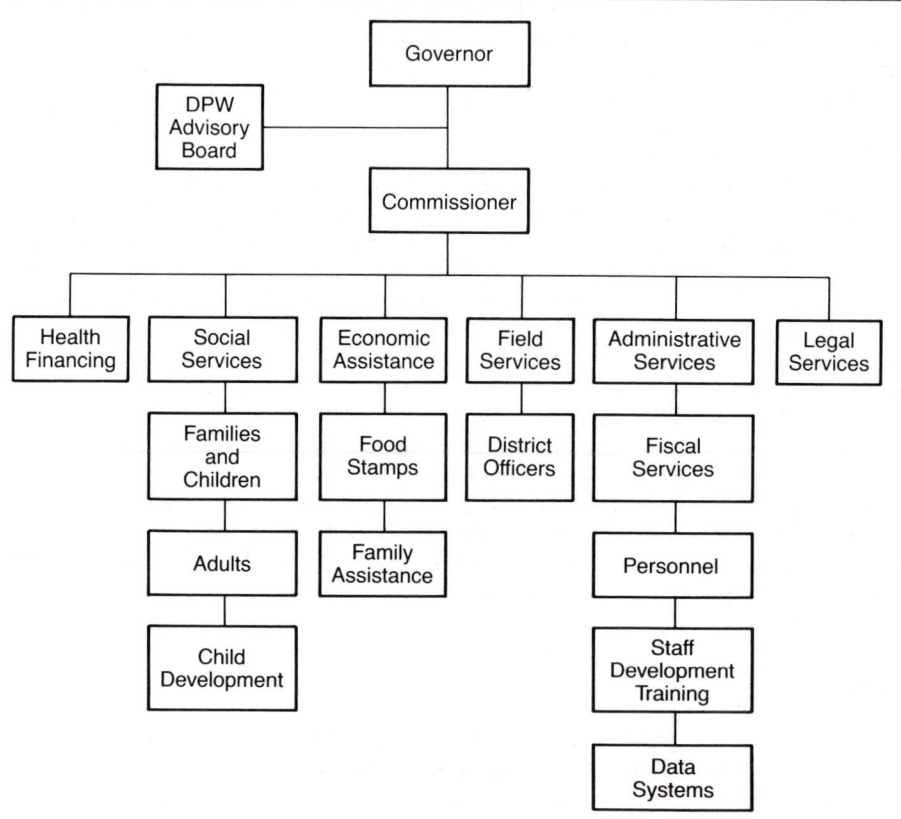

STAFF DEVELOPMENT AND TRAINING

Staff Development and Training (SDT) is a state-level office responsible for training and professional development of staff engaged in the delivery and supervision of economic assistance and social services. The personnel unit is responsible for training clerical and other support staff.

SDT administers an educational leave program for employees, provides orientation and in-service training, and administers funds for staff development (staff attendance at professional workshops, seminars, and meetings). The office is staffed by a director, three staff development specialists, and two clerk typists. One staff development specialist is responsible for the educational leave and professional development aspects. A second coordinates social services training and the third coordinates economic assistance training. An organization chart for SDT appears in Exhibit 2.

EXHIBIT 2. Staff Development and Training Organizational Chart

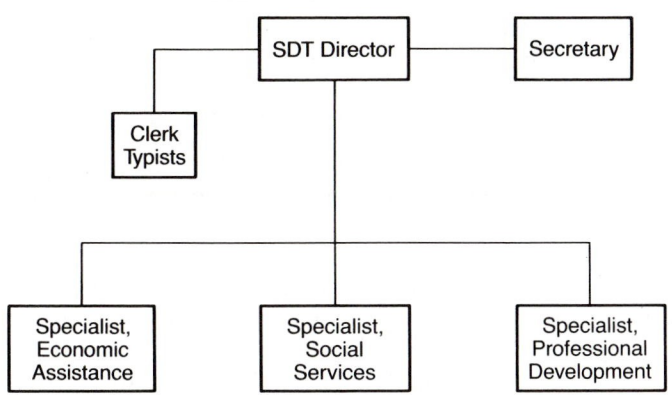

SDT's annual budget of approximately $1.3 million is administered by the SDT director under general guidelines established by the DPW. Some budget components are relatively fixed by priorities established on an agencywide basis. The use of funds for in-service training is at the director's discretion although training plans have traditionally been developed in concert with the service administrators and district directors. The SDT in-service training budget does *not* include trainee travel and salary expenses or expenses connected with a supervisor's provision of training to his or her immediate subordinates. These are, instead, covered in the unit budgets. The resource allocations for the current year (FY '80) and the projected allocations for the next two fiscal years (FY '81 and FY '82) are presented in Exhibit 3.

Training development and delivery is provided through a combination of DPW staff, consultants, and contracts with educational institutions.

EXHIBIT 3.   SDT BUDGET* FY '80–FY '82

	CURRENT FY '80	PROJECTED FY '81	FY '82
Educational Leave	$ 75,000	$ 75,000	$ 75,000
Staff Development	200,000	200,000	200,000
In-Service Training			
Economic Assistance	340,000	370,000	400,000
Social Services	600,000	660,000	660,000
Administrative Support	180,000	193,000	193,000
	$1,395,000	$1,498,000	$1,528,000

*Includes only direct costs of Staff Development and Training unit. Does not include prorata share of DPW central office expenses.

Training for economic assistance staff and social services staff is separately funded and is handled by SDT.

There is a basic one-day orientation program for all newly appointed staff. This video-assisted training package is provided in the district offices and is handled by the new employee's immediate supervisor. Any modifications of the content and format of the training package are developed and distributed by SDT.

Traditionally, most other training has been delivered according to the expressed needs of the districts. The districts have had different training priorities and have requested training in diverse areas in recognition of the need for a more comprehensive training plan for all employees.

The DPW commissioner appointed a task force to determine training priorities. The task force's recommendation formed the basis for FY '81 and FY '82 plans developed by SDT staff. These are outlined in Exhibit 4.

Traditionally, training sessions have been conducted during late winter and early spring. June, July, August, and December are the heaviest staff vacation months, and it is usually difficult to schedule training during these months. Training needs assessment, curriculum development, and program modification typically take place in the fall.

SDT usually engages outside consultants or the social work department of the state university to develop curriculum and conduct training sessions. When the proposed training program covers implementation of agency policies, such as the use of specific forms or new regulations, then DPW staff develop the content and/or work with the outside contractors.

EXHIBIT 4. Economic Assistance In-Service Training

TRAINING PRIORITIES FY '81

---

1. Development of a basic four-day training program, including training manuals, for line workers. Development should include a pilot training session and revision of the training content as needed. Sessions to include a maximum of twenty participants.
2. Distribution of training manuals.
3. Training of trainers to provide training for line workers.
4. Delivery of the training program to line workers. Priority to be given to new employees.
5. Development of a non-computer-assisted annual training evaluation plan.

TRAINING PRIORITIES FY '82

---

1. Basic job training for new line workers and for line workers not trained the previous year.
2. Development of a four-day basic training program, including training manuals, for supervisors. Development should include a pilot training session and revision of the training content as needed. Sessions to include a maximum of twenty participants.
3. Distribution of supervisory training manuals.
4. Training of trainers to provide supervisory training.
5. Delivery of training to supervisors. Newly appointed supervisors to be given priority.
6. Implementation of the evaluation plan designed during FY '81.

DPW FINANCIAL REPORTING PRACTICES

SDT financial reports are prepared quarterly by the Office of Fiscal Services and are distributed within thirty days of the close of each accounting period. Monthly financial reports are available upon request. SDT financial data are presented according to four categories: professional development, educational leave, in-service training, and administrative support. Within the in-service training category, the data are presented separately for economic assistance and social services. Indirect costs (a pro rata share of DPW central office expenses) are not presented on the financial reports.

Administrative costs are the direct costs associated with maintaining SDT as an organizational unit and are, for most financial analysis purposes, fixed expenses. They include salaries and benefits of SDT permanent staff (see Exhibit 4), travel costs associated with visiting the districts, general office supplies, materials, etc.

The financial reports reflect cash disbursements (monies actually paid out) rather than all expenditures (costs incurred because services or goods had been acquired). They reflect payments that were processed prior to or within five days of the close of the accounting period. (This five-day time period is extended at the end of the fiscal year.)

The financial reports compare cash disbursements with total budgeted amounts (authorized expenditures for the year) and with pro rata budget amounts for the accounting period. The pro rata amounts for the quarter are determined by dividing the annual budget by four and may bear little relationship to training activity.

CURRENT FINANCIAL SITUATON: ECONOMIC ASSISTANCE

In order to carry out the directives given him, Burke decided to focus first on the economic assistance in-service training program. He first reviewed the most recent financial report from economic assistance. This report had been prepared by the Office of Fiscal Services and covered the first half of FY '80. It is presented in Exhibit 5. Line items include salaries for DPW economic assistance staff who have engaged in curriculum development and delivered training, since monies are transferred from SDT accounts to cover their activities and contracts with independent consultants and educational institutions. These are in addition to printing, travel, materials, and facilities/equipment rentals.

Since the report reflected cash disbursements, Burke sought information on the unit's expenditures for the first six months, whether or not payments had been processed. The financial report which he developed using these data is presented in Exhibit 6.

Burke also reviewed the status of the contractual agreements for FY '80. He found that two contracts had been negotiated: a $38,440 contract with the state university to provide interviewing skills training and an $8,000 contract with a research consultant to study training evaluation

EXHIBIT 5. Economic Assistance In-Service Training Financial Report*
FY '80 (July 1, 1979 through December 31, 1979)

	TOTAL DISBURSEMENTS TO DATE	TOTAL BUDGET (AUTHORIZED EXPENDITURES)	BALANCE	PRO RATA	DIFFERENCE
Salaries/Benefits (Service Staff)	94,942	130,200	35,258	65,100	(29,842)
Consultants	22,774	59,500	36,726	29,750	6,976
Printing	23,834	62,860	39,026	31,430	7,596
Materials/Supplies	2,838	6,000	3,162	3,000	162
Travel	7,966	40,000	32,034	20,000	12,034
Facilities, Equipment Rental	814	3,000	2,186	1,500	686
Institutional Contracts	18,000	38,440	20,440	19,220	1,220
TOTALS	171,168	340,000	168,832	170,000	(1,168)

*As prepared by Office of Fiscal Services.

EXHIBIT 6. Economic Assistance In-Service Training Financial Report* (Revised)
FY '80 (July 1, 1979 through December 31, 1979)

	TOTAL ACTUAL EXPENDITURES TO DATE	TOTAL BUDGET (AUTHORIZED EXPENDITURES)	BALANCE	PRO RATA	DIFFERENCE
Salaries/Benefits (Service Staff)	99,878	130,200	30,322	65,100	(34,778)
Consultants	28,776	59,500	30,724	29,750	974
Printing	23,834	62,860	39,026	31,430	7,596
Materials/Supplies	2,838	6,000	3,162	3,000	162
Travel	12,956	40,000	27,044	20,000	7,044
Facilities, Equipment Rental	814	3,000	2,186	1,500	686
Institutional Contracts	18,000	38,440	20,440	19,220	1,200
TOTALS	187,096	340,000	152,904	170,000	(17,116)

*As prepared by Burke following review of services or goods acquired whether or not payment had been processed.

procedures. The evaluation contract was scheduled to begin in March 1980. The university contract had been in effect since the beginning of the fiscal year and provided for the delivery of twelve two-day training sessions to 240 workers in the two largest district offices.

THE CURRENT AND PROPOSED TRAINING PROGRAM

Most economic assistance in-service training conducted during the first six months centered on changes in DPW's eligibility procedures. The eligibility changes involved agency policy and DPW field staff provided much of the instruction. Fifty staff were trained in each session. One-fifth of the economic assistance eligibility specialists and supervisors had not yet attended the mandatory two-day training sessions. The interviewing skills training was proceeding according to plan. Five of the sessions had been conducted during the first half of the fiscal year. See Exhibit 7.

TRAINING COSTS

As part of the planning process, Burke sought cost data for the major training activities—curriculum development, training delivery, and training evaluation. Historically, cost data had been scanty with emphasis placed on line item expenditures and total project costs. Total project costs, however, bore little relationship to activity levels. During the current year, for example, one contractor was providing basic casework training for 120

EXHIBIT 7.　Training Content

ECONOMIC ASSISTANCE WORKERS

1. Interviewing skills and techniques
2. Human relations skills
3. Intra and interagency referrals
4. Agency policies and procedures
    Eligibility guidelines
    Completion of forms
    Support documents
5. Work management

ECONOMIC ASSISTANCE SUPERVISORS

1. General supervisory roles: support, teaching, administration
2. Work planning and management
3. Conflict resolution
4. Performance appraisal
5. Worker productivity
6. Teaching and implementing policy changes

EXHIBIT 8.   Training Cost Estimates*

I. TRAINING DELIVERY

a.   Trainer: $200 per day
b.   Training manual: $5 per copy
c.   Trainer travel: average of $ 20 per diem meals
                                $ 35 per diem lodging
                                $150 transportation per trip to training site
d.   Facilities rental: average per day $50
e.   Equipment rental: average per day $75

II. TRAINING DEVELOPMENT

a.   Curriculum specialist: $200 per day
b.   Video specialist: $1,000 per 20-minute segment
c.   Video materials: $60 per tape
d.   Travel for coordination purposes: same as training delivery

III. TRAINING EVALUATION

a.   Evaluator: average $300 per day
     (Cost holds regardless of phase—design, analysis, report writing—of the evaluation)
b.   Evaluation report: $3 per copy
c.   Travel: same as for training delivery

*Includes 7-percent costs increases expected for FY '81

social services staff for $30,000. A second contractor was providing basic casework training for 300 staff for $130,000. Nevertheless, Burke was able to obtain reasonable cost estimates through reviews of progress reports and financial records, interviews with training providers, and work sessions with SDT and fiscal staff. Cost data are provided in Exhibit 8. Estimates of

EXHIBIT 9.   Typical Resources Required for Development and Evaluation*

I.   Curriculum Development and Testing
     a.   Personnel
     b.   Curriculum Specialist   25 days
     c.   Evaluation Specialist   5 days
     d.   Video Specialist   5 days
     e.   Travel   3 trips per person
     f.   Supplies/Materials (tapes, reprints, etc.) $500
          Does not include printing of trainee manuals
II. Training Evaluation
     a.   Evaluator   5 days: evaluation design
                                         1 day for each training session delivered
                                         5 days final report
     b.   Supplies/Materials
          (Includes evaluation instruments)

*Based on four-day training program

typical resources needed for different training activities are presented in Exhibit 9.

ASSIGNMENTS

Given these data, Burke must now formulate sound financial plans for the economic assistance in-service training component of SDT.

Assignment 1

Analyze the financial situation with regard to the economic assistance in-service training funds at the end of the first six months. Prepare a recommendation that outlines how Burke can control expenditures and remain within budget for the remainder of the fiscal year. Use actual figures to support your analysis and recommendation.

Assignment 2

Develop a separate training plan and budget for FY '81 and FY '82 for the economic assistance in-service training program. Your training plans should be in narrative form and should describe the training that is to be provided and the number of persons to be trained. Present total training costs and costs for each of the following training areas: (a) curriculum development, (b) training delivery, (c) evaluation.

Index

DATE DUE

JAN 6 '98 S			
JAN 2 1 PAID			
GAYLORD			PRINTED IN U.S.A.